Advance praise for *From Presence to Power*

"Rashad Robinson is who you want with you in a foxhole. He'll see all the angles and devise a winning strategy faster than anyone. It's such a gift that this three-decade veteran of civil and human rights advocacy is sharing his methods precisely when we need them most. We all have something we want to change: in our schools, in our neighborhoods, in our country. But most of us worry that protest isn't enough. Using Rashad's principles for building power—and applying his engaging and incisive exercises to our own goals—we get a master class in real activism. This is the book to read for the fight ahead."

—Heather McGhee, *New York Times* bestselling author of *The Sum of Us*

"I'm sending this book to all my friends and family. Rashad doesn't just offer a diagnosis of the problems with how power works in this country; he offers clear, actionable ideas for how regular people can do something about it. I've been involved in activism a good part of my life, and Rashad gave me a new way of thinking about how power works. This is a must-read for anyone who wants things to change."

—Jane Fonda, actor and activist

"A book about winning and building power is a necessary tonic for the times when Donald Trump wields such power. Rashad Robinson has locked horns with the most powerful people on the planet. He expertly dissects how we can win, and where and why we have come up short. His analysis of roles, rules, and results is an essential framework for how to forge a path to power, moving us from analysis to action—a way out of the wilderness progressives find ourselves in today. This book is a must-read for anyone who wants to achieve lasting structural change, not just momentary victories and fleeting results."

—Anthony D. Romero, executive director of the ACLU

"Rashad Robinson is one of the most gifted and fearless leaders we have. In his eagerly anticipated and desperately needed book, *From Presence to Power,* he offers a detailed plan for how we can achieve true change by moving from visibility to vitality—from being seen to being felt. This is a strategically sophisticated book that teaches us how not to simply traffic in echoes and effects, but to be effective in our aims by amassing and then pulling the levers of real power."

—MICHAEL ERIC DYSON, sociologist, cultural critic, and *New York Times* bestselling author of *Long Time Coming*

"I've spent my career fighting for working people—for higher wages, safer jobs, dignity on the clock. And I've learned that the campaigns that get the most attention aren't always the ones that deliver. In *From Presence to Power,* Rashad names that gap with precision and shows how to close it: how to turn moments into the kind of power that actually changes the rules for workers and their families."

—APRIL VERRETT, president of Service Employees International Union

"To transform the world for the good, we must study power. As one of the most impactful activist leaders of our time, Rashad Robinson has taken on power—corporate power, media power, racist power—and won time and again. Even in losses, he won through learning. From all his wins and learnings, Robinson lays out a clear blueprint for making antiracist change."

—IBRAM X. KENDI, #1 *New York Times* bestselling author of *Chain of Ideas: The Origins of Our Authoritarian Age*

"*From Presence to Power* is an essential text for this moment: a how-to guide for winning positive change on a new political playing field, backed by decades of experience in the work of building power for progress. If you've ever despaired at the accelerating harms of the world around us and wished there was something you could do, this is the book for you."

—AI-JEN POO, president of the National Domestic Workers Alliance and executive director of Caring Across Generations

"Rashad has helped shape some of the most effective fights for justice in our lifetime—and I've seen that work up close. This book gives people the strategy and clarity they need to stop reacting and start winning."

—Angela Rye, legal analyst and political commentator

"Rashad Robinson's book is essential reading for anyone interested in creating meaningful and lasting social change. How fortunate are we that such a champion of justice is letting us into his mind so that we can make history and not repeat it."

—Jose Antonio Vargas, Pulitzer Prize–winning journalist and author of *Dear America: Notes of an Undocumented Citizen*

"I've been in movements all my life, and I know passion alone doesn't win—power does. *From Presence to Power* is a powerful and necessary book that cuts through the illusion that visibility equals victory and offers a real framework for changing systems, not just reacting to them. This is the book every new organizer needs and every generation should inherit. Rashad shows us how committed people turn frustration into leverage and energy into results."

—Tamika Mallory, author of *I Lived to Tell the Story,* co-organizer of the Women's March, and social justice activist

"Rashad Robinson has been leading successful campaigns for years, and now he has distilled all that learned experience into a crisp, clear, and compelling road map for others who want to learn how to build power and win. *From Presence to Power* is an invaluable gift to the movement; my only complaint is that I wish I had had it when I was twenty years old!"

—Annie Leonard, former executive director of Greenpeace (U.S.) and creator of *The Story of Stuff*

From Presence to Power

From Presence to Power

How to Take On the Fights That Matter—and Win

RASHAD ROBINSON

ONE WORLD
NEW YORK

One World
An imprint of Random House
A division of Penguin Random House LLC
1745 Broadway, New York, NY 10019
oneworldlit.com
penguinrandomhouse.com

Hardcover ISBN 9780593243565
Ebook ISBN 9780593243572

Printed in the United States of America

1st Printing

First Edition

BOOK TEAM: Production editor: Evan Camfield • Managing editor: Allison Fox • Production manager: Jennifer Backe • Copy editor: Janet Renard • Proofreaders: Susan Gutentag, Martin Schneider, Cindy Durand, Rachel Twersky

Book design by Kevin Quach

The authorized representative in the EU for product safety and compliance is Penguin Random House Ireland, Morrison Chambers, 32 Nassau Street, Dublin D02 YH68, Ireland. https://eu-contact.penguin.ie

I've been shaped by a life of learning and human
connection—by family, teachers, and friends.

This book is dedicated to my first teachers,
my parents, and to my first friend, my brother.

Contents

Introduction

Looking for Answers

The term *social change* evokes different images and ideas for different people. What comes to mind for many of us is the Civil Rights Movement of the 1950s and '60s, the women's liberation movement of the 1970s and '80s, the environmental, AIDS, and disability justice movements of the 1980s and '90s, the LGBT rights and anti-war movements of the 2000s, or the Black Lives Matter and Dreamer movements of the 2010s and '20s. The iconic images and stories from those periods of activism symbolize what it means to challenge injustice and change how society works—for the better.

Behind every iconic image of a past social movement, however, is a complex reality about how fights were actually won or lost. Relatively few people were involved in the Civil Rights Movement compared to the population, and yet it led to massive material changes in society, policies that didn't just impact Black people but that made the country a safer and more just place for us all. The Black Lives Matter movement sparked an unprecedented number of people of all backgrounds to take action, and yet it is unclear exactly what changed structurally and enduringly in society as a result. (And I say that as someone who was part of it and is committed to it.)

What is the deeper story behind the imagery of activism that can explain the difference between movements that win and movements that don't? What lessons do those stories tell us that can help us find our way forward today? I wrote this book to help answer those questions.

Those of us who are disturbed and wounded by what is happening in our country, and feel motivated to change it, face a central challenge. We must understand the many ways people thought about change and fought for it in previous decades that are still relevant and effective today, while also recognizing that what is needed from us now may look and feel very different—and even feel uncomfortable. Changing times require changing tactics, and being predictable often means being beatable. This moment requires all of us to think differently about how we fight for the future of our country.

In many cases throughout history, winning fights for justice and progress seemed impossible. Yet, despite the forces working against them, people banded together and won. More often than not, they surprised themselves (and society) by inventing new ways to confront forces that seemed too great to oppose and pursue dreams that seemed impossible to fulfill. In that way, social change is the practice of making the impossible possible. Making freedom possible. Making equality and equity possible. Making it possible for people to be safe, to live full lives and be their full selves, to afford what they need and pursue what they want.

And possibility is about one thing more than any other: power. Ultimately, making change isn't about how many people we mobilize to take action. It's about who we mobilize and what actions they take, and whether those actions create the kind of leverage necessary to force change. On the one hand, a small group of people who gain the right leverage can do a lot. On the other hand, millions of people who loudly express their desires but don't gain leverage can get stuck.

That's because *presence* and *power* are not the same thing. Presence is about getting visibility. Power is about getting things done. Power is about being able to change the rules for how things work.

Not every challenge to the status quo is an effective means for changing it. Visionary rhetoric can be motivating, as can staging big protests or trending on social media. But getting people excited and gaining attention often makes it seem like we've won things when we actually haven't. Achieving awareness and popularity can be an important first step, but it can also take us off course.

Visibility today comes with many rewards: the way big "like" counts on social media make us feel, the fundraising dollars that pour in from sending text messages to millions of people, the ad dollars that follow the viewer numbers on a video channel, the social status gained by being seen on every video podcast and news show, the confidence inspired by opinion polls that say a large majority of people agree with us, and even the pride that arises from writing a bestselling book. Our society rewards visibility, which is another word for presence.

But the one reward for achieving visibility that is most often missing is power. When we confuse presence and power, and focus on achieving the wrong one, we lose. And when people with agendas we don't like focus on achieving the right one, they win. The way to know the difference is to honestly answer one question: *Is what we're doing making something possible that wasn't possible before?*

There are forces working hard to make sure that movements for justice never make the transition from presence to power. They think they will lose if we win. The challenge for us now and in the years ahead is to become more powerful than those forces, not just more popular.

The Practice of Possibility

In the twentieth century, grassroots, people-driven movements profoundly transformed our country for the better. Many efforts did not win, much was left undone, and many injustices carried forward. But it is undeniable that those movements helped accelerate progress in many parts of our lives, while also preventing injustices that would have made our lives much worse. They also proved an essential point: There cannot be movement toward progress unless everyday people move to action.

More recently, however, leaders on the right wing have also realized the power of everyday people. As a result, they've flooded politics with people forging new roles for themselves, not just showing up at rallies but exploiting every resource at their disposal to advance their cause. They created new ways for outsiders to challenge established politicians and take over government offices. They created ways for students to help take down university professors and presidents, for radical ideologues to build alternative, fact-free media platforms that recruit more people to their side, and for passionate believers to take over social spaces—from churches to chat rooms—and use those arenas to push their agenda forward.

The right wing unleashed people's leadership and gave them a sense of ownership over their movements. And now we're living with the results. Of course, it helps that backing all of these efforts are billionaires and well-placed elites in corporations, government, media, and religious institutions—people ready to exploit seemingly popular movements for their own interests. But the right wing of today could not have turned itself from a fringe force into a dominant national power without everyday people participating in new ways. They may not be larger in number than we are, but they organized themselves in highly effective ways—focused on power.

Why can Donald Trump, large corporations, the right wing, and abusers of every kind get away with doing so much harm? It seems like morality, history, the vast majority of people, and even the law itself are often on our side, and yet we are still losing ground. If most people want progress, why aren't we winning more of it? It's because we don't have power on our side: We have not been able to force those with power to stand up to the right wing and stand with us instead. We have also not put ourselves in the position of *being* the people with power—using that power to reshape how the country works.

We can be highly active spectators of politics, but we need to understand the difference between spectator and player. Even the biggest sports fan—the one who knows everything about the game, shows up the most often, cheers the loudest, buys all the merchandise, and puts their money, heart, and soul into supporting the team—is still not a player on the field. That's because sports, theater, concerts, and other types of performances restrict the number of people who can take a place on the big stage. But politics doesn't. There is room for everyone on the field. The idea that there isn't is merely a self-serving story that serves one purpose only: letting our opponents take over.

Those of us who believe in fairness, justice, progress, and freedom need to embrace a different kind of participation in order to counter today's right-wing movements and their corporate, political, and media backers. Many of us have already made the transition from spectator to player on the field. But without changing the way we play the game, we will not get the results we want. It's not just about showing up; it's about strategy.

All of us, including those of us who have been part of social movements for years, must reexamine our approaches. And one thing is clear: The same politicians and political consultants who couldn't figure out how to stop the reelection of Trump are not the people who should be lecturing us on how to stop him now. They are not the solution. You are. You, me, and anyone committed to learning the hard lessons of making change that can help us see new possibilities and pursue them.

There is one positive result of the right-wing movement that brought Donald Trump back into office, inescapably turning every single part of our lives into a political fighting field. It gives each of us an incredible opportunity to play on that field—to fight back. Every school board meeting, hiring decision, course curriculum, healthcare choice, highway construction project, local tax or ordinance, government election and appointment, workplace policy, product purchase, and more has been turned into an opportunity to shape the direction of our country.

The debates that define national politics are not just happening far off in Washington, DC. They are right in front of us every day. Even wearing a mask to protect yourself and others during flu season is somehow a political statement today, defining what team you're on. The stakes of our individual actions (or inactions) have never been higher, and opportunities to engage are everywhere—both individually and collectively.

I've learned a lot in my lifetime of winning (and losing) fights for social change. Over two decades, I've tangled with Mark Zuckerberg, Elon Musk, police unions, prosecutors, Hollywood executives, and even Democrats in Washington, DC. Behind each of those clashes was a campaign aiming to make people's lives better: ending the injustices of the criminal justice system, protecting the rights and benefits of workers, protecting consumers from being exploited by big banks, making sure federal funds are distributed fairly, and making sure Black people and LGBT people have the same paths to opportunity as anyone else. These fights have forced me to develop tools and strategies capable of winning change when the odds look grim—lessons I can now share with you.

Trump could resign from office tomorrow, but we'd still be living in the country he exposed and exploited. It's a country in which too many of the rules shaping our lives enable people to profit from injustice, and too many of the safeguards we thought existed to protect us against abuses of power are not particularly effective at doing so (while those that work are being dismantled far too easily).

I believe the leadership of people working at all levels of society, not just the top, can change our course and transform this country. My hope is that this book will help you see your role in social change and also see how to raise your game—in ways that help us raise our collective game. I didn't write this book only to help you become a more observant spectator. I wrote this book to help make you a better player.

I Learned a Lot About Power When . . .

I was in middle school when an assistant principal at our local high school in Riverhead, Stephen Paskiewicz, made a decision that taught me a lot about my future in this country. The police wanted Black faces for a robbery suspect lineup, and Paskiewicz, a white man, was happy to oblige; he picked out seven Black students and served them up to the police as if he were a pharmacist happily filling a prescription. Apparently, there was no rule preventing him from doing so.

He didn't ask the kids' parents. He didn't give the kids a real choice. He didn't tell them they'd be dressed up in different shirts with baseball caps (turned backward) to look the part. He promised they would each get $15, an attempt to make something that was undeniably humiliating and coercive look legitimate, perhaps even beneficial to them. It certainly wasn't. He didn't think of what might happen to them or how this would affect their lives. They would be seen being picked up by police officers after school and being dragged into a police station. Police might decide to keep an eye on them afterward. It could mark them for life.

The way a lot of Black people in our community saw it, Paskiewicz was lending Black students out for compulsory labor, the same way people in power had always treated Black people in this country. At some level, he believed he owned them. "My boys," he called them. This was merely a temporary transfer of property from one white authority to another. The statement it made about who controlled whom in our town echoed loudly among Black people living there. We experienced the unique feeling all oppressed people know: shock without surprise.

This was early 1990s Riverhead, on eastern Long Island, so there was a passionate response to the assistant principal's decision. Black people all over the New York area had just lived through the false prosecution of the Central Park Five.[1] The legacy of the Civil Rights Movement was strong, and Black communities were proud, organized, and willing to make their voices heard. Pressure on the school board, local officials, and the news media to take this incident seriously came directly from the Eastern Long Island chapter of the NAACP and from the local First Baptist Church. Many in my family belonged to both. And both had built up a system over the years for responding to recurring moments of racism.

The Reverend Charles A. Coverdale, who just retired at the end of 2025 after nearly 40 years of service, was a leading pastor at the time. He knew how to rally people around a just cause. As a result, there was about as much attention on this incident as one could hope for. Racism was on full display, and lots of people were pointing at it.

But was that enough? To write this book, I had to think a lot about how and when I first learned about power. When did the difference between feeling powerful and actually being powerful become so clear to me? When did I become motivated to make sure the people who control how the country works face consequences for the injustices they create and benefit from?

There wasn't a single moment when it all became clear. But there were many moments that made me determined to figure it out. Seeing that assistant principal send those kids to a police lineup was definitely one of them. I grew up in an environment where racism was a very real factor in how society worked, and where survival, safety, and success depended on understanding how to navigate differences among people. I wasn't necessarily welcomed in everyone's home throughout my school years.

My family came to the town of Riverhead as part of the Great Migration, the exodus of Black people from the American South to the American North that took place in the 1920s and '30s. My dad's family came up from Goochland County, Virginia, and my mom's side came up from Cumberland County, Virginia. On summer road trips crossing back into the South to visit family still living out "in the country," I learned to reflect on that history: what was gained, what was lost, and what was not that much different at all for Black people north and south of the Mason-Dixon Line.

Long before "Make America Great Again" signs flashed across the lawns of Riverhead and hung inside many of its local businesses, many other painful signs communicated the relative value of different people in our community. A lack of Black teachers and Black elected leaders was a sign, as were the decisions people in authority so often made, and the attitudes they so often voiced—and felt it was acceptable to voice.

When outrage erupted after everyone found out what happened to those seven Black students, I learned something important: Black parents and community members (and the white allies who stood with us) had enough influence to force the recognition of a wrong, but not enough to make it truly right. The system could withstand our pressure. Our community did not have the power to shape how either the school system or the policing system worked, let alone the ways they worked together. So even though Black people suffered the injustice, we would not play a role in deciding what to do about it.

The power to define justice belonged to someone else. We could enjoy seeing ourselves featured in stories on TV or in the newspaper, especially in *The New York Times*—a big deal for people living off the last exit of the Long Island Expressway. But the rules existed to protect people like that assistant principal, even if people widely accepted that he shouldn't have done what he did.

The result was as predictable as the incident itself. The police faced no consequences at all. Paskiewicz wasn't fired by the district, either. He was merely demoted from assistant principal to a position they deemed less important: teaching history. When I got to high school, this man was my history teacher. He remained in a position of authority, and he would continue to make up his own rules for how to treat Black students because there were no rules to force him to do otherwise. I continued running up against those rules. At the time, I certainly wasn't able to change them. (For more about my high school history teacher and what those experiences taught me about power, see the online Appendix at rashadrobinson.com/book.)

Eventually, I moved on, resolved to find a way to change the rules that allow people in authority to hurt people who aren't. I began to realize that it all came down to power.

A Book About Power, a Book About Winning

My parents, most of their friends, and the vast majority of our family members of that generation never went to college, but they gave me an incredible education. Whenever we were in the car, they alternated between music and the news. They talked about the issues of the day at the dinner table, especially what affected our community. They not only voted but they took me to town council and school board meetings.

I would come to learn the effect one person's voice could have, especially when speaking on behalf of others. The rest of my extended family encouraged me to embrace that power by telling me I should be a lawyer, a politician, or a minister: the go-to roles in society for persuasive people, particularly in the Black community. In different ways, many of my relatives and my parents' friends—whether my god-parents or my grandfather who took me into the voting booth with him—influenced my social consciousness.

I was just a tween when, wearing a suit with a clip-on tie, I first spoke at a county board meeting, advocating on behalf of other kids for continuing the county's funding for 4-H (a skill-building program for youth that many parents relied on, similar to the Scouts). Because I was too short for the podium, they put me in a different place to speak. We won that fight: funding secured. The local TV news station ran a story: "The Kid vs. the County Exec."

My early experiences as an advocate, which my parents encouraged me to throw myself into, helped me figure out how to avoid getting put in places where others wanted to put me. They taught me to put myself where *I* wanted to be.

As I grew up and learned more about the ways in which other people were not free, my circle of concern expanded. I wanted to follow in the line of my parents, who were both builders—my mother built gardens and my father, who was an artisan and a contractor, built homes. My contribution would be building relationships, organizations, and other tools for making change.

I would face the same question over and over: Where did a Black gay man fit? The world was telling me I didn't. I needed to make space for myself to belong. And I knew that if I did, I would make space for others who deserved the same. The clip-on tie evolved into a bespoke style that would get me taken seriously when people might otherwise dismiss me, allowing me to set myself apart instead of accepting the pressure to blend in, and allowing me to feel confident and comfortable in spaces designed to do just the opposite.

From my earliest days, my parents helped me understand how the world worked and what that meant for people like us. I can't even remember the moment I first knew I wanted to change it.

My first adult jobs in the social justice field focused on student organizing, and then on electoral reform and voting rights. As I realized my passion for social change could become my career, I took a job at the advocacy organization GLAAD, which is focused on changing representations of LGBT people in news and entertainment media. Then I went to lead Color Of Change, an activist organization mobilizing people online to fight for racial justice, helping turn it into a national force that could accelerate progress for Black people. We used technology to mobilize people in new ways for a new era at a new scale, often taking on corporations when many other civil rights groups wouldn't. My goal was to help people make sense of what was happening whenever issues of race became major moments of focus and attention nationally or locally—and to give people something to do that mattered.

Working at both organizations, I knew that changing the way the country worked to make it safer and more promising for LGBT people of all types, and for Black people of all types, would have ripple effects: If we got it right, we would be helping to create a safer and fairer country for everyone on the short end of justice. But I saw clearly how we couldn't get anywhere by just popularizing our ideas. We needed to make ourselves powerful enough to implement them. And we did. Not always, not on everything, but we made an impact, and perhaps more importantly, we learned from every fight.

I love serving people by giving them ways to win something that matters for themselves and the people they care about. And I'm lucky to live a life in which I do that every day (or at least try to). If you're reading this book, whether or not that's what you do for a living, it's probably something you do—or want to do—too.

In this book, I share what I've learned. I wrote it to give you and other people who care about justice a road map to understand power more deeply, in ways that can actually make you—and all of us—powerful enough to win the changes we want to see in the world.

It's the book I wish I'd had, way back, to guide me as a young person learning to become an effective activist. It's also the book I wish I'd had in front of me as a social change leader in my adulthood, reminding me of the most important lessons about winning change that are so easy to forget in the heat of fighting for it. I aim to provide a way to understand why we win when we win, and why we lose when we lose, without boiling everything down to problems with messaging, get-out-the-vote operations, policy agendas, or other topics that are important but don't actually get at the heart of what it takes to win social change.

This book has three sections. Part I offers six key concepts for understanding what power is and how it works, Part II outlines five core practices for building power, and Part III brings it all together: a deep dive into four case studies from my work on the front lines of social change. Those stories demonstrate the importance of the fundamentals of power while also sharing behind-the-scenes insights from my experiences in taking on Big Tech, the criminal justice system, Hollywood, and the rise of Donald Trump.

Along the way, I offer activities so that you can experiment with some of the concepts and practices in your own life. One strong theme runs throughout the book: seeing and avoiding what I call the traps of magical thinking. That's when we fool ourselves into thinking that what we want to be true is the actual truth, ignoring compelling evidence to the contrary. In several chapters, I point to instances of magical thinking that clouded the judgment of people in politics and social movements—including my own—and got in the way of success.

If we are confused, understanding power brings clarity. If we don't know what to do, understanding power brings focus. Our challenge today is understanding how to fight back and become unignorable to decision-makers. The goal is to become the people setting the rules instead of the people suffering from them.

The right wing is standing on a foundation built over many years that makes what they're doing now possible, held up by tons of money, extremist followers, a system rigged to their advantage, and theories about social change that have proven very effective. To defeat them in a lasting way, we must stand on an equally strong foundation. It is a foundation built on the belief in justice, equality, and a profound understanding of how the world actually works so we can transform it into what we want it to be.

Many people coming together and taking action as part of movements for change have overcome a lot worse, across generations. As someone whose family lines trace back to slavery and the Jim Crow South, I know that all too well.

But if we think that just having the facts on our side, just having public opinion on our side, or just getting enough people to show up at big protests is going to make the difference, then we are ignoring the most important lessons those movements have given us. We must evolve to win.

PART I

How to Understand Power

What do we need to understand about power in order to effectively gain and use it?

1

Presence Is Not Enough

DEFINITION: Presence is about visibility, the ability to make something—a cause, an issue, a big new idea, a person, or an organization—widely recognized and popular. Achieving presence can include making an issue or idea trend on social media, landing a story on the front page of a newspaper, or motivating thousands of people to show up at a rally—that is, making your thing the thing everyone is talking about.

CHALLENGE: Achieving presence can make us feel powerful, even when we're not. It can be hard to accept that raising our voices doesn't automatically translate into increasing our power and impact. Presence, even at the most widespread level, doesn't necessarily lead to change. We live in a time when it's easy to get preoccupied with achieving presence and lose focus on gaining the real power we need to win the actual changes we want. To be powerful, we must know that presence is not power.

An Unnatural Disaster

There was a time when Kanye West told the truth. On September 2, 2005, he participated in *A Concert for Hurricane Relief,* a televised fundraiser that brought in millions of dollars in response to the ongoing destruction from Hurricane Katrina, which hit New Orleans and the larger Gulf (of Mexico) Coast just days before. Almost all of the celebrities participating in the benefit concert stuck to the scripted story about the devastating event that, even its first week, had already been designated the largest natural disaster in American history. Kanye did not.

The scale and impact of Hurricane Katrina revealed how little our country had changed over decades of nominal progress toward racial equality. The floodwaters quickly washed away any naïve notion that people in power care about everyone equally. People who call the shots in government agencies, news networks, churches, and corporations showed us exactly who they are—and whom they care about most.

George W. Bush had been president for four and a half years before the storm. During those years, he made decisions that would turn Katrina into a devastating force. Bush and those around him actually played a prime role in manufacturing a crisis that could have been avoided—and then pretending it was natural. As if it came out of nowhere. But Katrina was no surprise.

In 2003, Bush merged the Federal Emergency Management Agency (FEMA) with the newly formed Department of Homeland Security. That decision deprioritized disaster response. It drastically reduced the budget for addressing the oncoming threat of larger and more frequent storms that communities along the Gulf Coast were facing. Even Bush's own head of FEMA warned in an internal memo that budget cuts and other changes dangerously reduced its ability to respond to disasters, including by leaving it without the trained and experienced staff required to do so.[1] (The number of decisions being made by Trump today, setting us up for endless disasters to come in every aspect of life, is almost too large to count.)

When we look at the past, we too often get trapped in the story that people in the present want us to believe about it. One of the biggest lies they tell us: *We couldn't have known at the time.* In the case of Hurricane Katrina, local officials knew the dangers of not protecting the city from predictable weather patterns, and they warned the federal government repeatedly, making specific and clear requests for support.

People at every level of government knew the New Orleans levees, built to fend off storm floods of a much lesser degree, could never withstand a high-powered hurricane. They hadn't been quiet about it, either. Louisiana officials had asked the government for funds to strengthen the levees. They had documented very real threats and the very real need for $27 million in hurricane preparation and response funds.

Bush aimed to give them only $4 million for the entire year, the same amount that he and Vice President Dick Cheney's corporate contractor friends were getting *every twenty minutes* during the war they started in Iraq, based on fabricated claims about weapons of mass destruction. (Congress stepped in to help New Orleans, but that resulted in an allocation of merely $5.7 million.)

A flood of bad decisions turned Katrina into a disaster. And after the hurricane hit, more bad decisions kept coming. As just one example, basic evacuations were mishandled, creating barriers to survival instead of critical lifelines. Many of the deaths that resulted from Katrina occurred in homes. People who had survived the initial storm surge could not get to safety in the aftermath, and so they were swept away. They either were blocked from getting out of the city or had gotten out but returned to help family members and couldn't get back out again. Far too many Black lives were lost because the people whose job it was to give victims a lifeline couldn't have cared less about them.

A later investigation by a committee in the U.S. House of Representatives revealed that the Red Cross was also part of the failed response to Hurricane Katrina. According to the committee's report, "Many Black communities were forced to turn to 'churches and civil rights groups . . . dubbed "the Black Cross," . . . to provide aid in the absence of the Red Cross.'" The Red Cross later "acknowledged that its response to minority evacuees during Katrina and Rita was lacking, with some African American communities having less access to aid than white communities."[2]

Corporations turned their backs on the Black communities of New Orleans, too, with equal effect. In a targeted practice, insurance corporations made it nearly impossible for many Black residents to get homeowners insurance in the years leading up to Katrina. And, for those who did have insurance, those corporations failed to process their claims after the storm. That made the fallout much worse for Black people than for other people. It was a setup: They would not be able to rebuild, and many were forced to surrender their homes. State Farm was ultimately forced to pay the federal government $100 million in restitution for how it mishandled Katrina claims.[3]

The real disaster of Katrina was not the one nature created, but the one people in positions of power created. And it hit Black people the hardest, not only because Black people were living in the storm's path but also because they lived in the path of injustice.

At the time, of course, the prevailing story in the news wasn't that Black people had been abandoned by their government or victimized by people in power, but rather that they were not resourceful enough to help themselves.[4] (We heard this same rhetoric during the COVID-19 pandemic and in many other contexts.) News media and politicians didn't portray Black people as displaced disaster victims carrying supplies back to their families, which was how they portrayed white people doing the same thing. Instead, they decided to portray Black people as looters who needed to be controlled. The most influential public conversations about the crisis pointed to Black people's decisions, not the decisions that had actually created the disaster. That narrative was about unfortunate Black people who couldn't be helped because they were fatally flawed as a people. The narrative suppressed by most news outlets and political chatter was about the unjust actions of the people in power whose biases and choices caused the worst damage and suffering.

What is the logical conclusion of a story that makes us believe people's suffering is unfortunate rather than unjust? It's not a commitment to holding people responsible or creating change. It's an offering of charity. And so that was the story people in power needed to reinforce in order to continue deflecting the blame.

Cue the celebrity concert. And Kanye.

A Moment of Truth

It's hard to remember who Kanye was back then, given who he's become. He was starting to produce big hits like "You Don't Know My Name" and "All Falls Down." He was finding his voice, and people were listening. It made sense to put him on live television to help promote a charitable cause: enlisting millions of sympathetic viewers in raising relief funds for the people of the Gulf Coast.

I was on the road that week as part of my work with GLAAD, leading media trainings for LGBT organizations and activists across the country. That night, I landed in a hotel room in Washington, DC. I watched the benefit concert on TV in the very same city in which many of the decisions about the fate of the Gulf Coast and its people had been made. I knew the full story about Katrina wasn't being told. Would it ever come out?

During the event, Kanye went off script. Standing next to *Saturday Night Live* alum and comedy star Mike Myers, he declared, "George Bush doesn't care about Black people."

Hearing that shocked me. It was a different kind of relief. A real "amen" moment. He said the thing many of us Black folks knew well but talked about only among ourselves. All of a sudden, Kanye created a national audience for the truth.

He had the gall to suggest there was a cause for Black hurricane victims' widespread suffering other than bringing it on themselves. For a moment, he turned a story promoting charity into a story promoting change. And he pointed to the clear villain in that story: President Bush, the most powerful person in the country, who had denied Louisiana the resources it needed to prevent the destruction we were witnessing and who destroyed many Black people's lives as a result.

Kanye's statement was cathartic. We were not used to seeing the truth told in front of a national audience, with millions of people paying attention. For Black people across the country, it was a striking moment of resistance to the dominant, highly controlled story in the traditional news media landscape that dominated people's information intake at the time—one that let government officials, politicians, corporate leaders, and others off the hook. A strong symbol of the truths that needed to be told, the 2005 refrain "Kanye was right" echoed loudly in Black communities and beyond.

But was being right enough?

The Limits of Speaking Truth to Power

If Kanye's seven-word statement had become the story of the storm, if the news media had taken the cue to educate people about all the unjust decisions that led to what we were seeing in the Gulf, if anyone in politics had supported Kanye's statement and pushed the idea far enough that it could not be ignored until people in power changed course and owned up to their responsibilities, we might have seen a different reality play out in the weeks and months that followed.

But that didn't happen.

In the end, 8.5 million people watched the televised concert, which raised more than $66 million (in today's dollars). Two additional televised concerts raised another $67 million (in today's dollars) and nearly tripled the combined viewership. The dominant narrative quickly settled back into the status quo comfort zone: the classic story of Black people needing white people to save them from a mess they had gotten themselves into. It is a story that serves a purpose: helping people in power avoid responsibility for the problems they cause, and even worse, allowing them to be put in charge of solving them.

Kanye created a meaningful moment of dissent but not a fundamentally disruptive one. He gave us analysis, not action. Kanye could announce that President Bush didn't care about Black people, but he didn't have the power to *force* the president or anyone else to care about us—or at least do right by us, whether they cared about us or not. The act of "speaking truth to power" didn't make "power" very worried.

The people who caused the disaster and its far-reaching consequences would pay almost nothing for it. Unlike George W. Bush, whom Kanye explicitly challenged, most of them wouldn't even be named as responsible parties at all, not even once on TV.

Michael Brown, the head of FEMA at the time, resigned his post as the fall guy, taking the blame so that no one else would have to. He would be branded as the inept screw-up who mismanaged the whole thing. His resignation buried the fact that intentional and often cruel decisions had been made for years before the storm even hit, at the highest levels of government, showing a total disregard for our lives. Blaming a single person instead of exposing the whole system allowed the status quo to march forward, uninterrupted.

The people affected lost everything—their health, their homes, even their lives. None of us had the actual power to ensure that people in power would treat Black people with equal care and concern, neither in that moment nor in the months and years that followed. We could talk about how unjust it was—and Kanye could put a fine point on it—but we couldn't change it.

I lived through this episode of history in real time and remember feeling that painful reality creep into my heart. I eventually returned to GLAAD's office in New York. GLAAD focused on tracking and publicizing both fair and unfair representations of LGBT people across different media. It was a tactic to gain leverage with media corporations that did not want to have their public brand ruined by attracting negative attention for how they misrepresented us.

The data we gathered and published helped us gain leverage with decision-makers across the news and entertainment landscape, changing how they did business. Given the influence of American television and film on people far and wide, the changes they made in representing LGBT people could ultimately play a role in changing how LGBT people were treated in the real world. So we were constantly capturing clips from TV to help advance our work. We all had TVs playing in our offices, the small kind with the VHS tape slot built in. Images coming out of New Orleans filled the airtime for a long while. What we saw—and what we didn't see—was extremely discouraging.

From my time volunteering on Louisiana senator Mary Landrieu's runoff race in 2002, I knew many of the places in New Orleans where gay people went: bars, businesses, community spaces. That was the period in which I came out as gay, and I had been excited to start learning the terrain very quickly. Sitting in my office back in New York, I thought about the Black LGBT people of New Orleans, facing the compounding stresses of constantly being attacked for who they were and, now, facing a pain during this disaster that even white LGBT people wouldn't. I could imagine what they were going through: the stories that were not making it into the news, the needs that were being ignored or denied, the attacks and abuses not being reported.

Several other people working at GLAAD—especially the two or three other Black staffers—would come into my office to share how frustrated they were with the lack of any forceful pushback on the distorted reporting we were seeing. We ourselves worked at an organization with the word *defamation* in our original name: the Gay & Lesbian Alliance Against Defamation. GLAAD was very successful at challenging misrepresentations of LG (and eventually BT) people, but challenging inaccurate and dangerous anti-Black narratives like those we saw during Katrina was not the organization's work. And yet there was no response from anyone effective enough to change what was happening—all while Black victims of Katrina were being defamed and demeaned every day in the most stereotypical and self-serving ways by law enforcement, news media, politicians, religious leaders, and more.

Presence Is Not Power

It was not long after 2005's *Concert for Hurricane Relief* that I got the email. The subject line: "Kanye Was Right." The senders: James Rucker and Van Jones. The recipients: About a thousand Black leaders and activists across the country. The calling: To form an organization that would harness the newly emerging tools of digital organizing in order to rally Black people across the country to fight racial injustice—and to do so at a whole new level. The new organization would be called Color Of Change.

That email and those that followed were provocative. James and Van were two up-and-coming Black leaders who challenged us to see opportunity in a moment of devastation. James came from the tech world and had been playing a senior role at MoveOn.org, which had just made a name for itself by inventing a new set of online organizing tools that made an impact in the 2004 election cycle. Van was building a reputation as an innovator and founder of new enterprises.

The inclusion of Julian Bond, who lent his name to some of those early emails, was perhaps even more provocative. Mr. Bond was a legendary Black leader who helped found the Student Nonviolent Coordinating Committee in the 1960s and the Southern Poverty Law Center in the 1970s. Attaching his name to a call for building something new made a statement, connecting this effort to a fabled civil rights lineage. Even more so, it signaled a need for changing our approach. If Julian Bond recognized we needed it, we definitely needed it.

James would go on to lead Color Of Change through its start-up years. Of course, it was no surprise to a social change leader like James that the intervention of a celebrity hadn't sparked enough momentum to change the trajectory of the decisions that were causing pain for Black people during Katrina.

In the late 1960s and early 1970s, Muhammad Ali's star power helped him raise consciousness about the injustices of the Vietnam War and win his own case against being drafted. In 1968, sprinters Tommie Smith and John Carlos became bigger stars than they had been before by raising their fists in the air to make a political statement at the Olympics. Forty-eight years later, in 2016, quarterback Colin Kaepernick similarly became an even bigger star than he had been before by kneeling during the national anthem to protest police violence, sparking dozens more to do the same. But these defiant acts had movements around them: They provided a boost of attention to activism already in place.

They didn't—and couldn't—change anything by themselves. Kanye only highlighted how far we had to go. It was a moment of opportunity, but someone would have to seize it, build something out of it, and take it far beyond Kanye's single statement in order to make a difference. No one could.

Color Of Change was born in that moment. Years later, after I had become the head of Color Of Change and needed to tell its origin story, I got clear about what the nightmare of Hurricane Katrina had exposed: **No one was nervous about disappointing Black people.**

No one in power believed they would face any consequences if they let Black people suffer and die, not even with people on rooftops desperate to be saved, a national display of thousands of lives on the line. Not even in a city like New Orleans, in which Black people were an undeniable presence in every part of its history, culture, and life. Moreover, people in power knew that if they made money or achieved political gain by ignoring us, or even by making us suffer, we wouldn't be able to stop them.

George Bush didn't care about Black people because we didn't have the power to *make* him care—to create consequences for doing us wrong that would make him want to do us right. Having power means being able to compel decision-makers to do the right thing, and to prevent them from getting away with doing the wrong thing (let alone profiting from it).

Black people were present everywhere in New Orleans, but they were not powerful enough to control its fate—or their own. And that was a microcosm of the state of Black America overall. If we wanted to change that reality and prevent more disasters, we needed new organizations, new leadership, new strategies, and new tools—what I call a new infrastructure for becoming powerful. Saying seven words on national television wasn't enough on its own.

When James and Van circulated that email calling on Black people to be part of building a force that could challenge the status quo, I signed on. I also forwarded it to people in GLAAD who were looking for some way to participate in changing the conditions that allowed the disaster of Katrina to happen. It would rally many of us who wanted some way to engage. I liked the idea of building something new, and I also knew it would take time and serious work to realize the vision that James and Van had put forward.

They were just at the beginning of building something that would increase our power in society, and that would one day become a huge part of my own life.

Meanwhile, those who already had the power to exploit the situation and turn it to their favor didn't miss a beat. If it was ever unclear what profiting from our pain looked like, they made it clear immediately. Some of the country's most powerful people on the right wing—names few people had ever heard—came together to turn New Orleans into a laboratory for self-serving policies of privatization and endless corporate giveaways. Just one week after Kanye demonstrated the limits of presence, they demonstrated real power.

FIND YOUR POWER

Presence Versus Power

This brief activity is meant to help you translate the concept of "presence versus power" into concrete questions that you can apply to different scenarios you encounter—identifying different actions you and others might take to get beyond presence alone.

When have you assumed presence is power? Generally speaking, power is the ability to move something in a direction it would not otherwise go. Achieving presence is often an essential part of achieving power, but it isn't power in itself. In trying to determine the difference, the most important question to ask is this: Is a group of people's presence—the volume and visibility of their voice—redirecting how things are going?

If you see someone walking down the street, it's hard to tell whether they're going to stop at the end of the block, keep walking to the next neighborhood, or walk across the entire country. Most people would guess that a person walking down the street is not setting out to walk all the way across the country. Yet, in the realm of social change, we often assume that just because people are moving, they are going to go all the way.

When you're looking at the presence people have achieved for a cause, it's hard to tell whether or not they are on the path to power—ready and able to go all the way to impact. The same thing is true for any organization you are part of, or even your neighborhood or town: You can get people talking about a problem like the quality of what your company is producing or something that's causing health issues in your local environment, but that doesn't necessarily lead to change. In fact, sometimes a culture of constantly talking about a problem is exactly what *allows* the status quo to continue unchanged, especially if the talk is more about expressing feelings than banding together to build momentum for change and leveraging that momentum to achieve a specific goal.

Think of a time when you saw someone raise a problem for discussion and it got people thinking and talking, but the conversation didn't go anywhere. It may be a time when you did this yourself. What was missing? Think about what might have made that presence a step toward power, rather than just an end in itself:

- Would having talked to people ahead of time helped, for instance, getting them aligned to build off what the first person said to raise the stakes, demanding a specific change?
- Would following the statement of the problem with a clear and tested plan of action for creating a solution have made sure the conversation progressed to the next step?
- Would having had a plan to become so present as to be unignorable—perhaps raising the issue repeatedly over days and weeks, in a way that made the status quo feel unbearable for all those involved—made a difference?
- Would having anticipated what the people who dismiss the problem or oppose the solution were going to say, and having prepared clever responses that neutralized their positions and put them on the defensive, made a difference?
- Would having already marshaled certain resources in service of making change—like having raised some

> money, pulled together some evidence, gathered signatures or statements from other people, amassed some of the resources needed to make the change—helped create momentum and prevented the conversation from merely spinning in place?

In some sense, the first step of converting presence into power is about being ready for taking the next step. Remember what I mentioned earlier in this chapter: Kanye's statement during the celebrity benefit wasn't tied to a group of people that could use it as a springboard and take it to the next step of action, but Colin Kaepernick's act of kneeling was more connected to an organized movement that could. How are you, or the people working to advance issues you care about, readying themselves for the next step? How is the effort of presence tying into forces that can build real momentum for tangible change? If you achieve presence, have you figured out how to go all the way to power—and to impact?

2

Power Is Making (or Breaking) the Rules

DEFINITION: Power in its highest form is the ability to change how things work—to control the written and unwritten rules that govern how people make decisions. Those rules determine which problems are taken seriously, who gets to be in charge, who gets resources and privileges, and what behavior gets punished or rewarded. Power can operate out in the open or behind the scenes. It can focus on changing the rules for a small organization, for big parts of the government, or for entire industries.

CHALLENGE: One of the great challenges of social justice is to win the big rule changes that positively affect large numbers of people, while making it as difficult as possible to reverse those changes. Winning big rule changes requires an accurate and honest assessment of how to gain the right level of power: motivating the people whose voices and actions can change what the rules are and how (or if) they're followed.

DC After Dark

The Heritage Foundation, a right-wing think tank, became famous during the 2024 race for president by bringing together conservative and far-right leaders from every domain to create a blueprint for the second Trump presidency, which they hoped could make all of their policy dreams come true. It was called Project 2025. And they got exactly what they wanted: Only eight months into Trump's second term, the administration had already implemented half of the ideas the plan laid out.[1]

It was a true exercise in power: finding a precise way to motivate and equip the Trump administration to reshape almost every aspect of how America works, as quickly as possible. Trump had already radicalized the court system in his first term. With Project 2025 as the blueprint, he and his team would now change the rules for job hiring and college admissions, international relations, the economy, workers' rights, gender and race, corporate and environmental regulation, immigration, and much more. The authors of Project 2025 had a clear vision for transforming our society, and they knew that putting an actionable blueprint in the hands of the right decision-makers would increase their chances of winning that change. They had it ready well before Trump won the election.

Twenty years earlier, however, the same organization that would go on to produce Project 2025 had, without any fanfare, rehearsed its strategy for taking over society—very much behind the scenes. New Orleans was its laboratory. What the Heritage Foundation and its allies did back then can help us understand what is happening now and why so many different people, in so many different sectors, are going along with it.

On September 13, 2005, eleven days after the televised concert for Katrina, the lights stayed on long after dark at the Heritage Foundation, just a few blocks from the U.S. Capitol. There was no press for this after-hours meeting because it hadn't been publicized. No one put out a press release. Yet, one by one, a who's who of Republicans took their seats. Indiana congressman and future vice president Mike

Pence—at the time, the head of the influential House Republican Study Committee—hosted the meeting. The topic was the aftermath of Hurricane Katrina and the opportunities it presented.

Those present at the meeting began mapping out the future of New Orleans. They aimed to remake the city in the interests of corporations and also in service of right-wing values, whether the people who lived there liked it or not. The day before the meeting, Heritage released a quickly-pieced-together report that demonstrated just how ready it was to pounce. It wasn't subtle: "Private entrepreneurial activity and vision, not bureaucratic government, must be the engine to rebuild."[2]

While Kanye's statement had been heard across the country and lingered as a topic of conversation, Pence, Heritage, and their co-conspirators stayed under the radar. It would be easier if the report was kept quiet: Avoiding any presence was a key to their power.

Weeks after Hurricane Katrina hit shore, the suffering of the city's communities, especially its Black communities, was still on full display. The fatally inadequate government response to Hurricane Katrina allowed for more than 1,400 deaths, $170 billion in damages, out-of-control police violence (including an order to shoot "looters"),[3] white vigilante violence, and a flood of misinformation and scapegoating aimed at Black people across the state and country. Most news media were still clouding any public understanding about who and what was responsible for the level of destruction that had taken place.

While most conservative political players and corporate leaders lacked any interest in the city before and during the storm—especially when it came to protecting its Black residents, institutions, and culture—they were more than happy to exploit its devastation afterward. Black communities were consumed with meeting emergency needs, which left them less able to defend themselves against a well-organized political assault. It was open season for the right wing. Mike Pence and his crew took aim.

Billionaires once hated government until they realized how much they could gain from leading government agencies and setting up multibillion-dollar government contracts to make themselves even wealthier. Similarly, Republicans once wanted to stay as far away from

"Black cities" as possible, until they realized the rewards they could reap by taking them over. The 2000s represented a new era of opportunism for Republicans, and they got started with New Orleans.

There Was a Plan to Change the Rules

Major social change—changing the course of our future, the conditions we live in, the realities of our lives—happens only when well-organized forces work to make it happen.

Efforts to rebuild New Orleans via "private entrepreneurial activity" had begun even before that one night in DC. In the immediate wake of Katrina, President Bush suspended rules requiring federal contractors to pay standard wages, waived affirmative action guidelines for federal contractors in the Gulf region, and marginalized Black communities and leadership. (By October 2005, only 1.5 percent of the $1.6 billion that FEMA awarded in contracts went to minority-owned firms.) Meeting no formidable resistance only gave Pence and his colleagues the signal to keep going.

"The desire to bring conservative, free-market ideas to the Gulf Coast is white hot," Pence told *The Wall Street Journal* after the meeting at the Heritage Foundation. "We want to turn the Gulf Coast into a magnet for free enterprise. The last thing we want is a federal city where New Orleans once was."[4] The *Journal* allowed Pence to talk directly to the audience he wanted to reach while staying off the radar of anyone who might cause him trouble. The racially coded meaning in Pence's words also conveyed a very clear message for Pence's Wall Street audience: *This is a majority Black city, but don't you worry about that. We're going to clear the way for corporate executives and investors like you to take over New Orleans. Get ready to join the party.*

The Wall Street Journal summed it all up very clearly in that same article: "Congressional Republicans, backed by the White House, say they are using relief measures for the hurricane-ravaged Gulf coast to achieve a broad range of conservative economic and social policies." Pence and the people at that September 13 meeting hatched a plan: thirty-two regressive policies, all aligned with what journalist Naomi

Klein calls the "shock doctrine" and the "disaster capitalism" playbook.[5] Privatizing the city was one of their key aims, and nothing was too big to fit in their laboratory: schools, healthcare and hospitals, housing, policing. And it was clear what they wanted out of it: a steady stream of profits and political control.

That's not how New Orleans was set up to work before, but these would be the new rules that governed how people made decisions across the region. They would control which decisions were encouraged and which were discouraged.

Generally, power is the ability to make changes that wouldn't otherwise happen and prevent changes that otherwise would. In the context of major social change efforts, power is about controlling the rules that shape how society works. Having power means being able to change rules so that a system starts to produce more of the outcomes you want and fewer of the outcomes you don't.

Power isn't only about the written rules that state how things are supposed to work; it's also about the unwritten rules that determine how things actually work. Being able to control both is power at its highest level. (I dive more deeply into written and unwritten rules in chapter 5.)

The Heritage Foundation, its backers, and everyone in league with it had a thirst for power and a vision for changing rules. But they also had what they needed to execute that vision: the infrastructure of power. They had relationships, policy expertise, resources, a way of getting organized to launch attacks on the city's independence from different angles. That's what enabled them to put their plan into practice instead of just publishing it as a paper that sat on people's desks and went nowhere. (In chapter 8, I discuss the idea of infrastructure at length.)

As a result of the ideology they put into practice, thousands of public housing units were demolished and replaced. The new housing stock was unaffordable to the previous tenants, even those largely unaffected by the storm damage. Residents didn't just passively lose their homes; they were driven out. And while they were gone, their homes were stolen by real estate speculators, corrupt contractors, and banks acting like vultures feeding on dead prey. There might have been systems or at least attitudes and customs in place to prevent that before, but no longer.

For thousands of people, the idea that the city was their home—that they belonged there and that any recovery effort should make it possible for them to return and recover—was completely erased from the newly hatched right-wing recovery playbook. The rules of the game had changed so much, so quickly, that everyday residents of New Orleans were no longer even welcome to play the game.

Big results followed big changes in the rules. Before Katrina, forty-one thousand rental units had been designated for low-income individuals, the lifeblood of the city's history, culture, and economy. After those units were restored as part of the recovery process, the new economic rules that had been set in place by all the corporate power players raised the average rent from $461 to $836—almost double. People were priced out.

Many people were forced to live in trailers provided by FEMA, in some cases for years. Though each trailer itself cost only about $14,000, FEMA paid its subcontractors—including the construction giant Bechtel and Vice President Dick Cheney's Halliburton—up to $229,000 in total, including unnecessary storage and maintenance fees related to the mismanagement of the project overall—the very definition of waste and fraud that conservatives claim to care about.

The Government Accountability Office "found that over a seven month period, FEMA made a total of $30 million in improper or fraudulent payments for trailer maintenance alone. The investigators also found examples of phony inspections, rigged bids, and excessive payments."[6] Needless to say, if each family had been given that $229,000 originally, instead of Bush's FEMA giving that money to Republican-favored corporations and exploiting the situation for profit, they would have been back in their own homes already.

The influence of the many different ideas coming out of the Heritage Foundation strategy pervaded local politics as well. Writing about New Orleans in 2014, researcher Paul Kadetz gave a specific example: "The City Council unanimously voted in 2007 for the destruction of 4,500 low-income public housing units (of the total of 5,100 pre-Katrina units), thereby eradicating the possibility of public housing for a majority of low-income forced migrant families."[7]

That's when it's clear the rules have truly changed: Everyone is playing by them, and few are questioning them—even the people who may have once opposed them. Everyone has fully internalized the rationale behind the new rules, citing it as the reasoning for their own decisions as if it's the most natural thing in the world. It no longer matters who or where they came from, or the agendas of the people who set them in place.

The ideas coming out of the Heritage Foundation, backed by the infrastructure it had to advance them, established a new normal for the way things worked in New Orleans. The think tank's highly biased ideology became a kind of conventional wisdom—a new common sense—that everyone embraced as a long-standing way of thinking and behaving that should not be questioned, even if it had never been proven (and made no sense at all).

Heritage knew the upside of being able to rewrite the conventional wisdom. Its original team had gained momentum for seeding radically conservative ideas starting as far back as the 1970s. The following decade, they greatly influenced the economic playbook for the Reagan administration. The ideology of privatization was already dominant headed into the 1990s and the Clinton administration (which fully adopted it), as were several other core principles that would eventually be grouped together under the banner of "neoliberalism." But New Orleans was still a special opportunity and it required its own strategy.

Of course, all the jobs, economic security, and prosperity that Pence and others promised would result from their policies never materialized. That's the hallmark of many right-wing policies, which Donald Trump represents better than anyone: endless promises to improve people's lives and make government more efficient, followed by corporations funneling public money to themselves and an endless stream of negative effects on people's lives, all while making government less effective, useful, and responsive to its own people. It was another element of an interconnected right-wing vision.

Money had poured into local churches to support relief efforts during and after the storm. And so did interest from well-organized white evangelical groups, seeing an opportunity. Just as Pence and the rest of the Heritage crew used the recovery for their own ends, national religious institutions exploited rebuilding activities during the recovery period to establish a wider footprint in the region, aiming to make Christian life more politically conservative. The dynamics changed: There was now a platform for right-wing evangelical Christian movements to become more influential.

And all of this opportunism—political, corporate, religious—focused on changing how the region worked and would undermine the ability of local communities to control their future.

It's easy to see who has the power to shape the rules by looking at the people who benefit from them. In this case, the coalition that created a federal, corporate, and social takeover of New Orleans gained very clear benefits. Privatization in New Orleans meant transferring power from public authorities and community leaders to corporate interests and right-wing political radicals. The results ranged from privatizing schools, to creating tax breaks that undermined public budgets and programs, to allowing the oil industry to expand their drilling and refining operations, to giving free rein to contractors like Halliburton, Bechtel, and Blackwater that had been raking in billions from their work in Iraq.

Looking at the results of the Heritage Foundation's experiment in New Orleans twenty years ago, we can see where Project 2025's plans for the entire country are headed twenty years from now. The Heritage Foundation, the network its leaders have built, and all the interests they represent, have very clear goals in mind for transforming how our country works.

They had the power to implement their plan in 2005, and no one had the power to stop them. They experimented with changing the rules to control the fate of a largely Black population, and soon after they were experimenting on everyone else.

Why did the federal response to the 2008 financial crisis favor corporations instead of everyday people, even under Barack Obama? How did Donald Trump let corporations raid our government treasury and get away with causing so much harm during his first term in office, and how did his attempted coup in 2020 come so close to destabilizing our entire democracy? The corporate right wing turned many of their strategies from "experimental trial" into "proven method" in the aftermath of Hurricane Katrina. The evidence was clear in who benefited: rich people, military contractors, right-wing religious institutions.

In many ways, Kanye seemed to be a powerful player during the post-Katrina period: He was well-known and rich, and he made tracks people around the world knew word for word. But while that enabled him to get his statement about Katrina out on a scale that most of us cannot, the catharsis of speaking the truth wasn't the same as changing reality.

Kanye's comment was probably the most visible sentence spoken about Katrina. In today's terms, we would say his statement got more likes and views than anything else during that time. But it changed nothing about the agenda for a post-Katrina world. Presence without power.

On the other hand, the Heritage Foundation meeting received little coverage, but what was decided at that meeting changed everything. It was real power at work, without the need for presence.

Donald Trump, of course, brings the two together: He has figured out how to translate celebrity and media presence into political power: gaining control over people's decisions, and establishing new rules for how politics, government, and business work. Presence can be a major tool in gaining power, but only if used in the right way.

Breaking Down Power

It's hard to think about power without veering off into magical thinking. We may sometimes hear people say they are powerful because they can turn thousands of people out to a march, or reach a lot of people on social media, or buy a politician. Those are individual powers, but they don't necessarily add up to the overall power to change the rules. It's possible to have a lot of very strong, very impressive *capabilities* and still not have the *power* to win anything. For instance, confusing the ability to turn out people to a march with the ability of that march to influence decision-makers is a mistake that many social movements make.

Gaining power requires getting past magical thinking: If we're not meeting our goals of real and lasting change on any given issue, then we either don't have the individual capabilities we need to win or we are not using them in the right way. And yet the incentives influencing the approaches of many social movements too often encourage leaders, participants, and followers to claim they're doing everything right—and winning—even when they're not.

I have felt the pressure myself to claim that the powers my organization or coalition put in play added up to more consequential leverage with decision-makers than they actually did, or added up to some kind of long-term, systems-change impact that they clearly didn't. That is one of the unwritten rules of the game: To gain the support from members, media, and especially philanthropic funders that is needed to drive important work forward, every organization needs to find a way to stand out. The system rewards stories of success and punishes stories of failure (whether or not those stories are accurate). Any social justice leader who tells you they haven't felt this pressure isn't telling the truth.

Success comes from honestly looking at the powers we have and don't have, and understanding what more we need to build in order to change the rules for how things work in a lasting way—in a way that changes lives for the better.

The infrastructure that the post-Katrina Heritage Foundation crew had built over decades gave them many individual powers. They used them to gain the overall power required to transform the rules for how New Orleans worked:

- **Narrative power.** Convincing a critical number of influential people in authority with the lie that what they were doing would benefit everyone.
- **Administrative power.** Manipulating regulations and standards to allow themselves to implement their plan unstopped.
- **Brand power.** Convincing enough everyday people to believe that the politicians, corporations, and conservative churches could and should be trusted.
- **Legal power.** Writing and shaping new laws and policies in ways that could be easily adopted by government officials and defended well in court.
- **Political power.** Incentivizing politicians and other decision-makers to change their thinking, see their self-interest, and buy in to the program.
- **Implementation power.** Having people on board with the right resources, know-how, and instincts to move from planning to action—building the new housing, taking over the schools, and doing everything necessary to execute the plan.

Strategy is about having a realistic, actionable plan to use all of those individual powers in the right combination—in the right way, at the right time—in order to achieve a goal. When people talk as if "changing the narrative" is going to lead to big wins on its own, that's magical thinking at work. When people act as if the words in a brilliantly written press release or an inspiring mission statement are going to jump off the page and go do something in the world on their own, that's magical thinking at work. Strategy, in contrast, is about knowing what you can actually go out and do effectively to gain power.

It's the world around us that determines the level of the power we need to make change. A boulder doesn't move because we've done the best we can do. It moves because we mustered the force that its weight requires to move it, no matter how much lighter we wish it were.

Dominating in the realm of each of the individual powers listed above, far beyond the level that any community opposition could muster, gave right-wing politicians, corporations, and churches power over the rules of the entire system. That's how they won. They knew how to get people to ignore their opposition, while becoming unignorable themselves. They knew what real power was and wasn't. They knew which capabilities mattered most—and in what combination—for gaining the power to change the rules.

Changing the Values of a System to Change Its Rules

One trap we fall into is talking about political power as the influence one person or group has over another person or group. In this view, it is all about the ability to force people to do things, even when they do not want to do them. That is often what power looks like—but not always.

Do corporations like ExxonMobil, Bank of America, DraftKings, Pfizer, Meta, or members of the crypto lobby use their campaign contributions to pull the strings of members of Congress to get them to vote this way or that on a certain bill? Absolutely. That's one kind of power. But it is not the most significant power those corporations hold.

Corporations, like any of us, are most powerful when they don't have to pull strings at all—when they can ensure that everyone is already moving in the direction they want them to go, without having to use force or make sacrifices. The less effort required to achieve their goals, the more it shows how embedded they are in our lives—and how much power they have.

That is because corporations engage in a whole set of strategies aimed at establishing their needs, values, data, and perspectives as the standard to follow—the norm everything revolves around. It's also because they create a whole set of social, personal, and financial consequences to discipline any people who deviate.

That is true of anyone who aspires to change how things really work. As someone who launched and led advocacy campaigns for a living, I knew that I had the most power when I didn't need to run a campaign against a politician or corporation to get them to act, either because they had come to believe in doing the right thing (or at least came to see the reward in doing so) or because they did not want to deal with the problems our campaign would cause them if they didn't act. When our campaign took certain decisions off the table for them, I knew we had real power. The goal was being able to define and limit the field of their action.

Power is not about influencing one decision. It's about influencing the values that guide every decision. It's about holding sway over how every decision-maker looks at a problem and therefore determines the best solutions for it. The greatest power a social movement can have is the ability to make its values the norm, changing the rules society lives by to align with those values. That doesn't mean that everyone embraces those values, but it means that those values guide the way the system works, defining its rules.

Gay people being able to marry is now a norm. Not everyone likes it, and there may even be a resurgence of resistance to it. But generally, the rules in society now support the deeper value shift that allows two men or two women to marry and have societal legitimacy in their partnership, alongside opposite-gender couples. Same-sex marriage is recognized in companies' human resources policies, including health plans. It's written into how memberships work, from libraries to gyms to frequent-flyer programs. It counts as part of many people's unwritten "plus one" rules for inviting people to weddings and other events. It would take a lot of power to uproot those values, now that they have been widely established (though the right wing, the conservative Supreme Court majority, and the Trump administration certainly have the power to rewrite those written rules, as a step toward displacing those values).

It takes a lot of work influencing individuals before it becomes possible to influence an entire value system—and all the people operating within it. Changing the rules to create positive consequences for upholding those values, as well as negative consequences for violating those values, is long-term work. As is establishing new ways of thinking that people accept as intuitive and natural to follow. It takes place on many fronts. But that's how values become the norm.

Big corporate banks were "educating" politicians for ages. Their executives built strong relationships of influence with elected officials, sometimes while attending the same prep schools as kids. They identified many different levers of influence that allowed them to establish the banks' way of thinking—and the rewards of following that way of thinking—as dominant. Politicians accepted that way of thinking, not always believing they were taking sides as much as believing it's just how the world works (and believing the banks knew their industry best).

Most people in power, from journalists to policymakers, turn to banks for guidance on what to do in a financial crisis—even one caused by the banks. It becomes an unwritten rule: This is who journalists are supposed to listen to for analysis. This is who politicians are supposed to listen to for information. If they don't, they can be punished for it: their credibility attacked, their voices ignored, and worse. The influence runs so deep that it's embedded into the very identity of their own profession.

So when the 2008 financial crisis hit, after the major market crash resulting directly from all the reckless mortgage games that those very same banks had been playing, there wasn't even a debate among the key decision-makers in Congress about bailing them out. No one else was trusted to show the way forward. No one else had power. (That's not to say there were no objections from a few, less powerful members of Congress.)[8]

As it was with Katrina, people in power during the financial crisis bore no responsibility for the problems they created and yet gained maximum authority for solving them. It did not matter whether better solutions could be found, or even if no real evidence supported what the banks were demanding. The banks made money through all the bad decisions that led to the economic crash, and then after the crisis hit they cashed in again. That constitutes real power:

controlling the rules for how everything works, including how people make decisions, while never being threatened in any real way by opposing points of view. In this value system, the banks had caused a disaster, but the bigger disaster would have been not listening to them when figuring out how to respond to it. And that value system was in control of all of our lives.

Power is about motivation: incentivizing people to make decisions in line with the outcomes we want, whether people feel themselves being incentivized or it's done in far more subtle ways. Changing someone's value system makes it less necessary to use explicit incentives. When people feel something is the norm they must follow, they don't need much prodding to make a decision—they act in accordance with the norm.

FIND YOUR POWER

Three Questions for Seeing Power Dynamics

This activity is meant to help you assess the different forces and factors you need to navigate as you think about getting someone in power to make the decisions that will bring about positive change—or prevent negative change.

These three questions about power dynamics—i.e., questions for gauging the types of action that will be effective in challenging people in power—offer a simple first step for getting beyond presence alone. They can work at any scale. They can help you become more effective as an individual change agent, help your community group better pressure local politicians, businesses, school board members, or others to make meaningful changes, and even help you push a social change group you care about to expand its approach.

Think about a problematic condition or wrongful pattern of behavior taking place in a given context you are in, one you have been trying to change. Then ask the following:

1. Who is directly responsible for the problem, and whose intervention could stop it?
2. How have you gone about engaging and influencing either of those people?
3. What worked, what failed, what wasn't tried, and therefore what should you do next?

It's helpful to consider whether, up to this point, you have been telling yourself a story about the situation that plays to your biases but isn't exactly accurate, and therefore makes your efforts less effective. For example, are you assuming someone is on your side on this issue, but forgetting that they have a stake in the status quo on this particular issue (i.e., something valuable to lose) that makes them an unreliable ally?

Map out the problem and the solution (i.e., what's going wrong and what/who can change it) and your own role in the solution (i.e., what you can do to intervene or force the hand of people who can intervene). Then see if there's anything you're missing or leaving out. Try to map it out again but from a different vantage point, or by imagining not all of your assumptions are correct, and see if you get the same result.

A Sample Scenario

Let's say you're in a community where, suddenly, parents who you've never seen at school board meetings before are showing up to attack books you love and remove them from school libraries. They are loud and they're getting louder. They are gaining momentum. Other people disagree with them, like you, but they're scared to risk speaking up. What can you do?

First, do some research on the group to understand where they came from and what their strategy for achieving their goals may be. And then, even more importantly, do the best research you can to determine who is actually the final decision-maker. Let's assume it's the schools superintendent—that the school board itself is not going to make the decision but will defer to the school leadership to do so. Then work through the following steps:

1. **Engagement.** How can you get the superintendent to respond to you? What are you willing to do to build leverage and force them into a negotiation, if they are not immediately open to listening to you or adopting your arguments to make their decision? Is there someone else they need to hear from instead, or is there a way you could marshal voices

to support your goals that would outweigh the voices the superintendent is hearing on the other side?

2. **Incentives.** How can you make it in the superintendent's interest to negotiate with you? If simple persuasion or the demonstration of your presence isn't enough, how can you create consequences for them either ignoring you or stalling you endlessly and favoring the other group? How can you change their perception of you, in a way that motivates them to make the right decision? What consequence can you create that they cannot afford to bear? At the same time, is there a way to weaken the hold that your opposition is gaining over the superintendent? How can you lessen your power, in order to increase your own relative power? Last, are there outside forces influencing the superintendent that you can tap into, counteract, or change?

3. **Real solutions.** If you're moving in the direction of getting them to take action, is it the right action or is it a distraction meant to give lip service to what you are demanding while ultimately siding with the right-wing parents group? Are you playing into their appeasement strategy or neutralizing it? Are you accepting anything less than what it takes to actually change things?

4. **Power.** If you're getting stuck, is it because you do not have enough power to either force a negotiation or force that negotiation to move in the direction it should? What type of power, and how much of it, would it take to get a different result? Do you have any relationships or resources that you are not using? Are there other people you can enlist in your effort? Who might be able to create leverage with the group that you presently can't?

After asking the questions on the above list and mapping your answers, try to develop a strategy that will create the impact you want. Keep these questions in mind and keep coming back to them as you move forward.

3

How to Make Injustice Unprofitable

DEFINITION: Profiteering is benefiting from injustice—creating, increasing, or exploiting an injustice for profit. The profits I refer to in this chapter are often financial, but profits can also include increased social status, professional advancement, access to special privileges, and the ability to control others. It's not just money. People with power often change the rules of society to make profiteering easier to get away with—reducing the consequences for it and even encouraging it outright.

CHALLENGE: The challenge of social change is to make injustice *unprofitable*. And making big changes in the rules is the way to do it. Many of us are motivated by moral arguments, but that doesn't mean the decision-makers whose behavior we're trying to change will be compelled by morality. The system of rewards and punishments they operate within, which lets them get away with what they do, will not change simply because we prove that what they are doing is wrong. Ending the ability of politicians, corporations, and others to profit from injustice requires gaining the power to create serious consequences for profiteering while reducing the opportunities to do it.

The Most Obvious Profiteering

On January 20, 2025, a team of right-wing ideologues entered the White House and began handing their re-inaugurated boss a series of executive orders to sign. An executive order allows a president to instruct government agencies to conduct business in a particular way—enabling the president to dictate a wide range of government policies without needing to pass a law.

Seated at a large table as if ready to feast, with a pile of orders each bound in a leather case, Trump looked like he was surrounded by a stack of oversized Greek diner menus, the kind he probably held in his hands often while growing up in the Queens borough of New York City. Who was behind getting all of these orders ready for day one? Trump loved playing the "master," but it was hard to believe that he alone was also the "mind."

In fact, none of it was the result of a single mind at work. The pile of executive orders represented the collective will of a small but powerful group of people motivated by clear goals, ranging from ideological to financial. Many in that collective were people from right-wing policy circles whom the Heritage Foundation brought together to create Project 2025. But they also included businesspeople, politicians, church leaders, and media personalities who had long fought for conservative causes and saw that moment as their best chance to finally advance them by leaps and bounds. Every order was cashing in on the opportunity of this presidency.

The ceremonial signing of executive orders, and the many radical moves the administration enacted in the weeks and months that followed, served a purpose beyond their specific content. Trump and his team knew that they wanted to change the rules for how America worked, far beyond the typical changes that any new administration makes. They also knew that maintaining the power to do so required them to feed specific groups of people what they wanted—in fact, so much of what they wanted that they would not interfere with the larger project of Trump taking over everything else.

Every executive order served a purpose, appeasing a certain group:

- Feeding the populist appetite for seeing Trump do something radical and seemingly productive on issues like immigration.
- Feeding the bloodthirsty drive among his core supporters to destroy liberal causes, like racial equity, and stick it to the people those causes represent.
- Feeding self-serving corporate executives and wealthy individuals the profits they craved through deregulation and corrupt government contracts, people who would see Trump as their path to unearned, unlimited wealth, privilege, and total financial dominance over everyone else.
- Feeding both his political opposition and responsible news media outlets more than they could respond to effectively—to the point of paralysis.

The right people holding the right type of power could engineer the dismantling and reconstituting of our government, nearly overnight. One secret to gaining that power was ensuring that no one in the larger conservative coalition was in their way: They would be either overwhelmingly enraptured by the profits they could gain under the new regime or overwhelmingly threatened by the consequences (financial and otherwise) of not playing along.

Team Trump needed to signal to everyone in the world of business, media, religion, law, civil society, and mainstream conservative politics who might cause them problems that the occasional pain they might experience with such a radical reworking of America was nothing compared to the profits they would eventually be able to reap. Trump would give away anything if it meant getting praise and support in return.

For those who hoped to profit, every injustice and absurdity the administration was going to manufacture would present opportunities that would keep them very, very happy. Rich with money and resources. Rich with the power, privilege, and permission to do whatever they wanted. Rich with followers. Rich with rule changes that could create a new value system for America based on their extremist ideology.

As long as we allowed there to be rewards for injustice, there would be long lines of people ready to step up and claim them. Those people are called *profiteers*.

Cracking down on immigrants in vicious and unjust ways meant huge profits for contractors that build detention centers and for technology corporations that build weapons and surveillance. It also meant lucrative new enforcement jobs for right-wing vigilantes (granting legitimacy to their thirst for violence) and dramatic, high-traffic imagery and videos for media corporations to exploit.

Environmental deregulation, along with a host of grossly unfair advantages given to the fossil fuel industry, meant that renewable energy competitors would be driven out of business and dirty energy corporations would be able to continue profiting from pollution, price gouging, and every other wrong for which they had just started getting penalized under President Joe Biden.

Our confidential data held by the government was for sale. Our public property was for sale. The tax revenue we get from wealthy people would be taken out of our national budget and returned to them with a bonus. Our healthcare costs would spiral out of control. Our foreign policy would be warped to focus on real estate deals that enriched Trump's friends, and giveaways that won him favor with international leaders, rather than anything related to American security.

But raking in cash is just one form of profit. Canceling diversity, equity, and inclusion (DEI) policies meant that already privileged white men might no longer need to compete with qualified women and nonwhite people. They could get in the back door at colleges that might not otherwise accept them, get loans and contracts that might not otherwise go to them, and get jobs at workplaces that might not otherwise hire them. With no more DEI, those people would be free to practice discrimination against everyone else. Undeserved and unfair privilege, gained at the expense of others, helps certain people rise up in society—whether in status, access, authority, wealth, or all of the above. They profit from discrimination, which makes them profiteers, too.

The burdens of protecting us from collapsing bridges, polluted water, viral pandemics, social media emotional manipulation, cryptocurrency scams, unrestricted discrimination, and racist violence—all of these were going to shift dramatically. The responsibility would no longer fall on a strong government and regulated corporations but on our own largely defenseless selves. We'd be on our own. Not that the government was protecting us nearly enough—or that corporations were nearly regulated enough—beforehand. But it was going to get a lot worse. And it has.

Putting in place one set of rules for himself and his allies, and another set of rules for everyone else, represented the height of power Trump was aiming for. It's the definition of injustice and the foundation of profiteering.

Trump pardoned the violent right-wing rioters who had tried to stop the certification of the 2020 election, talking openly of revolution, attacking police, breaking into and ravaging the Capitol, and threatening to assault or kill members of Congress and his own vice president. But he harassed, attacked, and prosecuted peaceful protesters advocating for modest, legal changes in society, whose views he didn't like.

He authorized raids on certain factories in certain places, under the pretense of cracking down on workers without work permits, but not in the industries or states that would cause problems for his friends. He promoted people with no experience (many of whom were white) to positions of great power, while firing people who actually knew what they were doing (especially people of color). He canceled federal spending on lifesaving research and instead spent hundreds of billions of dollars on wasteful contracts and tax breaks for Elon Musk and a long line of other profiteers.

If there was a chance to make money or get ahead by squeezing American people in some way, that opportunity was open to the highest bidder or biggest Trump ass-kisser.

The big lie: Trump will run the country like a business and make it more efficient and fairer. The big truth: Trump is a vindictive, corrupt profiteer of the highest order. He and his administration are destroying many people's lives and destabilizing the very foundation of America in order to enable a very few people to profit.

Even in a short amount of time, the results have become very clear. The Trump family alone, just in the first seven months of his second term, made an estimated $3.4 billion for themselves through "five Persian Gulf mega-projects, a luxury jet from Qatar, a sprawling resort in Hanoi, half a dozen projects peddling crypto, and MAGA merch."[1] Supporters who buy all that merchandise often think they're contributing to a cause, but they are merely handing money over to Trump himself. Every single country Trump visited on his first trip outside the United States had Trump-branded projects in the works. In the first year of his second presidency, and perhaps for the first time in his life, Trump stopped talking about how rich he is—a strong sign he doesn't want anyone looking at what he and his family are doing.

The more profits there were to gain, the more people rushed to Trump's side. Even business leaders who had been Obama fans and were supporters of Kamala Harris (or at least stayed relatively neutral during the race) quickly changed their position and aligned their corporations to ally with Trump—especially the tech CEOs.

But it's not the Trump family, incarceration and military contractors like GEO Group and Palantir, and foreign governments alone that are exploiting the new Trump regime. It's also individuals, at every level. It's the head of a federal agency that could pump money into its own businesses, like major government contractor Elon Musk leading Trump's so-called Department of Government Efficiency (DOGE), or Chris Wright, former CEO of the fracking company Liberty Energy, leading the Department of Energy. It's a wealthy person getting a specialized tax break or getting a pass from the IRS on tax dodging. It's a middle manager freed up to hire their best friend and fire someone much more qualified who didn't look like them, or a business dumping pollution into a public water reservoir in order to save a buck. Everyone could cash in, one way or another.

Adding up the impact of canceling environmental protections and workplace standards, kicking people off health insurance and taking us back in time on vaccine and other health policies, and siphoning away billions from both research and aid related to urgent health crises, estimates place the expected Trump death toll in the many millions—including the mine workers Trump disingenuously championed during his campaign. All in service of fulfilling the wish list of corporations and right-wing ideologues.

Unlimited profit, no matter who pays the price, was the promise Trump made to the people he needed to fund his reelection campaign and to enable his hold on power. Profit for some in the form of money, next-level status, social media followers, or congregation sizes. For others, profit in the form of being in charge of big agencies and institutions, or gaining control over other people's lives and lifestyles. For still others, profit in the form of assets—such as land or classified secrets or our personal data—which lead to more money and more control. At the highest level, it is profit in the form of a permanent pardon of their worst behavior: being able to commit any crime or do any wrong, without any restraint or responsibility, no matter how many people got hurt.

If Trump could guarantee that promise to the right people, he could guarantee his own personal profits and his own political power, nearly forever. That is why Team Trump's first big step was to fire many of the top people who investigate corruption and hold people accountable for stealing government money: inspectors general, federal prosecutors, IRS agents.

That is also why they fired the people who investigate corporations and hold them accountable for cheating people and hurting people: the head of the Consumer Financial Protection Bureau, financial regulators at the Securities and Exchange Commission, and the head of the Federal Trade Commission.

In their place, and at the top of every other agency, they put corporate leaders in charge: people who would grant contracts or make rules related to their own corporations. They quickly took steps to prevent any oversight that would uncover all the ways they were stealing public money and resources for themselves.

While the Trump-invented DOGE initiative widely publicized its efforts as ending waste and fraud across the government (which, in reality, it completely failed to do), the real Trump legacy will be increasing waste, fraud, corruption, and abuse at the highest level imaginable.

It all started on Trump's Day One: January 20, 2025. But the plans had been in the works for years, before Trump was even on the political scene. He certainly didn't get there alone, nor would his presidency have looked the same without the influence of the particular forces in society he chose to align with to get there. The Heritage Foundation was planning for this. Many billionaire-backed conservative think tanks, corporate trade associations, politicians and political clubs, media influencers, religious leaders, and others were building toward this moment, too. They captured Trump, and Trump captured them.

While step one was transferring huge sums of wealth from millions of everyday people to a very few billionaires, Trump delivered for more than just billionaires. He gave people power who don't deserve it, putting them in positions to advance their ideological agendas. He made people famous who shouldn't be, giving them a platform to spread lies and promote violence. He gave people all over the globe access to sensitive information and technology—and it's still unclear how much of American security he undermined by doing that.

Power and Profiteering

There is another side to the story, however. The only reason Trump could make injustice so immensely profitable, and build an entire administration around doing so, was that he was not afraid of the opposition: us.

The power he was leveraging to change the rules, at the highest level, towered over the power of any of his opponents to foil his plans. Our challenge has been so difficult not only because we need to overcome Trump's political power, administrative power, and legal power (the latter granted by having a Republican-controlled Congress and a conservative Supreme Court at his side) **but also because we must reverse the fortunes of all those who are profiting from Trump and don't want to give up those profits.**

We're facing the challenge of overturning the deeply rooted interests of profiteering in America. Long before Trump took office, that has been the challenge for those of us who care about justice, equality, and safety. Of course, the mechanics of power are hazy by design—people in power benefit from everyone else not knowing how those mechanics really work. That's why winning requires us to think about power at a much deeper level—and it requires us to question our assumptions about what it takes to win.

For instance, public opinion doesn't have the effect we often think it does. Constantly, advocates for different causes talk about how "most people support the right to have an abortion," or "most people want safe water and air," or "most people don't want the police to harass them," or "most people don't want to let everyone have guns everywhere all the time." The people who say these things build campaigns on the assumption that they have the wind at their back, and just getting people to vocalize their majority opinion will force politicians to change their votes. But politicians have no incentive to act according to public opinion—especially now, when right-wing media outlets can make public opinion seem like it's whatever they want it to be, giving those politicians even more cover to ignore people's actual beliefs and desires. In fact, one definition of the authoritarianism that Trump's government increasingly represents could simply be: making decisions without any concern for public opinion at all.

By basing their strategies on public opinion statistics, advocates overlook the role of power in making political change, as well as the entrenched nature of profiteering's grip on the rules we live by. As a result, they often express surprise when we do not get the public policies that reflect the majority's preferences. And they leave their supporters surprised, having told them that they were in the right and that what's right would inevitably win out.

Social change isn't about people's preferences. It's about profits. Winning social change is not merely about winning in the opinion polls, getting record attendance at a march, or writing a public policy research paper that proves our ideas are right. It certainly helps to have majorities of people who believe in a cause and are ready to act in ways that generate the power needed to make change. But minority opinions with a power analysis behind them can often go further than majority opinions without one.

Social change happens only when it is no longer profitable to keep the status quo in place. If we make injustice unprofitable, we can change the rules that allow it to continue. Several big changes illustrate this point: Across the country, we created consequences too great to bear for politicians who had been continually denying the right of gay and lesbian people to marry. California created consequences too great to bear for corporations that would have otherwise been happy to pollute. Black people and all of our allies in criminal justice reform created consequences for prosecutors who set the goal of incarcerating as many people as possible—ultimately kicking several of them out of office.

Winning means gaining more power than the people who currently control the rules, in order to be able to change those rules. We can make issues popular and represent the preferences of the majority and still lose. We can operate under the radar and win. The tactics for winning social change can vary, but the goal is always the same: making it unprofitable for people in power to permit or exploit injustice. ("Unprofitable" in the way I defined it above: creating a cost too great to bear, whether it's a cost related to finances, reputation, privileges, or anything else.)

Injustice is big business, and it has enormously diverse revenue streams. It is part of the magical thinking of our movements to assume that if we simply prove that most people agree with us, an imaginary referee will step in and declare us the winner. That is not how it works.

(And racial profiteering has always been especially formidable and durable in America, across every domain of society.)[2]

It's helpful to think about injustice as a product, not a by-product. It's *the* product. And those who manufacture it can make a lot of money by selling it. Those who sell the injustice of hunting down immigrants, not unlike the depraved slave catchers of the 1800s, can make a lot of money. And that is what they are doing right now. They depend on injustice for profit.

We may feel this is unacceptable, but our feelings will not stop it. One of the biggest, most impactful rule changes we can ever win is a rule that makes profiteering not okay at both a social level and a legal enforcement level, with real consequences for violators and with millions of people ready to stand up and defend that rule so effectively that no one can undermine it. As long as profiteering is okay, our communities will not be.

Holding Profiteers Accountable: The Case of ALEC

As I demonstrated in chapter 2 in the case of the Heritage Foundation, right-wing profiteering depends on gaining power, and gaining power depends on building strong infrastructure—systems, assets, relationship networks, and organizations. Ending profiteering often requires taking on that infrastructure, either weakening it or becoming more powerful than it.

Long before Trump, but even more so during his time in politics, the right wing has invested greatly in infrastructure. Outside of the Republican Party itself, the most well-known infrastructure helping the right wing win is in the realm of media: Rupert Murdoch and Fox News, Elon Musk and X (formerly Twitter), conservative Christian churches and their media networks, Rush Limbaugh (and his dozens of online imitators today), small but influential channels like Newsmax and Sinclair stations, websites like Breitbart and relative newcomers like Larry Ellison. Right-wing forces have also freely exploited platforms like Meta and Google/YouTube—ultimately getting their CEOs to bend to their will. A lesser-known but influential media platform for recruiting young people to the right wing is PragerU, which, since its founding in 2009, has been infiltrating school systems with conservative video content—a process the Trump administration is now enabling it to accelerate.[3]

These media corporations are in it for the long game. They may even take on financial losses up front, knowing how much they can make on the back end in terms of tax breaks, policy changes, and other benefits when their media influence achieves its goals.

But it takes a lot more infrastructure than that: lobbying, leadership development and talent pipelines, election coordination, policy development, content and message development, donor networks, grassroots organizing (mobilizing everyday people), grasstops organizing (mobilizing elites and people in authority), social platforms (forming relationships and circulating persuasive content by means of anything from dating apps to in-person social clubs to niche social media channels), and so on. They all reinforce one another, and depend on one another, too. For instance, PragerU is part of the media infrastructure, but it requires political and advocacy infrastructure to get its content into the school system. The following are some other examples of right-wing infrastructure:

- **Insider think tank, legal, and advocacy organizations focused on developing policies and strategies that either bring right-wing people into power or help them use their power once they gain it.** These include the Heritage Foundation, the Federalist Society, the National Rifle Association (NRA), the American Israel Public Affairs Committee (AIPAC), Alliance Defending Freedom, the Institute for Justice, Americans for Prosperity, the Judicial Crisis Network, the Marble Freedom Trust, the America First Policy Institute, and the Conservative Partnership Institute.
- **Donor networks and committed-at-all-costs individual donors ready to spend millions to advance right-wing causes.** These include the Rockbridge Network (co-founded by J. D. Vance and backed by Silicon Valley investors), the Na-

tional Christian Foundation, the Donors Capital Fund, the Koch network (headed by Charles Koch), the Council for National Policy, the Lynde and Harry Bradley Foundation, Leonard Leo, Miriam Adelson, and Robert Mercer and his daughter Rebekah Mercer.

- **Political forces working at the state level.** These include the State Policy Network, the Republican State Leadership Committee, the Rule of Law Defense Fund, and the State Financial Officers Foundation.
- **Organizing and talent pipelines.** These include Turning Point USA, the Leadership Institute, American Moment, and the Teneo Network.

Every day, it seems like a billionaire (e.g., the hedge fund manager Bill Ackman) or an ideologue on a mission (e.g., the anti-affirmative-action activist Edward Blum) establishes a new initiative or organization that only adds to the right wing's infrastructure of power. The money of those individuals can attack long-standing laws and principles that people fought tirelessly to establish—often paying for them with their lives. As part of the larger power network, they can do even more damage than they can by working alone.

I once tangled with one of these organizations. Understanding how profiteering worked was instrumental to undermining its power and reducing the harm it caused.

The American Legislative Exchange Council (ALEC) is a right-wing policy shop co-founded by the conservative activist Paul Weyrich in 1973, the same year he co-founded the Heritage Foundation. ALEC's enduring goal is to make America a fundamentally conservative nation in every realm of public policy. While the Heritage Foundation pulled together a coalition of people and organizations to produce Project 2025 as a master plan for the Trump presidency, ALEC has been working in parallel at the state level for decades.

Almost entirely outside of public view, ALEC writes right-wing legislation in a fully ready-to-adopt format, and then trains its network of Republican state legislator members to push it through state legislatures across the country. Whenever we see right-wing laws being passed in multiple states at the same time, often sharing the exact same language, it's usually because ALEC is coordinating a campaign to do so behind the scenes. Voter suppression. Environmental deregulation. Life sentences for nonviolent crimes. Incentives for private prisons. Shielding corporations from lawsuits. You name it. The laws arising from ALEC's campaigns enable corporations and right-wing politicians to profit from injustice.

By the early 2010s, ALEC had helped pass so-called Stand Your Ground laws across the country, using the template legislation successfully advanced by the NRA in Florida in 2005. The legislation shifted the legal standard related to gun violence: Instead of gun users having the legal responsibility to retreat from a conflict if they are able to do so, they can kill people at will as long as they claim they feel threatened, no matter the situation and whether or not deadly force is necessary. Of course, these laws encourage vigilante violence and embolden gun users to believe they can kill people without consequence—because they can. And that's exactly the future that the biggest supporter of these laws, the leadership of the NRA, wants for our country. The NRA is one of the most active members of ALEC, using ALEC's extensive political infrastructure to advance its agenda.

In Sanford, Florida, in February 2012, that Stand Your Ground mentality was in effect when George Zimmerman stalked, confronted, and ultimately killed the newly seventeen-year-old Trayvon Martin, who was walking through the neighborhood of his father's fiancée on the way back to her house. He had been picking up some candy at a nearby convenience store.

I had been running Color Of Change for barely one year when this happened, and it was clear that we were going to need to help our members respond in a way that was both meaningful and powerful.

The horror of this crime was made worse when it became clear that law enforcement could and would do nothing to bring George Zimmerman to justice because his claim of self-defense invoked Florida's Stand Your Ground law. Though Zimmerman was finally brought to trial the following year, he was acquitted.

No matter how many times I have thought about Trayvon, and no matter how many times I have imagined what happened when that man hunted him down, every time I step back into that moment I am left haunted. Just as many other Black people are, in ways that many non-Black people still do not fully appreciate. The way that Ava DuVernay brought this moment to life in her 2023 film, *Origin*, is even more chilling, and certainly helps viewers come closer to understanding what our children face.

Stand Your Ground laws had always been unevenly implemented. The laws' roots trace back to the period following the Civil War, when laws were passed in the United States to legalize the murder of Black people by white men, in particular, under the ruse of self-defense. Back then, the laws relied on what was referred to as the "true man" principle, invoking the idea that a "true man" would not retreat from a potential threat. Of course, it never worked the other way around: a Black person acting in self-defense was usually charged with murder. ALEC continued this tradition.

The killing of Trayvon by a vigilante allowed us to put ALEC on the map for our members at Color Of Change. But it took work to connect the dots, given how the organization had been operating underground—by design. Our members intuitively understood that this killing of a young Black teen was not a one-off incident, but rather part of a pattern of anti-Black violence in America. But what wasn't clear at all was that it was the result of a coordinated campaign by the NRA and white nationalists, made possible to scale across the country by ALEC, to arm and amp up racist vigilantes (who were excellent gun customers) and then protect them from legal accountability.

We told a story that connected the dots between the killing of Trayvon Martin (which was highly visible and emotional) and ALEC (which was behind the scenes and technical, but tangible). Millions of people across the country had been activated, and they were ready to do something about those who had played any role in the killing—or were playing a role in enabling such killings to keep happening.

This is exactly the moment when the ideas of presence, power, and profiteering all converged in one story—and one strategy. How were we going to convert presence (the widespread awareness of Trayvon's killing) into the power it would take to stop the kind of profiteering that led to his death? Advocates had taken on ALEC before, and had taken on Stand Your Ground legislation before, both without success. How could we do something different this time and win?

We could mobilize people to demand justice in Florida, but we weren't going to change how Florida worked. And we could rally people to challenge the NRA, but the NRA stood on a financial, political, and social foundation that was hard to shake. We saw only one real opportunity in our power analysis: We could take on ALEC with a new level of leverage, in order to prevent these and many other ALEC laws that harmed Black people from spreading further.

Once our members saw the effect ALEC was having in the world when it came to anti-Black violence, we could bring them into the work we were already doing to stop the targeted, anti-Black voter suppression laws that ALEC was effectively moving through state legislatures at the same time. The work to stop ALEC's voter suppression campaign—laws to implement voter ID requirements, prevent formerly incarcerated people from voting, purge voters from the voter rolls, and more—had hit a wall. Even though we knew these laws were designed to reduce the participation of voters who voted against conservatives, that immoral fact wasn't enough.

With new energy and a new surge of people involved, I believed a new level of accountability could be possible. But that accountability wouldn't be the result of merely getting ALEC exposed in the news or getting crowds of protesters to chant its name. In the midst of all the public furor related to Trayvon, we needed to take the first rule of social change to heart: Focus less on the big presence our issue was achieving, and focus more on the way to achieve real power relative to our target.

Point and Pivot

We made a key strategic shift. We realized that we could never make right-wing politics unprofitable for a right-wing policy shop. That's what some progressive organizations concerned about ALEC had been trying to do for quite a while, and it wasn't working. But we could make supporting a right-wing policy shop unprofitable for its corporate funders. We shifted our emphasis to where we had leverage.

We found out from Lisa Graves and her team at the Center for Media and Democracy that 98 percent of ALEC's funding (and therefore a big source of its power in the realm of state policy) likely came from its corporate sponsors—Coca-Cola, Kraft, State Farm, AT&T, UPS, all the pharmaceutical corporations, and dozens more household name brands. That enabled us to see a viable path to accountability.

Instead of merely pointing at ALEC's wrongdoing, we pivoted to target the corporations that made it possible. Corporations made ALEC what it was: By funding most of its budget, they enabled the harmful role it played in the world. At the same time, dozens of those same corporations depended on Black consumers for their own revenue.

In the same way corporate leaders have aligned with Trump (even those that had previously supported Democrats), corporations fund ALEC to get specific policy outcomes that generate more profit for them. They look the other way when it comes to anything else ALEC is doing—regardless of who is getting hurt. Our challenge back then was to make corporations lose more by supporting ALEC than whatever profit they gained from it. We had to make it unprofitable for them.

Which would they choose: profiting from ALEC's unjust policies or profiting from keeping their Black customers? The moral argument wouldn't work, but the business argument might. As we shifted focus to holding corporations accountable for spending their money with ALEC, I would often say: *You can't take Black people's money by day, and then take away our freedom to vote and our freedom to be safe by night. You can't host a Black History Month celebration and then play an instrumental role in harming Black futures.*

We were clear about how to engage them. If we launched a public campaign and got into a public fight from the get-go, we would not be able to negotiate—there would be nothing for us to give up in a negotiation. But in private conversations, we could show them how we would create consequences for them, showing what our campaign would look like (its message, its reach, its influence on people), and demonstrating our ability to rally our members and create a media storm they would not survive unscathed. Showing what a force our members could be, and how motivated they were, also gave people who agreed with us on the inside of these corporations new leverage for influencing the decision-makers they worked with every day.

We gave them the chance to do the right thing, and to gain something by leaving ALEC rather than losing something by staying. I remember very clearly being on the phone with some of these corporate executives, telling them how outraged it would make our members if they found out that a brand they routinely buy (like Kraft cheese for making mac and cheese) was pumping money into the organization that led to Trayvon's death and was now trying to suppress our votes.

They would often connect me with their highest Black executive (who wasn't always too high up) to try to talk me down and show me they loved Black people. But I made clear that there was only one way to show they cared about Black people in that moment: leaving ALEC. Balancing behind-the-scenes and out-in-public tactics was always essential in clarifying the stakes for decision-makers. That's true whether you are trying to push Coca-Cola to do the right thing, or push your local principal, business owner, or boss at work to do the right thing.

My team and I also knew that spotlighting a few key brands at first was critical: Once the corporations most concerned about their reputation with Black consumers committed to leaving ALEC, we could leverage that with others to create a domino effect. As certain brands like Coca-Cola made very public exits, the situation became even more potentially unprofitable for those that hadn't. Most did not stick around to find out how hard those consequences would hit them. As a result of our campaign and its ripple effects, with other organizations jumping in, too, more than a hundred major brands left ALEC. Many of them were eager to make sure we were the first call they made to share the news they were leaving.

For a time, we changed the rules that determined what crossed the line for corporations in terms of the political organizations they supported. It was the first real defeat for ALEC in decades, the first pressure it felt, and the first consequences it faced for all of its bad behavior.

Eventually, of course, corporations crawled back to ALEC. Eventually, ALEC's voter suppression work spun back up. The corporations were seeking profits through what they could achieve with ALEC, and that outweighed the losses they might face for funding an organization promoting voter suppression. We had created a rule and forced powerful organizations to play by it, but we didn't have the dedicated infrastructure or the means to adapt to ALEC's evolving power strategies to make that rule permanent.

Racial Justice as a Strategy

Color Of Change was founded in 2005 because no one was nervous about disappointing Black people, even in the dire moment of Hurricane Katrina. By 2012, we had made some corporations nervous about disappointing Black people, so much so that they took the actions necessary to stand with us (or at least not stand against us).

Even more so, we had made it clear how racial justice could break through in a way that other approaches to taking on ALEC couldn't. During that time, I worked closely with the "pro-democracy" crowd of progressive, mostly white organizational leaders who had been alarmed about ALEC's role in attacking election reform and campaign finance reform but had not been able to create a way to stop them.

Many of them saw Black people as beneficiaries of the noble work they were doing, but not drivers of it. And they acted accordingly. They didn't realize that they had benched their best players: Black leaders and communities across the country who weren't just foot soldiers in the fight over voting rights but had strategic ideas about how to gain power and how to take power away from ALEC and reduce its influence—that would prove crucial to winning accountability.

I faced a similar challenge during the fight to win the policy of net neutrality during the Obama administration, a policy that would ensure corporations could not create a pay-to-play scheme for the internet, slowing down access to independent websites in favor of speeding up access to sites they controlled—and from which they profited. Many of the white advocates who focused on these types of policies, which determined how the internet was regulated, treated race as a side issue—one that would only prevent them from creating a more "universal" coalition needed to win the policy fight. But as the leader of Color Of Change, which not only cared about racial justice and tech policy but also saw the connection between them, I took a different approach.

It turned out that framing net neutrality as a policy that would ensure Black people could freely use the internet to connect and organize was what secured the votes necessary to win—peeling key members of Congress away from aligning with the telecom industry's interests. Putting race at the forefront was good strategy.

In particular, the legendary congressman John Lewis saw the connection. He began to talk about the value an open internet would have had for him as a young activist helping to build the Civil Rights Movement, and how important it would be to protect it. That helped neutralize prominent Black voices the telecom corporations were depending on for support.

Racial justice has a special role to play in any challenge to profiteering, especially given the two deepest roots of profiteering in America: the mass theft of Indigenous land and genocide of Indigenous people, and the establishment of slavery and genocide of African people. Black people are still the target, or at least the collateral damage, for some of the worst profiteering there is. And yet Black people also have one of the longest histories of fighting back, changing rules, and taking on profiteers as successfully as any group ever has.

It is not easy to take on profiteering: Corporations that hurt people, directly or indirectly, usually have a lot at stake in continuing those practices. It's too much to give up, unless we consistently make them pay a price for it. After the violence of January 6, 2021, many corporations said they would no longer support politicians who participated in or supported the attack on the Capitol. A new rule or just new rhetoric? Their commitment didn't last long: We were not able to make it unprofitable for them to break that commitment, so most corporations resumed their donations to those politicians within months.

Not even one year before that, corporations made endless commitments to address the racism running rampant within their organizations and at the core of much of the way they do business. A new rule. It lasted long enough for some real changes to take place. But as soon as it became unprofitable for them to follow that rule—whether due to the cost of what it takes to make real change or due to the punishment they would later face from the Trump administration—they quickly broke it. And again, we have not been able to create consequences for either their backtracking on racial justice or their support for Team Trump's most harmful actions.

One reason is that we are in a constant battle of perception about the nature of injustice itself: whether people's suffering is seen as an injustice manufactured by people for some form of profit, or whether it is seen as a reality that is simply the natural order of things. It makes all the difference when it comes to whether people accept the rules that produce suffering or rise up to change them.

FIND YOUR POWER

Seeing Racial Justice as a Strategy

This activity is meant to help you see the ways in which racial justice is not just an outcome of fights for social change, but an essential strategy for pursuing and winning them.

Since 2020, tens of millions of people have leapt forward in their awareness of anti-Black racism and the dangerous role it plays in the life of our country, from healthcare to job discrimination to policing and the justice system. They have become aware of the effects of both individual and structural racism in terms of the toll it takes on Black lives, as well as how it functions to cover up and enable injustices in society overall—affecting everyone. Racial justice now ranks among the big changes many people want to see (or even help fight for) in our country and in our world.

Yet, most people who have experienced this new consciousness still think about racism as an outcome: where we are trying to go, not how we get there. The idea of racial justice as a strategy still lags far behind in acceptance, including among people leading social change efforts. In fact, many people who sign on to the idea of racial justice still don't like talking about race at all. They don't think about race as an entry point to issues like democracy, the environment, the economy, or healthcare. They want to talk about those ideas in a "neutral, universal" way, without "making it about race," because they believe that if we win on those issues then racial justice will follow. In my experience, there are many cases (such as the cases of ALEC and net neutrality) that prove the exact opposite: If we get racial justice and other forms of justice right, then progress on the larger issues becomes possible in a way it wasn't before.

These are three questions to ask, which can help determine whether leveraging the power of racial justice as a strategy may, in fact, prove more effective than other strategies:

1. Will leading with issues of race bring a constituency into the fight that may have more leverage with people in power than the people who would become the face of the issue if race is downplayed or ignored? For instance, does a corporation see the need to respond to charges of abusing Black workers more than charges of abusing workers in general, for fear of the legal consequences?
2. Will implementing solutions focused on the standard of eliminating adverse racial impact set the highest standard for justice, across all affected people? For instance, is the standard of eliminating environmental racism the best standard for reining in the worst practices of polluters and other abuses of our environment?
3. Are there key people who can influence decision-makers and the overall outcome on an issue who see themselves as representative of a racial group and will feel more motivated and obliged to intervene to help accelerate change if the fate of that group is at stake—for example, choosing to side with advocates of change instead of a corporation whose influence might otherwise sway them.

What does this mean for people organizing to make change?

Sometimes, a group led by mostly white advocates,

working on an issue they associate with being interesting to mostly white people, will assume that the main relationships they need to forge in order to win policy change are relationships with elected leaders and officials whose support could translate into support for new laws and regulations. But in many cases, the relationships they may better focus on first are relationships with nonwhite community organizations and leaders who will be able to lead a different kind of strategy—better understanding the power dynamics, bringing many more people into the cause, creating stronger leverage, and being able to get decision-makers to make different decisions than they otherwise would.

4

Perceptions Define Solutions

DEFINITION: Perception is how people understand a given reality. The way people perceive reality either leads them to accept it or motivates them to take action to change it.

CHALLENGE: It is difficult to motivate people to fight an injustice if they don't perceive it as an injustice—if they perceive it only as an unfortunate but acceptable part of life. Those who profit from harming others invest a lot in managing our perceptions, knowing that it can influence whether people accept or oppose those harms. Overcoming their influence over people's perceptions is challenging but often necessary in order to win.

The Battle of Perception: Unfortunate Versus Unjust

In January 2025, I read an article about the Los Angeles County wildfires devastating the area at the time. It said they would likely turn out to be the costliest "natural disaster" in American history. Seeing that headline, I felt a hard punch.

Calling disasters "natural" never felt right to me. Destructive wildfires. Overwhelming floods. Havoc-wreaking storms. They all have something to do with nature, but that doesn't make them natural. As we know from Katrina, there is a distinctly human hand behind many of the disasters that we are told to call "natural."

The choices our leaders make often determine how much or how little we prepare for disasters (or try to prevent them), how we do or don't respond to them, and therefore how much damage they do. People in positions of power all across society choose to ignore and accelerate climate change, which has made floods and fires much more frequent and destructive. Untamed and unmaintained power lines often spark fires that affect hundreds of thousands of people. If we do not create consequences for people in power whose decisions lead to disaster, why would they act any differently? People are not always motivated by what's best for others. They are mostly motivated by the rules—the system of rewards and punishments—they're operating in.

In just two weeks in early 2025, fires in and around Los Angeles destroyed more than twelve thousand homes and entire communities, including the historic Black middle-class community of Altadena. It took generations of hope, sweat, and struggle to build that community, which started as a landing place for people excluded by the racial redlining in nearby Pasadena. It took only days to destroy its homes and landscape—and deeply damage that hope. But under the embers and rubble was another truth: People made decisions that enabled those fires to get out of hand, and they abandoned those communities once they were torched. Leaders at the electric utility that defied warnings (a pattern for Pacific Gas & Electric).[1] The new federal administration that defied its responsibility to its citizens. According to *Politico,* "Former White House advisers said Trump hesitated as president to provide disaster aid to California because of the state's Democratic leanings."[2]

It had been nearly twenty years since Hurricane Katrina destroyed thousands of lives and brought Color Of Change into being. In January 2025, I had just left Color Of Change after nearly fourteen years of leading and building it. Had anything changed in the perception of what causes these disasters and who is responsible?

Back in 2005, Katrina was talked about as being the costliest "natural disaster" in American history. In Louisiana, especially in New Orleans, it was largely Black communities that would be forced to pay those costs. The people responsible for letting Katrina get so far out of hand would bear no responsibility at all. Was it all playing out much the same in Los Angeles? Rich and poor communities, and communities of all backgrounds, were paying the price in L.A. But they would not all pay *the same* price—it would not play out evenly. Were we supposed to believe that disparity was "natural," too?

I actually like nature a lot. I love the beach. I love the food that comes from my mom's garden. I do not believe that nature has it in for Black people. Whenever we fall for the story that an injustice is part of the natural order of things, we are less likely to confront the people who actually cause it. That's why they keep using the term *natural disaster.*

Time and again, people who benefit from the way things are use the idea of "nature" and "natural" to explain away the injustices that they themselves create and perpetuate. It's a story that lets them off the hook.

Black people are naturally inferior, they say, *so however corporations, police, and politicians exploit them is their own damn fault.*

Being gay is unnatural, they say, *so however churches, schools, or corporations discriminate against them is exactly what they deserve.*

Women are weak, they say, *so it's natural for men to push them out of the way because men are strong.*

And the people who benefit from all of this discrimination? *Well,* they say, *that's natural, too.* These are powerful stories that people invent to convince others—as well as themselves—that certain so-called realities are unfortunate but not unjust.

That's the connection between perception and power. What's the logical conclusion of thinking that a bad situation is unfortunate rather than unjust? The conclusion is to give up on the fight for changing the systems that produce that condition, and to let the people in charge reproduce it over and over, no matter who gets hurt. The status quo wins with that story: *What people are going through may be sad, but what can you do?* When something is unfortunate, we blame life—fate, nature, the world. When something is unjust, we blame people. Profiteers never want to be blamed. Irresponsible leaders who make bad decisions never want to be blamed. They care about perception. They invest in managing it.

"Unfortunate" realities lead to charitable solutions: consolation prizes for victims of injustice rather than solutions that prevent those injustices from happening and give people the restitution they deserve for experiencing them. And that lets people who cause those injustices off the hook.

They might persuade us to think, for instance, that sending water bottles to Flint, Jackson, Cleveland, Detroit, or any other city with high levels of lead in its drinking water will solve the problem caused by the governments and corporations that enabled the poisoning of people in those cities. But water bottles are *charity*. Replacing lead pipes and compensating people for the injuries they suffered is *justice*. The part of President Biden's 2021 Infrastructure Investment and Jobs Act related to clean drinking water was an act of justice: It forced local governments to replace lead pipes and stop poisoning their own people. That is, of course, one of the federal mandates and allocations of money Trump and congressional Republicans have tried to cancel.

We cannot progress as a society and improve our lives if we invest only in charitable solutions to structural problems. Nothing is wrong with charity inherently. Helping people in need is a good thing. But when it serves the purpose of letting injustices persist, we need to question the people who are telling us that charity should be our only focus. And one of their biggest tools for misdirecting us is controlling our perception: making us think the problem is merely unfortunate and not unjust. When we believe in "unfortunate realities," we get reentry programs to support people leaving prison instead of reducing the unjust policies and practices that put them in prison in the first place. We get celebrity concerts after the hurricane has already hit and wrecked people's lives instead of levees that could have prevented disaster. Charity is just a consolation prize. We are being trained to think we need to live with injustices rather than believing we can eliminate them. We are being duped into thinking people are victims of life itself rather than victims of people in power.

On a related note, if we demand that bad actors simply apologize for the harm they cause, rather than change the practices that led to that harm, we've internalized perceptions exactly as they want us to. (For more on using apologies to stop perpetrators of injustice, rather than allowing them to use apologies to continue profiting from them, see the online Appendix at rashadrobinson.com/book.)

In July 2025, seven months after the Los Angeles County wildfires, flash floods in Kerr County, Texas, hit a string of riverside summer camps and killed more than a hundred people (more than thirty of whom were children), while causing a lot of damage and pain. It was all "thoughts and prayers" from Governor Greg Abbott. Back when Abbott took office in 2015, however, local officials in Kerr County started petitioning for funds to replace their outdated early-warning system for floods. They never stopped asking for those funds, and Abbott never stopped denying them.[3] When the floods came, everyone responsible played the same old game: *Blame nature for something so unfortunate; don't look at the decisions we made that were so unjust—and deadly.* The governor's power to control the rules for dealing with disasters was directly related to his ability to control how people perceive them.

It's hard to look around today and not feel like we're losing the struggle for justice. But fighting for justice isn't a fight with nature. It's a struggle with people. And a struggle with people is always a struggle we can win—with the right strategy and the right infrastructure backing up that strategy. It's a commitment to become powerful enough to challenge the people who thrive from creating injustice, and to prevent them from being able to do whatever they want no matter who gets hurt. It's the power to create consequences for harmful decisions.

It starts with understanding the perceptions that can motivate people to action, and preventing perceptions that breed inaction,

defeatism, and misplaced blame from taking hold. That's why the distinction between *unfortunate* and *unjust* is so important.

As the events played out, I could not shake the comparison between the floods of 2005 in New Orleans and the fires and floods of 2025 in Altadena and Kerr County—not to mention all the disasters in between. What power did any of us have, individually or collectively, to prevent such bad decisions and the disasters they lead to? What power did we have to make sure disaster recoveries no longer left out Black communities or other people whom corporations and politicians have a habit of leaving out—in service of making sure their friends can siphon off billions in disaster recovery funds for themselves? Twenty years later, did we have enough power to control the rules for how disasters worked?

Maybe not, but there were important differences. In 2025, with Trump taking office again, we were generally moving backward. But after years of educating people about structural racism, building tools for accountability related to it, and changing some of the value systems that govern how California responds to community needs, were we moving forward in any ways at all?

The perception of who and what is to blame, and what is an unjust outcome versus an unfortunate one, was very different in 2025. We didn't see the type of blame-the-victim narratives take hold in the way most news media covered what was happening to Black people in Altadena as a result of the fires. We didn't see state authorities criminalize people desperately trying to survive—let alone give orders to shoot them. We did see a lot more coverage and concern for the role corporations may have played in contributing to the wildfires and the role the government played in letting them get out of control. (Of course, the fact that criticism of the local government was much more forthcoming during the fires in L.A., when a Black woman mayor was in charge, may say just as much about how far we've come as it does about how far we have to go.)

Importantly, however, we also saw more public attention paid to how the history of unchecked corporate-led and government-enabled redlining and bluelining set up Black people in Altadena to experience more pain and negative impact from disasters than others—and, in general, more attention paid by news media, academics, advocates, and others to racial disparities in both the response and the subsequent recovery. Outside of the right-wing media ecosystem, we heard a lot about the injustices at play instead of merely hearing the events cast as unfortunate.

That was presence: the visibility of a different value system and a genuine change in how people perceived what was happening, as well as the pressure that change put on decision-makers across government, media, and elsewhere to be on good behavior and tell more accurate stories. But that wasn't the real test of the commitment to equality and racial justice.

When it came to the power required to determine what the rules of recovery would be for Altadena compared to other places, there was not nearly as much progress. Years of unequal treatment by insurance corporations making coverage less available, and by government officials withholding resources for preparedness infrastructure, left the people of Altadena at a structural disadvantage before the fires sparked. One typical sign of that injustice: Billionaire Rick Caruso could hire private firefighters to protect his own shopping center while leaving everyone else to deal with the largely inadequate public infrastructure of response and recovery created by public policies advanced by billionaires.

It would therefore take a highly proactive approach to equalize outcomes for recovery. But we have not yet seen presence translate into the power to change the rules at that level.[4] And, as one report uncovered, profiteering seems alive and well: In Altadena, "nearly 70% of severely damaged homes show no observable action toward recovery. . . . In addition, investors have purchased two-thirds of the homes that have changed hands, raising concerns about displacement and affordability."[5]

Perception is powerful. Even when there is more recognition than ever about racial injustice, and how that plays out during a crisis like the wildfires, the ability to accept unequal outcomes as an unfortunate part of life can lead to sympathy and charity in place of making the changes that would deliver the justice people need and deserve. People being motivated not only by seeing a problem as unjust rather than unfortunate, but also by believing they can join with others to do something about it, is critical in determining what changes are possible. While opinions may reflect general attitudes, it's perceptions that drive behavior. That's why capturing perception is so important for any movement, right or left: It's what makes people align with a cause and it's what drives them to act in service of it.

Profiteering Relies on Perception to Survive

The business investor Devon Archer defrauded a Native American tribe (the Oglala Sioux Nation) and several pension funds. The founder of an electric truck company, Trevor Milton, defrauded his own shareholders. But within two months of taking office in 2025, Trump pardoned them. Before the end of that same year, they were each let off the hook by Trump's Securities and Exchange Commission, which dropped all efforts to force them to pay their penalties.

By court order, Devon Archer and Trevor Milton were, in sum, slated to pay hundreds of millions of dollars in restitution to their victims for the many crimes they committed. But aside from some legal fees and time spent in a legal process they eventually undermined, they got away with all of it. Stealing from people in the way those two men did is now partially legal. That's due to an unwritten rule: Loyalty to Trump allows certain criminals to get away with almost anything they want to do. There are dozens of Archers and Miltons wreaking havoc on people, and they grow in number every day that Trump remains president.

In addition to ceasing investigations against alleged perpetrators of major financial crimes, he has pardoned those already convicted, shielding them from having to pay millions that the courts determined they owed for their crimes: David Gentile (fraud), Changpeng Zhao (money laundering), Juan Orlando Hernández (drug lord), Ross Ulbricht (money laundering), Paul Walczak (tax cheating), Marian Morgan (fraud), Henry Cuellar (bribery), and the list goes on.

All the victims of these crimes, who were set to get back some degree of money that was stolen from them, have been left out to dry. Now they get nothing. Trump sold them out for his own personal gain: loyalty, favors, business deals, and who knows what else. Together, victims of the people Trump pardoned have been cheated out of more than a billion dollars in payments that had been awarded to them.[6]

This is more than corruption being normalized. It goes deeper than that. At the heart of it is a change in perception. The politicians, journalists, government officials, members of professional associations, everyday voters, and others who could intervene to prevent this kind of corruption from running rampant have changed their perspective in two ways.

First, for some, profiteers who are allies of Trump are now perceived as protected people, much like someone in the mafia is regarded as a protected person. If a prosecutor or regulator goes after them, they are essentially going after Trump. And that comes with consequences. At best, you could get reassigned or fired. At worst, Trump's government (and followers) could turn around and come after you. It's risky. The cost of doing one's job has skyrocketed, beyond what most can afford. That shift in perception turns an injustice that can and should be stopped into an "unfortunate reality" of the new normal. A president associating with criminals was once perceived as a liability. Now criminals associating with a president is perceived as an asset, and everyone acts accordingly.

Second, and increasingly prevalent, these profiteers, rather than the people they hurt, are perceived to be the real victims. Archer, Milton, and others like them claim to be victims of government regulation, victims of an anti-business climate, or victims of the previous administration (that is, unfairly targeted by Biden's Justice Department). Trump's White House spokespeople rationalize the pardons by making those very claims in their defense. They should be celebrated, the argument goes, not punished. In this perception, government interference is the real injustice, while damage caused to defrauded people is merely the "unfortunate cost" of having entrepreneurs in our society.

Accused of stealing millions? That's "unjust persecution." Accused of stealing a backpack, like sixteen-year-old Kalief Browder? That's the "real threat to society" and someone like that should go to jail and die. (Browder was arrested in 2010 and held at the Riker's Island jail in New York City, without trial, for three years, during which time he maintained his innocence. He spent almost eight hundred days in solitary confinement. Two years after his release, he committed suicide.)

Just as many believe the increasing numbers of gun deaths (accidents, murders, and suicides) in the United States are the regrettable but necessary cost of Second Amendment freedoms, an increasing number of people on the right wing believe that people being scammed or defrauded is simply the cost of businesspeople doing their thing. They claim that we need businesspeople to be free in order for America to be free, and restraining them or holding them accountable would be anti-American. That's another change in perception that MAGA world has successfully brought about: The suffering may be unfortunate, Trump's followers say, but it is not unjust. In fact, it's what freedom is all about. And of course, all of this is self-serving: Trump making fraud into a heroic act helps excuse his own crimes, influencing people to perceive the prosecutions against him as the greater injustice they should care about.

Profiteers have always depended on the rules of society letting them get away with what they do. Long before Trump, they knew to invest a great deal of resources in countering any effort that might create rules that work against them—any rules that might limit their ability to profit from injustice. Profiteers aim to ensure that any of the people capable of stopping them either don't know what they're doing, don't think it has much of a negative impact, or believe it's part of the natural order of how things work, which either cannot or should not be stopped—even if it's wrong.

Threats to profiteers begin with perception. Trump has greatly used his power to accelerate and widen this shift in perception, but profiteers are always working on it. It doesn't necessarily matter that a ton of people see right through it and refuse to fall for it. He may not shift perception among a majority of people; all he needs is the relatively small set of people whose specific actions and decisions enable him to do what he wants to do, who can prevent the majority from taking control away from him.

To be powerful enough to control the rules society lives by, one must understand the perceptions that are most important to control. Remember from chapter 2 how Mike Pence and the Heritage Foundation crew positioned their takeover of New Orleans as offering a promising future, rather than undermining the progress the city was making and dragging everyone back into the past.

The right strategy isn't always about the most obvious perceptions. For example, many liberals and news organizations point to the fact that Trump is unpopular, by virtue of his low (and often sinking) approval ratings. That is just one perception: whether people believe he is doing a good job. Trump, and the Republicans and corporate executives he brought to heel, figured out long ago that his public job approval is not actually the most important perception for maintaining his—and their—power. The far more important perception: whether it is possible to beat him (that is, to win a public battle with him, get any wrongdoing to stick to him, and break his hold over people's loyalty to him). And even if it is, whether it is worth the risk. This is the perception Trump is always trying to manage, not his popularity. In fact, sometimes one goes up while the other goes down. **When Trump's opponents focus on the wrong metric of his power, they focus on the wrong strategy for increasing their own.**

If people do not believe it is possible to effectively challenge Trump, they will not stand up to him. Members of Congress may not even vote against his policies if they think living under his authority is merely a new fact of life. The Senate minority leader Chuck Schumer famously said that all the Democrats needed to do was get Trump's approval rating down. But it's unclear what actions merely having a negative perception of Trump would lead people to take, and whether those actions would limit his power. **The "beatability" perception, however, is the one that drives people's actual behavior—the decision they make about whether or not to try.**

We criticize the many so-called leaders across society who have sold out to Trump—as we should. But not many people would risk getting into a fight they know they can't win. In fact, many people rise to positions of authority—and stay there—by being very careful about the fights they get into. Manufacturing the perception that Trump is unstoppable, popular or not, is what has enabled him to get away with so much, and break through so many previous limits on a president's power, which in turn has enabled all the people profiting from the Trump presidency to get away with what they do.

We often think that by demonstrating what someone is doing is wrong we will shift perception in ways that prevent them from doing it. But even if something is perceived as being wrong, it is not always perceived as being necessary to change—or even changeable at all.

Opinion is not the same as motivation. We all know painfully well that a behavior (such as withholding life-saving resources from communities vulnerable to disaster, or defrauding consumers, investors, or shareholders) can be widely regarded as wrong and still persist because not enough people feel motivated to challenge it. No matter what scale we're working on—taking on Trump and corporate profiteers or taking on a local business or politician—the perceptions that motivate the right people to action are those we need to be able to influence. An essential facet of power is controlling the perception of what is and isn't acceptable.

5

The Written and Unwritten Rules

DEFINITION: Rules are about behavior; they define what actions are acceptable in any given context by creating positive consequences for following them and negative consequences for violating them. *Written rules* are stated explicitly in the law or in another official form. *Unwritten rules* exist as unstated or unofficial expectations that we internalize and feel we need to live by.

CHALLENGE: The written rules of policy are often less important than the unwritten rules of culture, which can influence decision-making a great deal more. When we gain the power needed to change the written rules but not the unwritten rules, we often find ourselves failing to achieve the impact we want.

Changing the Rules That Matter

Everything that happens or doesn't happen in society is the result of people making decisions. What's taught in schools. What food is inspected, and by what standards. Who the police target and who they let run free. How we pay for healthcare, and what is even recognized as healthcare. Who can harm people and profit from it and who gets punished for it. Whether there are different sets of rules for different groups of people.

All decisions made in society are based on both written and unwritten rules. Some rules are explicitly stated in the form of official policies and laws—those are the written rules. Some rules are implicitly conveyed through our culture; it's the way we're trained to act by the people around us—those are the unwritten rules. Unwritten rules show up in our deeply embedded instincts and understandings about how we think we're supposed to act. They define our calculus of "how things really work" when it comes to making decisions: the actual consequences we face in the real world for doing or not doing something. They also shape our sense of right and wrong.

The height and width of the front door of a building is usually governed by a written rule of policy. Whether or not you hold that door for someone walking into a building is governed by an unwritten rule of culture.

Often, it's the unwritten rules that govern whether anyone takes the written rules seriously. A city law on the books stating that marijuana is illegal is a written rule. A police practice of arresting Black twenty-year-olds for smoking marijuana but not arresting white twenty-year-olds for doing the same thing is an unwritten rule.

When and where a written rule gets enforced is usually a rule that no one writes down, but it's the one they live by. And it's often extremely biased and unfair.

Whether drug use is treated seriously as a crime and a major threat to society in one context, while being dismissed as a harmless youthful indulgence in another, depends on the unwritten rules of drug enforcement. But it is compounded by other unwritten rules—for instance, those that teach drug-law enforcers to think that Black men are a threat when they break rules and that white men are "just like us" and should be given a break.

Not saying (or doing) anything about injustice, and letting police departments and mass incarceration profiteers get away with it, is another unwritten rule. It's one that countless mayors, prosecutors, and other people in authority lived by for decades—and that ruined countless Black and Brown lives, while countless white people benefited from the privileges granted to them by that disparity.

Written rules and unwritten rules are not always aligned. In fact, they may be driving toward opposing results. In those cases, it is usually the unwritten rule that wins out.

No better example is the government under Trump. One unwritten rule has always allowed presidents to get away with lying—even lying to dupe people into supporting a war, whether the Vietnam War, the decades-long "war on drugs," or the 2003 invasion of Iraq—as well as many other injustices. Another unwritten rule, however, has constrained presidents in their use of power, even when the written rules might allow them to exercise more of it. Trump has changed those rules. Under Trump, passing a law that authorizes funding for a certain program is now no guarantee that the president will actually spend the money in the way Congress mandated. People in the current administration are choosing not to enforce laws about corruption that would affect Trump, his family, and his friends. They are also leading or encouraging actions that clearly break any number of laws on the books related to free speech, protections for citizenship, and other constitutional rights.

The rule that matters in government right now is a very clear unwritten rule: Give the president whatever he wants. That rule may be whispered in some corners while not even being stated at all in others, but those are the expectations large numbers of decision-makers have internalized and feel they need to live by. People are reading the power dynamics and the incentives they are operating in—the consequences of standing up for the rule of law versus the consequences of being obedient to the rules of Trump.

That is how important the unwritten rules of culture can be: Seemingly overnight and without any effective resistance, like floodwaters rushing through a chain-link fence, they can pass right by official policy, completely deactivating massive investments and long-fought achievements focused on changing the written rules of law and policy.

Failing to understand the incentives and power dynamics that determine the unwritten rules in any given system means failing to win real change. We can spend decades working to get written rules on the books but then fail to reinforce them with unwritten rules, which are what would make them come to fruition in reality.

Not all written rules require such extreme fortification by unwritten rules in order to be realized. But any rule that affects our lives in a big way—whether a corporation cheats us, whether the government denies us our freedoms, whether we're treated unfairly and unsafely when we're at work or anywhere else—is a factor of the strength of the unwritten rules.

That's why power in society comes from controlling the unwritten rules: defining the actions and behaviors that are acceptable (or even expected) in practice, and those that are not. If the power required to change the written rules is too great, but you are able to change the unwritten rules, you can often win the changes you want. In such cases, you don't even need to change the written rules—you simply render them irrelevant.

Written and Unwritten Rules Working Together

Culture can make policy irrelevant by deprioritizing or disincentivizing its enforcement. A great example of this is the policy written into the deeds of houses that originally prevented Black people from owning property in one particular neighborhood of New York City: Harlem. Despite that fact, Harlem became one of the most important Black communities in the country. (For a deeper dive on the back-

and-forth between the written and unwritten rules and how that played out for Black people in Harlem over a century, see the online Appendix at rashadrobinson.com/book.)

But sometimes, written and unwritten rules work together. Written rules can help establish, reinforce, or increase the power of unwritten rules. One clear example is wage theft, the profiteering practice by which employers steal or withhold money they owe their employees, underpay them, or deny them benefits they've earned. It's rampant, from the local nail salon to Walmart, McDonald's, and other corporations. It affects millions of people, including people whose lives rely on every single dollar they earn.

How can we stop it? First, we need to get official laws on the books that make the various forms of wage theft illegal—creating official and painful consequences for them. Second, we need to create a political culture in which the agencies required to enforce those laws are fully funded and staffed to do so, and in which the people in charge of enforcement are incentivized by government leaders and other influential forces in society (news media, civil society, voters) to pursue investigations and prosecutions aggressively.

In many parts of the country, and with respect to many types of wage theft, the first has been achieved but the second hasn't, which is what allows these injustices to persist. There must be a strong set of incentives that drives all the people involved in preventing wage theft to maintain an interest in it and take it seriously, both within government and among employers. Employers must feel they can no more get away with wage theft than restaurant owners feel it's both a good idea and easy to get away with adding poison to their customers' food.

Some of the most important rules have to do with the industries that shape our overall culture. Thanks to many years of dedicated advocacy and activism, written rules at corporations like Disney generally prohibit TV shows from broadcasting homophobic language and lesbian and gay stereotypes (if not always bisexual and trans stereotypes). When followed by major media outlets over time, those written policies shape the unwritten conventions of our real-life culture. Millions of people in the real world might start to believe that using homophobic language or invoking those stereotypes would violate an unwritten rule of culture in real life, and so they refrain from doing it. Working together, the written and unwritten rules might even make people less passive and more vigilant about identifying and challenging homophobia when they see it—that is, promoting and enforcing the unwritten rules wherever they can in their lives. That rule isn't written down anywhere. They learned it from the world around them—including the media they consume. And they learned that part of the rule is not just abiding by it but promoting and defending it actively.

At GLAAD, we were always playing the written and unwritten rules off of each other. We knew that written rules can change the behavior of people with influence, which can then change everyday people's behavior in the real world: establishing unwritten but equally influential cultural rules that move people to change their behavior. We also knew that unwritten rules of culture—embraced by communities whom media corporations felt they could no longer continue to disappoint without consequence—could help us build momentum and pressure toward changing the official rules of policy.

Without doubt, written rules and unwritten rules can be in conflict. Rules are not stable. Power means having the ability to control or amend the rules and, where there's a conflict among rules, to make sure the rules we believe in—the rules that benefit our cause and lead to the outcomes we want—become the dominant rules that determine how things work. Sometimes that's using the unwritten rules to negate the written rules to get the outcomes we want. Sometimes it's about creating a reinforcing loop between the two, which drives each of them forward until we see the outcomes we want.

Understanding the relationship between the two is critical to achieving any social change goal. Many social justice movements and liberal institutions have focused so much on changing written rules that when we're faced with a political leader like Trump who has no respect for them—and is not bound by them—we don't know what to do.

Black Elves: A Story of (Im)Possibility

When we change rules for the better, we can affect society in one of two ways: raising the floor for what's acceptable or raising the ceiling for what's possible. Rule changes can raise standards for behavior, making certain bad behaviors no longer acceptable. Rule changes can also eliminate constraints, creating possibilities for better behavior. The biggest impact requires doing both.

Rules run deep. They can run so deep that they prevent us from even thinking in certain ways, despite all evidence or common sense. Case in point, as I mentioned before: turning to banks as the trusted experts for dealing with an economic crisis they themselves caused.

Some ceilings are glass ceilings: We can see possibility through them, even if there's a barrier preventing us from reaching them. But other ceilings are solid: They are so effective at conditioning our thoughts and vision that we can't even imagine anything on the other side of them. I often think about a story a friend told me about Black elves—a story that may seem trivial but that represents real impact on people's lives.

It was a cool, late night in L.A. and I was listening to a comedian friend tell me a story that summed up everything about how the entertainment industry works. A year before, my friend, who is Black, had been out on a similar night and wound up talking with a group of white men who were scripting a new movie, a fantasy film that was going to feature a lot of elf characters.

"I know some actors who would be great for it," he shared with the group around the table.

Without thinking, one of them quipped, "Are they Black, too?"

"Yes, like me, they are also Black. What's the problem?" my friend replied.

"Well, you know," they all agreed in unison, as if singing along to a karaoke set for people drunk on ignorance, "elves aren't Black."

A great performer, my friend was used to leaving people speechless, not *being* speechless. He showed me how his face had frozen in the "What?!" position in front of them for an appropriate moment, and then for even longer, and then for even longer until they realized he wasn't joking.

Wondering whether he was in an argument he had already lost, or in the middle of a teaching moment they would never forget, he put this simple question to them: "How can you say that Black elves don't exist when elves themselves don't exist? All of it is fiction. It's all made up. If we can make up elves, why can't we make up Black elves?"

Now they were speechless. Someone—perhaps many people directly and indirectly over a long time—had defined the story of elves for them in a way that prevented Black elves from ever existing. They started to realize that story wasn't the truth, but rather a self-serving fiction they had been taught to accept and promote. They had internalized that story as an unwritten rule, a rule they were playing by as they were making decisions about casting and envisioning their movie. The rule was so deep they didn't even know they were following it. They just followed it. Obediently.

You can have elves that fly, elves that do magic, elves of different sizes, elves with all sorts of fantastical physical variations. Elves had already been reimagined in twentieth-century America, hundreds of years after appearing in Norse and Germanic mythology, as the industrial workforce of Santa's North Pole factory. Elves can be anything. Just not Black, according to the screenwriters sitting at the table with my friend that night and according to everyone across Hollywood they represented. Even in a fictional world in which nothing actually existed at all, the unwritten rules said that Black elves could not exist.

An imaginary world that insists on all-white elves has nothing to do with something inherent to elves. It has everything to do with the authors who have imagined and reimagined that world. It has everything to do with what they want their world to be about, and not about, and how they pass on their vision to all the storytellers that follow.

People in certain circles ask me often, "What are people talking about when they say there's a problem with 'whiteness' in society?" It's not about white people. It's about a system of rules that certain white people have built up around themselves, which they use their power to force the rest of us to live by.

In that context, racism, patriarchy or any similar system of rules is a ceiling that reduces possibilities in the world. That's what it is. That's its function. It shrinks our collective imagination about what is possible. When people talk about "whiteness" in this way, they are referring to a system of rules that makes it impossible for certain nonwhite people (and even many white people) to belong. To take part in all parts of society. To contribute to society. To benefit from society. My friend and all his Black actor friends hit that ceiling hard in Hollywood, over and over again.

People created rules for this fantasy world of elves, rules that run so deep they don't even need to be articulated in a conscious way because they are reinforced all around us in a cultural way. When someone violates the rule, the rule may be articulated. But rarely does it need to be. Not any more than the rule we follow that makes us act as if pink is for girls and blue is for boys. We know and internalize those types of rules by living in the world created by them, as if they are forever rules, eternal rules. Natural rules. There goes "nature" again, taking the fall for injustices human beings have created.

In truth, these rules are merely part of a story originating in people, not in nature. In America in the early 1900s, *blue* was for girls and *pink* was for boys. Those colors had a whole different meaning, the opposite of what they mean today.[1] Similarly, and more seriously, the unwritten rules of culture have trained us for centuries to act as if women are less intelligent and capable than men. This bias showed up in written rules preventing women from voting and in unwritten rules that made people oppose the movement to let women vote. It's all about controlling what makes sense and feels right, and therefore what we think is possible and good—just and unjust.

Today, MAGA culture is creating a new possibility: *taking away* women's right to vote.[2] First, they change the unwritten rules to make the conversation about denying women's rights acceptable. Then they change the written rules: They are actively promoting laws that will take away millions of women's right to vote (though not promoting it directly as such), on the path to something even more extreme. Their ability to build a culture around these ideas is rooted in establishing countless stories in which women either do not belong at all or belong in an inherently and permanently inferior role. This particular faction is worried about how women voters could affect the game of politics in the long term, so they want to change the rules of that game.

Like all rules, the unwritten rule about elves needing to be white was created to preserve a form of privilege. In this case, the purpose was to ensure that the story of elves, wherever it may be told, would continue to express the worldview that its dominant authors (and audiences) believed in, could identify with, and could feel comfortable with. The privilege it preserved made it impossible for nonwhite actors to play elves, for nonwhite writers and producers to own an elf story, and for nonwhite audiences to see themselves represented in certain imaginary worlds. It might seem funny, but it's no joke. Rules like these are all around us.

The perception is that allowing Black people to be elves somehow harms the ability of white people to be elves—the question is evaluated in terms of how it affects possibilities for white people. I often hear such complaints in the course of my work in Hollywood: *It's impossible for white men to get any writing jobs these days.* People were saying things like that even back at a time when 80 percent of TV writers were white men. "No Black elves" is just one example of rules that result in unfair exclusion and therefore inequality.

The sum of all the rules like this one that pervade decision-making in Hollywood explains how in 2025, five years after Black Lives Matter became one of the most participatory movements in American history, we can still wake up to see this headline in *TheWrap:* "Over 90% of Series Streaming in 2024 Were from White Creators, UCLA Diversity Study Finds. White actors accounted for nearly 80% of leading roles in the most-watched streaming comedies and dramas of 2024."

Changing the rules about who can be part of a profession is a threat only if people want to hold on to an unfair advantage and don't want to live in a truly equal world. That is, if they think their own opportunity depends on denying opportunity to others. If they think they would not be able to succeed if they were forced to compete against everybody, equally. But no one is saying there won't be any more white elves; they are just saying there shouldn't be a rule that there can *only* be white elves.

For the white men around the table that night with my friend, it was going to take a long time to see the unwritten rules, recognize their harm, not get defensive, and understand that fighting for a fairer way of making decisions would ultimately benefit everyone—even them. Moments like that are important, but they need movements behind them to result in any real change.

Rules Create Hierarchies

Many rules create a hierarchy—a social order that assigns a value to different people based on their different backgrounds, social identities, and social realities, and then ranks their privileges in society according to that value. Hierarchies open up possibilities for some people while shutting down possibilities for others. Racial hierarchies. Gender hierarchies. Class hierarchies. And more. The imbalance of power leads to imbalances in wealth, health, opportunity, freedom—everything.

In this hierarchical system, certain people's lives, needs, dreams, opinions, and talents are ranked as being worth more than those of others. The rankings are not based on the value of those dreams, opinions, or talents; or the urgency of those needs; or the uniqueness of those lives. They are based solely on the value the hierarchy assigns according to an identity, regardless of anything else. It's a set of rules we internalize and play by.

Being a certain race or gender. Being part of a certain family line or having a certain financial status. Being from one neighborhood versus another. Being disabled or not. Being "normal" versus not—whatever that means. In America, people in power, as well as the systems they oversee, often assign the value of a life in ways that make it all too easy to predict who will succeed simply by looking at where they're born and to whom.

Hierarchies are based on rules that turn natural differences into artificial divides. These hierarchies are so deeply embedded within us that we often enforce their rules without even thinking about it or knowing that we're doing it. Even feminist parents might lapse into treating daughters differently from sons when it comes to how late they can stay out and other things they are allowed or expected to do.

The unwritten rules of hierarchy justify injustice because they create a story for it that makes it seem like the natural order of things (just like the story that turns something unjust into something merely unfortunate and therefore acceptable). And those rules would not be possible without a deeply entrenched story that says, for example, that Black people are failing their society instead of their society failing them. That story makes disparity seem like it makes sense, even though it's complete nonsense.

The Rules of Racism

The story about Black elves also illustrates the important difference between *individual racism* and *structural racism*. Individual racism is what people in power want people to believe racism is at its worst. It's the idea that individual hateful people do individual hateful things. And it's a lot easier to live with the fantasy that only terrible people do terrible things. But that is not the worst form of racism.

The worst racism or hierarchy of any kind, in terms of impact on people's lives, is when an entire system of rules results in generally decent people playing along and making decisions that make certain things possible for one group of people that are not possible for anyone else—often, not even noticing they're doing it, not feeling they can do anything about it, or even becoming addicted to the privileges that come with it.

Structural racism is when the basic rules of a system establish and reinforce racial inequalities. In the United States, structural racism creates advantages that allow white people to profit by excluding or harming people of color. The rules are usually deeply entrenched, promoted, and enforced by people's everyday behavior, whether or not they intend to be racist or even understand the impact of what they are doing. The result is a hierarchy so well established that it seems like the natural order. But it is very much human-made.

And we will live with it until we see it for what it is—and then create the power to change it. My father is a tile artisan and a residential builder. Growing up, I got to see the choices people made about the way structures were built, and that always made me think about myself in the world in a certain way. Living in the world, I often felt like I had moved into a house that was built a hundred years ago, for someone else, but was then forced to live with all the decisions that were made back then about how to live—accepting every part of that structure as a mandate for how to live in that house, even if it didn't fit me. The world that the architects and builders created when they built that house is now my world. I'm living by their rules, until I can change whatever supports those rules and prevents other rules from emerging.

Structural racism is what makes the idea of a world without Black elves seem perfectly normal. It's also what makes the idea of sending a Black man to death row when it's not even certain he killed anybody, while giving civic awards and million-dollar bonuses to executives whose corporations kill hundreds or thousands of people every single day. It's about how systems are set up to produce injustice, like factories that churn out injustice at a scale that individual people can't do on their own. It's about written and unwritten rules, combined.

All of us have a choice about whether to play by the rules. We can use the rules as an excuse; we can say our hands are tied and there's nothing we can do. But to be clear: If we are not part of dismantling the structure of racism and changing its rules, then we are part of reinforcing it.

To a Black actor, it doesn't matter what the intention of a producer or a casting director is, or what their excuse is, or whether they wear a BLM shirt while casting the next white elf. What matters is whether or not they hire that actor.

And to anyone who is on the losing side of the rules of a hierarchy—whether those rules merely create annoyances or go so far as to ruin their lives—the question is always this: Who is going to join me in fighting to change these rules, and how are we going to win?

FIND YOUR POWER
The Rules in Your World

This activity is meant to help you see the rules that shape the different environments you live in, identify rules you want to change, and develop an approach for trying to change them.

Think about a social environment you know really well—a "world" you spend time in often. It could be your work world. Or the world of a place you frequent, such as the supermarket, the gym, or the club. Or the world of a religious community or a hobby group you're involved in. It could be the world of your family—or even your own home.

1. Pick just one world to start.

What are the rules of that world? What are the rules that truly govern the behavior of the people who spend time in that world, including yourself? Some are likely written down or stated regularly. Others probably exist as unwritten rules that somehow everyone knows—or is supposed to know—even if they are never formally stated.

At the gym, it could be anything from a policy against taking pictures in the locker room (a written rule of safety) to how loud people can be when they're talking on the phone while working out on a machine (an unwritten rule of etiquette).

Of course, rules are not functional unless there is some kind of reward for playing by them and/or some kind of consequence for violating them. That's what makes them real.

Think about the rewards and consequences you see play out in that world.

2. Write out some of the written and unwritten rules of that world.

Then write out the rewards and consequences for each of those rules.

Now choose one of those rules that you don't like—a rule you want to change. You might choose a high-stakes rule that would take a great deal of time and effort to change. But it's okay to start with something simple, like a rule making everyone do "Taco Tuesdays" at work every week even though not everyone wants it.

3. Write down the rule.

Then write down the different ways that rule is communicated to people, both formally and informally.

Write down the different ways it's enforced (rewards and consequences), to whom it applies, and what makes it wrong in your eyes. Write down how you would go about changing this rule.

Put what you've written aside for the moment. Come back to it after you have read through this book (or at least Parts I and II) and revisit your instincts about how you might go about changing this rule. See if there's anything you would alter in your approach.

Then answer the following questions:

- What individual power do you need in order to change this rule?
- Is this the only rule you need to change in order to get the outcomes you want?
- What are your leverage points, especially given whether it is a written or unwritten rule and the nature of how it's enforced?

- What opposition to your efforts might you be underestimating, especially coming from anyone profiting in some way from the status quo in the form of money, status, or anything else? (For more on profiteering, see chapter 3.)
- What perception might you need to change? (For more on perceptions, see chapter 4.)
- What belief might you need to cultivate in yourself or others? (For more on beliefs, see chapter 7.)
- What infrastructure might you need to tap into or build? (For more on infrastructure, see chapter 8.)
- What role might you need to change first? (For more on roles, see chapter 10.)
- What magical thinking might hold you back? (For more on magical thinking, see chapter 11.)

4. Write out your plan.

Think about how to get other people involved: those who are negatively impacted by the rule, as well as those who identify with people who are (even if they themselves are not particularly affected). Consider whether you'll pose a stronger challenge to the rule by working together.

Try it out. You'll make mistakes. But keep trying: not just until the rule is changed, but until the outcome you don't like is changed and you've achieved the outcome you want. Or, if you cannot find a way to win, try to analyze why.

You may need to do more than simply eliminate the rule—you may need to replace it with one or more new rules, practices, customs, or enforcement measures that ensure the world you've chosen generates the outcomes you want instead of the status quo.

Everything you learn about changing the rule of this one system you're part of is something you can apply to changing the rules in the bigger systems we're all part of.

5. Take stock.

Note what you're good at as you go through the process (and the skills, support, and infrastructure that you needed to tap into as part of your strategy), and what that tells you about the role you can play in advancing bigger social changes.

Don't forget to celebrate: No matter what happened, you learned something you can take with you, and that is always worth appreciating. It's your starting point for regrouping, defending what you won, or taking on the next (and bigger) fight.

6

Outsmarting the Blame Game

DEFINITION: Blame is the story we tell about why things are wrong and who is responsible for them. It's one of the most powerful justifications of the written and unwritten rules that govern how decisions get made at every level of society. It makes them seem to make sense.

CHALLENGE: Blame has defined American laws and culture for generations. If we keep losing the blame game, or getting caught up in it ourselves, we will never be able to build the largest possible coalition of Americans ready to bring about change. But that is what's necessary for putting an end to the injustices of profiteering and building a country that is safe and free for all of us.

Redirecting Blame: The Secret Power of Profiteers

So far, I have talked about five fundamental ideas about what power is and how it works. None of these lessons are academic. They are drawn from the many big wins and tough losses I have experienced over decades:

- Presence is not power.
- Power is about changing rules that govern the decisions people make.
- Profiteering is the machine that keeps injustice going.
- Changing perception is essential for motivating people to take on profiteers.
- We must change both the written and unwritten rules that enable profiteering—replacing rewards with consequences.

There is one more fundamental principle of power I must address here in Part I, and it may be the most difficult to reckon with.

It should be clear to anyone watching what is happening in and to our country that dissent doesn't make change on its own. We can't merely express our opinion and expect to win. To move from dissent to disruption—that is, to change how things actually work and not just what people think about them—we need to gain real power. Yet the path to power for people who care about justice is full of detours. Misunderstanding presence as power works as one detour. Magical thinking can take us on many detours. Another detour is not understanding how profiteers use race to divide us and keep the rules exactly as they are: by playing the racial blame game.

The deepest, most influential stories humans can tell are fictions that we experience as facts—fictions-as-truths that we think were always true from the beginning of time, are still true, and will never not be true. That's how stories shape reality: We think they *are* reality, and we accept them as unchanging truths. And anyone with the power to control some of the rules that determine how society works has been successful at convincing people of a story about the nature of the biggest problems we face and who is responsible for them.

For example, even a person skeptical of information coming from our corporate food and health industries might believe that fat in our food is a huge problem, and that rule changes targeting fat are good solutions. They might not know that the sugar industry spent a great deal of time and millions of dollars introducing and reinforcing that idea—vilifying fat far beyond its justifiable risks—in the hope that making fat the villain of our health stories would take the heat off sugar, which is a far worse health-destroying villain.[1] We were all played. The sugar industry executives, and all the savvy marketers working for them, were so good at their jobs that we think the lies they planted in us are natural, eternal truths. When they said, "Forget about sugar, focus on reducing fat," they managed to get their ideas so deeply embedded in our beliefs, attitudes, and instincts that we didn't even question them.

The stories people in power tell about what the problem is (and who the villain is) are a big part of what makes rule changes seem to make sense and feel urgent to people who are not in power. Rules rely on strong narratives (a topic I will delve into more in chapter 9). Challenging and rewriting those narratives is one way to begin challenging and rewriting those rules.

As I discussed in chapter 4, profiteers don't only invest in spreading the "unfortunate reality" perception. They are just as adept at manipulating the "unjust" narrative to their own specific ends: They love defining injustice and redirecting blame when it gives them a chance to gain power. And whomever or whatever we blame for what's wrong convinces us what needs to be done to make it right. Owning the story of blame is powerful. Profiteers of all kinds greatly benefit from the perception that they are the victims and that government regulators and tax collectors, their own workers, social justice warriors, or anyone else they can get people to blame are the perpetrators of injustice against them. The perception of something being unjust, and the story of blame that goes along with it, is highly motivating. It makes people want to cheer for the victim, to fight back, or to give resources and authority to people who will fight to take control of a situation on their behalf.

Post-Katrina New Orleans provided a perfect example of how profiteers used the "unjust" perception to their advantage. With no shame, given how many of the Bush administration decisions played a role in creating the disaster of Katrina, Mike Pence, the Heritage

Foundation, and their allies set about creating the perception that leadership was the problem—not their leadership, but Black people's leadership. Central to their strategy was to position themselves as saviors who could do what Black leaders couldn't. In ways both subtle and crass, their answer was to take the most consequential decisions about New Orleans out of the hands of the people of New Orleans, either co-opting or marginalizing Black community, business, and government leaders. (We can look at the marginalization of Black teachers, as just one example.)[2] It was almost a colonial approach, with the promises of bringing civilization to savages. It was the same argument used to justify apartheid in South Africa: *Yes, perhaps ideally the country would be governed by its overwhelming majority, but Black people simply aren't ready or capable to govern, so white people need to stay in control for the benefit of everybody.*

The pattern of post-Katrina New Orleans has been common in cities across America. Just about the time that Black people come into power as mayors and city councilors, and as heads of institutions that traditionally influenced the course of events in a city, we see national and state forces undermine the very authority of those positions. Federal and state politicians move money out of their hands, corporations take decisions out of their control, national media put them under intense (and often unfair) scrutiny and undermine their legitimacy, and the federal government attacks them. It is all highly racialized.

That's not to say that truly corrupt and ineffectual Black leaders should not be held accountable; Black communities are often first in line for the march against them. But what is noteworthy is the attack on *effective* leaders, specifically because they're effective at starting to change the rules in ways that pose a threat to profiteers, while changing the perception about the kind of leadership that we need.

Undermining Black people in authority, just as they reach new levels of authority, is a continuing political practice. As soon as Black women became prosecutors, for example, conservative legislatures and governor offices across the country took action to reduce their budgets, reduce their authority, and even take cases away from them. In 2023, Florida's governor, Ron DeSantis, took the extraordinary step of suspending Monique Worrell from her position as a duly elected state attorney in Orange and Osceola counties specifically because she was so effective at driving reform. To get her position back, she was forced to run for it again the next year, winning her race against the person DeSantis appointed to replace her. Every Black woman progressive prosecutor faces attacks of varying degrees, aimed at undermining their authority, that their predecessors never did. And while attacks on Black women are particularly vicious, the effort to undermine anyone fighting for justice is never mild, even when they are white and well-off.[3]

It is a response to the specific reforms those people were advancing (which threatened the status quo, including the ability of police to write their own rules and the ability of profiteers to benefit from mass incarceration), as well as the diversification of power and control that those Black people represented.

The idea that Black people take over something, inherit intractable problems from white predecessors, and then get blamed for all of a sudden making it no longer the thing it once was, is often referred to as the "hollow prize" problem. It is a term popularized by academics in the late 1960s to describe the phenomenon related to Black mayors such as Carl Stokes in Cleveland, Coleman Young in Detroit, Maynard Jackson in Atlanta, and Tom Bradley in Los Angeles. Trump loves this tactic. He is clearly threatened by Black people in leadership and puts a special target on their backs. Black leaders Trump either fired, tried to fire, or otherwise persecuted just in the first months of his second term included Lisa Cook at the Federal Reserve; Letitia James, the New York attorney general; General Charles Q. Brown Jr., chairman of the Joint Chiefs of Staff; Gwynne A. Wilcox, chair of the National Labor Relations Board; and Charlotte A. Burrows, commissioner and chair at the Equal Employment Opportunity Commission. It's a pattern that's unmistakable for anyone being honest about his record.

It is also no accident that Trump takes action against Black people as a way to build up confidence in himself and rally his supporters—he sees Black people, Black cities, Black countries,

and everything and anyone Black as eminently blameworthy. For everything. He is tapping into a deep-seated perception in America about whom to blame when things go wrong. His followers eat it up and his allies know how to exploit the opportunities it opens for them. His opponents often let him get away with it, due to their own hang-ups related to race.

It is all made possible by a perception long embedded in American culture: Whenever something goes wrong, there are Black people to blame. The role of this perception in the corporate takeover of New Orleans was clear: making it seem logical that decisions about the future of New Orleans should be turned over to white-led institutions, even though it was the indifference, incompetence, and racism of those very institutions that were responsible for outsized damage that Hurricane Katrina caused.

The blame started early on during Katrina: blaming Black people for looting (while white people engaged in the same behavior were "bravely scavenging" and "struggling for survival"), blaming Black people for lacking resourcefulness (while George Bush generously outfitted mostly white storm survivors in Florida with everything they needed), blaming Black people for resisting police orders (while the police were committing violent rampages). Our communities might as well have been blamed for the weather itself.

Almost everything about how New Orleans marketed itself was rooted in Black culture: the music, Mardi Gras, the costumes and fashion, the food, the street parties. But that didn't make anyone think twice about blame. It reinforced a truism of race in this country: **People can love Black culture but hate Black people at the very same time.**

We were not able to battle back effectively—that is, in a way that would result in a different outcome. And yet, while this blame game played out in public, the meeting that Mike Pence organized was private. The blame game was both a justification and a way to distract people from the power grab that was taking place. Blame is not only a profitable business; it is essential for profiteering.

One of the Original American Blame Narratives: "Black People Are a Problem"

W.E.B. Du Bois opened his 1903 book, *The Souls of Black Folk,* with a profound and provocative statement: "Between me and the other world there is ever an unasked question: . . . How does it feel to be a problem?" He was naming how both white Americans ("the other world") and the American system of rules for running society treat Black people as a problem—an object to be managed—rather than seeing racism as the problem to be solved. This has always influenced me and stayed with me when I look at our culture.

America has some really bad habits. To succeed in creating a world that produces more justice than injustice, we need to change those habits. But it's not easy. Our collective bad habits as a country run deep because the narratives driving those habits run deep.

The power to embed stories deeply within us and affect our behavior—millions of people at a time—is concentrated in too few people's hands. And they're the wrong people. Even before people like Rupert Murdoch and Elon Musk controlled much of our media landscape, there were people in control of the major news networks, national and local newspapers, movie studios, and other influential media who are not household names but who have perpetuated the same injustice of miseducating people. The narratives that shape our thoughts and feelings didn't get inside us by accident. They were put there. They serve a purpose. Usually, they serve a profit. Whether that profit is financial gain or political gain, the protection of social privilege or the strengthening of social loyalty, the narratives we internalize are often profitable to someone.

Why do some people think crime is going up even when it's going down? Why do we give tax breaks to people who don't need them, but ignore people who do? Why would someone experiencing a medical emergency on an airplane refuse help from a doctor who happens to be Black? Why do so many people think that activism doesn't change anything, and is not time well spent, when there are so many instances that show activism can be effective in overcoming injustices and transforming our lives for the better? Most of all: Why do we blame Black people for everything that goes wrong in society? And why are we allowing the right wing to use the well-established template for blaming Black people as a weapon against trans people, immigrants, poor people, and others?

Why do so many people still maintain a deeply internalized story that tells them to think and act as if Black people are the problem? What does that make possible and impossible? What would replacing that narrative do for all of us? When I talk about this, many people immediately get defensive. I understand that. But stay with me a bit longer. As someone who sees this blame play out in politics every day, I can promise you that I am not overstating the situation.

Democrats lose an election? Blame Black voters. Our school system is failing? Blame Black parents. Kids today are violent? Blame Black kids. Corporations aren't making enough money? Blame Black workers. Gay rights legislation didn't pass? Blame Black preachers. Poverty still exists? Blame Black culture. Big banks crash the economy? Blame Black victims of their predatory loans. You stub your toe and it hurts real bad? Some Black person out there is responsible, and you should curse their name. People in power can get away with almost anything if they effectively blame other people for it; often, they can gain even more power by doing so.

The blame game isn't only about focusing on the wrong problems and solutions. It's about ignoring or failing to see the right problems and solutions. That is, it's not just morally wrong to misplace blame, it's strategically wrong—and often factually wrong.

Black men who voted for Trump in the 2024 election is a perfect example. According to the data we have now, 75 percent of Black men voted for Kamala Harris. That's a far greater percentage than any other voting group—except, of course, Black women. A much higher percentage of Black men voted for the pro-immigration candidate, and against the immigrant-bashing candidate, than Latino voters or Asian voters. A much higher percentage of Black men voted for the pro-choice candidate than white women voters. Black men voted for the pro-union and workers' rights candidate at a much higher rate than white working-class men. A lot of people were blamed for Harris's loss, yet it was striking to see Black men blamed more loudly and often than others because it's clear that people assume the numbers will back up that blame—without even looking at them.[4] There was an endless stream of news and opinion articles focused on the "problem" with Black men, as if they were the main problem for Democrats—as opposed to men in general, white women, or any other group.

What are Black men supposed to think when they hear political pundits blaming them for an election loss that was not their fault—when they showed up and did their part better than all other men? But again, misplaced blame is not just morally wrong but also strategically wrong: If we obsess over "what's wrong with Black men," then we overlook the voters whose choices we actually need to focus on addressing most. And we will also fail to hold the Democratic establishment responsible for the many bad decisions they made during the election cycle—so they are free to keep making them. We shouldn't abandon voter engagement for Black men and take them for granted. That is certainly not my point. In fact, it's surprising how well Black men performed given how neglected they were (and have been) in terms of outreach and engagement. But we certainly make a big mistake if we think Black men were the problem with the 2024 presidential election results.

(To learn more about how the racial blame game works, with examples, see the online Appendix at rashadrobinson.com/book.)

"A Problem" Versus "The Problem"

The narrative that Black people are "a" problem is distinct from the related idea that Black people are "the" problem. The narrative that Black people are "a" problem frames us as a threat, a danger, a challenge to be neutralized, and a dilemma that authorizes and excuses all manner of violence to contain and control. The even deeper idea that Black people are "the" problem leads people to assume that Black people are the cause of every adverse condition, the responsible party for every bad outcome, the people to blame for anything and everything that goes wrong in America. If it were a movie, Black people would be the antagonistic force that makes life hard for the protagonist, the frustration that gets in the way of the hero achieving their goal. In the story of America that many people carry in their minds, that's the character Black people play.

The story isn't just that we threaten all that's good, it's that we're the cause of all that's bad. The former manufactures fear, but the latter manufactures blame. Together, they burn our humanity from both ends. One justifies denying us opportunity because we can't be trusted to do good, while the other justifies punishing us because of all we've done that's bad.

Fear and blame are deeply related. On the right wing, they often lead to the same conclusion in terms of motivating people to get behind ideas that discriminate against Black people, and ultimately undermine public services and safety standards, let corporations get out of control, and allow people in power to do things that ultimately hurt everyone except for the wealthiest and most elite people. But it can be a dangerous pattern among liberals, too, as in the case of blaming Black people for an election loss, or blaming conversations about race for making an issue less "universally appealing."

Blaming Black people protects systemic racism in the most powerful way of all: by pretending that systemic racism isn't actually discriminatory (i.e., that it's not racism at all) but is merely a series of rational and necessary actions and policies—the way things should be. In this deeply embedded narrative, racism isn't wrong—it's "justice." And that worldview is promoted and reinforced in our textbooks and TV shows, our policy debates and moralizing pundit rants, our workplaces and social media feeds, our conventional wisdom and pseudoscience and police quotas. Everywhere. It trains us to go looking for a problem to solve and a cause to fight that doesn't even exist. It also trains us to accept everything that this idea makes possible: the systematic punishment and exclusion of Black people and issues of race across society.

The story that "Black people are a threat" is one story that justifies targeting Black people, controlling us, and taking away our freedoms.

But really, the blame narrative that "Black people are *the* problem" behind everything that goes wrong runs much deeper and is more widely effective. It gets even more people involved in the story than those who simply fear Black people. It practically gets anyone involved who even knows Black people. And that is exactly the weapon of misdirection that people in power need to get away with what they do.

We All Lose the Racial Blame Game

Both blame and fear narratives are powerful. They help those who wield them effectively to change the rules for how society works. They allow people in authority to implement systems of control that enable them to punish, exploit, and exclude people for their own self-interest—justifying creating one set of rules for some people and another set of rules for others. And these systems of control are applied to anyone who is somehow associated with Black people or any attribute historically melded with Black people in the long narrative history of the United States. That includes poor people who are not Black. That includes anyone wrapped up in laws that were intended to control Black people, such as laws that treat powder and crack cocaine differently, laws that try to prevent Black people from voting through felony disenfranchisement or voter ID, corporate practices that deny people healthcare or prey on people's health conditions, food deserts, and lack of legal representation or political power. (In her 2021 book, *The Sum of Us: What Racism Costs Everyone and How We Can Prosper Together,* Heather McGhee illustrates in great detail how racism creates realities in which many different people lose out.)

The result? Instead of placing blame where it belongs—on bad policy choices made by politicians, illegal or immoral acts committed by corporate executives, incentive structures that put profits over people—our society too often points to some specific Black person or group of Black people messing everything up, ruining everything for the rest of us. We see that person or group as needing to be chastised, humiliated, and punished. And of course, it is easy and profitable to extend that blame to other people, such as immigrants, Native Americans, or LGBT people, also holding them responsible for the injustices they face and blaming them for problems people in power have created. When we fall for the racial blame game, we allow rule changes that hold us all back and miss opportunities to make rule changes that could help all of us move forward.

PART II

How to Build Power

What are the practices that allow us to end profiteering and change the rules in favor of justice?

7

Building a Culture of Belief

DEFINITION: A *culture of belief* is a mutually reinforcing feeling among people who are fighting together for a specific change—the feeling that winning is possible. That feeling allows us to reject the idea that we are forever stuck on the losing end of power and motivates us to take the disproportionate but necessary risks required to win.

CHALLENGE: A culture of belief is necessary: It allows us to see that the tools for change to which we have access at any given time are enough to build winning momentum, if we can use them well. The challenge is being bold enough to believe that our actions matter without indulging in the magical thinking that all risks are good risks and all forms of action are strategic action and will lead to winning change.

Stepping onto the Field

The field of social change is like any other field. It has its great thinkers and model practitioners. It has its conceptual side and its technical side, its raging debates about how to do things, and its raging competitions about who does them best. One book cannot cover every topic, let alone do so in depth, when the collected wisdom from effective leaders of social change can fill a library. My challenge in writing this book has been to choose the lessons and concepts that I think are most important for taking our social change game to the next level, given the ways we've gotten stuck and the ways the field we're playing on has changed. In Part I, I presented six fundamental concepts about power that encourage taking a different approach to understanding it.

Part II shifts from helping you understand power to helping you build it—whether you are advocating for change at your local school, in the White House, in climate-related policies and practices, or while learning to be an agent of progress for the very first time. In this and the next four chapters, I highlight just a few of the tools and strategies that can help you become more powerful. And the very first tool that any successful movement for power starts with is the belief that change is possible.

It is not always easy to find that belief within ourselves, let alone to help others find it. You might be discouraged right now if you are looking uphill at an authoritarian government rolling high-impact boulders down at you and others in your community, feeling it will never stop. But we must not see change as a prize waiting for us at the top of an insurmountable peak. The truth is that we are always on a horizontal (if uneven) playing field that millions of people before us have found ways to navigate. We are in a fight with people who wish to do us harm, but they are nonetheless just people, like us. They may have more resources, or more control, but they are not greater than we are. They are not above us. And they can be defeated. There is always a way through them, and there is a way to make progress toward bringing about the world we want to live in. History gives us plenty of evidence to prove it.

Of course, that's easy to say. But the challenge of belief and motivation isn't about lining up the right historical facts. As I pointed out before, it begins with perception—including our perception of ourselves, of the people on our side, and of the people we're up against.

A Belief Greater Than Risk

I was born an optimist. I was also surrounded by signs of hope early on, from the images in my parents' copies of *Jet* magazine, to a home transformed by my father's handiwork, to a yard transformed by my mother's gardening. Jazz played constantly throughout our house, a living lesson about the importance of creativity, improvisation, and what it means to strive for something new.

I was inspired rather than (too) disappointed that my parents took the money we were going to use for a trip to the Great Adventure amusement park and put it into Jesse Jackson's 1988 campaign for president. That was hope. In high school, I saw a path to stopping Rite Aid from barring teenagers in our town from shopping there; I believed we could band together to fight back and win—which we did. That was hope.

Belief has a lot to do with belonging, too. Being part of something, being connected to people, can make us far more likely to believe that we can make it—whatever *it* is. But as I grew up, it also became clear that the world was not built for me. Clothes weren't made for someone my size that also made sense for my age. Leadership roles and paths to success weren't made for me as a Black man, let alone a Black gay man. My parents would make clear that I would need to work twice as hard just to overcome the inherent unfairness of how the world worked against us, and though I might roll my eyes, I would also see them doing that double-time work themselves, and I eventually felt how real that was. I did not always believe that anything was possible, neither for the country nor for myself.

Sometimes, I saw a ceiling limiting the possibilities of progress for the people and issues I cared about, and it was glass. I could see through to the other side. I could believe in getting there. Other times,

I simply lived my life under a ceiling that was solid and never even considered there was a change waiting above it to be claimed. Many people think it was inevitable I would come to lead a national organization, but there was no precedent for someone like me growing and running a national racial justice organization. In fact, some of those same people who now think it's as natural as the sky is blue for me to have risen to that position were doubters all along the way, or don't appreciate what it took to get there. I had to believe a lot to get there. I didn't always realize it, but I had to risk a lot, too.

It's so easy to look back and think that our victories at GLAAD and at Color Of Change were inevitable (or even miss the fact that there was a long, hard struggle to achieve them). That's a testament to how deeply people now believe in the causes we have championed. But the far more challenging belief is seeing yourself on the other side of that ceiling even when you can't see through it—even when everyone is telling you it's as hard and unbreakable as rock.

When it came to same-sex marriage, I never predicted we could raise the ceiling of possibility so quickly. I believed it would happen one day, though I could relate to people who thought it would never happen. That's what it felt like for the many gay and lesbian people in Alabama, where GLAAD sent me in the 2000s to lead media trainings for community members as part of the fight to make progress on gaining cultural acceptance for same-sex couples, as a step toward policy change.

Getting local newspapers to publish the marriage announcements of gay and lesbian couples was one of our strategies. Representation matters: If we aren't seen in the news, it is like we don't exist, and if we don't exist, how can we win anything for ourselves? It was meant not only to show our existence and normalize it but also to build support for us—to get us in the newspaper in a way that encouraged gay and lesbian people to continue coming out and sharing our lives in public, and to help straight people both relate to us and also see that the world wasn't falling apart just because we are being recognized as equal. (Not everyone agreed that "normalization" was the goal, if it meant assimilation. That was a big debate at the time, and it still is today.)

The New York Times, following a meeting between GLAAD and its editorial board, published its first same-sex wedding announcements in 2002. In a special edition to honor the progress underway, it published forty-one of them on May 23, 2004, the same week that Massachusetts began issuing marriage licenses to gay and lesbian couples, becoming the first state in the country to do so. (For a deeper explanation of the connection between culture change strategy and policy change outcomes, and a story about how we got *The Today Show* to accept gay and lesbian couples as part of their very popular wedding contests, see the online Appendix at rashadrobinson.com/book.)

Then, in 2006, GLAAD published a manual I put together for engaging people working in the news industry, and we would bring copies of it to our seminars and workshops in order to empower more people with the tools they needed to change the rules of representation in their local media outlets.

In Alabama, there was a long way to go. Every year, lawmakers in Alabama filed dozens of bills in the statehouse targeting gays and lesbians, such as bans on schoolbooks containing any reference to homosexuality. In 2006, a statewide ballot initiative amending the state constitution to ban same-sex marriage passed overwhelmingly. President Obama did not publicly declare his support for same-sex marriage until 2012. Many others took a lot longer than he did. While the reaction to our movement in states like Massachusetts was to make same-sex marriage legal, and in other states to create compromises like "civil unions" and "domestic partnerships" that at least represented a step toward legitimacy, the reaction in many other states was to ban it entirely. Where there was progress in one state, there was backlash in another. It was not at all clear at the time which would win out overall.

Same-sex marriage didn't become legal everywhere in the United States until the Supreme Court overturned the state bans in 2015, fully eleven years after Massachusetts began issuing marriage licenses to gay and lesbian couples. And there was no guarantee the court would come down in our favor—it was not inevitable. (There are justices on today's Supreme Court—perhaps a majority of them, in fact—who are looking for ways to overturn that decision.)

During the time it took to win that fight, visibility brought freedom and protection for some but required great risk and even brought danger for others. For most same-sex couples whose wedding announcements were published in *The New York Times,* it was a step forward and a reason to celebrate. Yet for same-sex couples in states like Alabama, having their wedding announcements published in local papers was a step forward on a much more dangerous path. Some who published their announcements were fired from their jobs and not subsequently hired anywhere else. LGBT people could be fired in most states for putting their wedding photo on their desk. Others were threatened or even attacked. Still others were shunned by family members and social circles that had tolerated them in the closet but would have nothing to do with them once they stepped out of it. Cake bakers and numerous other businesses shut the door in their face. They were kicked out of church. Moves were made to take their children away. They didn't even feel safe walking home at night. The choice to participate in a campaign that required going public was not an easy one.

The unwritten rules for how gay and lesbian people were allowed to live—not only in places like Alabama but also in certain areas of California and New York—were hard to break. Imagine winning some form of progress for yourself and then seeing the reaction of everyone with power around you being to overturn that win and try to put you back in your previous place—doing everything they can to take your newfound freedom away. It hurt.

For some, the right to marry was the one big privilege they were denied in an otherwise privileged life. Both the board and the staff of GLAAD, anchored mostly in New York City and Los Angeles, were fully stocked with this type of person—mostly white, mostly economically secure. They knew they deserved marriage and acted accordingly. In some ways, I admired that sense of entitlement. For others, of course, the right to marry was one more freedom denied in a long line of injustices they faced: the ability to work at a good job with fair wages, the ability to live in a healthy environment, the ability to get a good education, the ability to be treated fairly regardless of race and gender. That was the world I stepped into in Alabama.

Asking gay and lesbian people in Alabama to organize themselves and push their local newspapers to recognize them publicly was a double-edged sword. They would get cut. And there was no guarantee it would be worth it: How could sticking their neck out in a public wedding announcement possibly lead to winning the legal right to marry and gaining all the freedoms that came with that right? They, like all of us, needed to believe they could win in order to take those risks and suffer that pain. But it wasn't just that they needed to believe in the strategy. They needed to believe in themselves—to see themselves as winners, to see that they belonged to a community of people who were going to win, even if they themselves took a lot of hard losses.

Fighting for rules that protect us means standing up to rulers who attack us. The belief that winning is possible and necessary—that we can do it—is the only force that can motivate large enough groups of people to take those risks and suffer those consequences. That is why any social justice movement begins with building a culture of belief.

Seeing and Believing

Thanks to all the stories about the very real risks people took as part of the Civil Rights Movement of the 1950s and '60s that I knew so well growing up, and the many other stories of social progress I was learning all the time, my understanding about the role of belief was always in the back of my mind. But that didn't mean I knew how to practice it when I landed in Alabama. I thought that all the technical support I was there to provide through my media skills training would give people confidence and help them believe. We'd had success at GLAAD with major newspapers in big cities. Now we were pushing the strategy into more difficult terrain. I thought the stories of our success would be encouraging.

I had called Howard Bayless, a local activist in Birmingham, to ask if GLAAD could support the work that the organization he chaired was leading, a small organization called Equality Alabama, the main statewide LGBT organization. He wasn't sure what to make of the overture. At the time, gay and lesbian activists in Alabama weren't used to getting attention from national organizations. Howard later told me that when he got calls from people in my position at national organizations, it was typically because someone was looking to poach his donor database and contact list. National groups mostly thought of Alabama as a lost cause, not a real priority. Engaging gay and lesbian people in Alabama was about channeling local energy into larger national fights, not channeling limited national resources into local fights that were perceived by national organizations to be unwinnable.

I had a chance to take a different approach. I wanted to help Howard and his organization stage and win fights over local news media practices. We wanted media outlets to update the words reporters and anchors used to label gay and lesbian people, rotate in authentic images of gay and lesbian people, and rotate out the cliché B-roll that usually accompanied news segments about LGBT-related issues (such as the video of men in jean bootie shorts dancing with rainbow flags that it seemed every local news station in the country played in the background no matter how irrelevant to the story being covered). And of course, we wanted to convince the local papers to publish gay and lesbian wedding announcements right alongside the straight announcements.

I flew to Atlanta, rented a car, and drove to Alabama with Alex, a GLAAD staffer who came with me on the road trip—an enthusiastic, straight, white media strategist in his twenties who was eager to be involved in a major civil rights effort. We held our Birmingham media training in a room at Birmingham AIDS Outreach, which had become Alabama's first AIDS service organization in 1985.

Howard didn't really know what to expect. Typically, if ten people showed up for an LGBT meeting, that was considered a huge success. But about forty people came to the training. Some were from the community, some were undoubtedly allies, but all of them wanted to hear what we had to say. The meeting sometimes got lively, and not everyone there agreed with GLAAD's approach.

But after several training sessions across Alabama—in Birmingham, Montgomery, Mobile, and other cities—something happened. People started talking. People at the training sessions shared the information with their friends. Those friends told their friends. Pretty soon, people started speaking up and contacting members of the press to get their stories into the paper. They saw their own personal leadership, even in small steps, as instrumental to the larger fight.

These were everyday people getting involved, believing in what they could do together. Knowing that the local newspapers had serious influence—the ability to shape how people thought about issues—they believed that getting their very human and relatable stories into the paper would get them into people's minds. They believed they could do something that mattered, something worth their time, energy, and risk. They believed in the strategy. What really made them powerful, however, was their belief that coming together and acting collectively would eventually lead to some kind of change. All the strategies and tactics followed from there, helping the local activists manifest their belief in ways that pierced through the blame game that so often targeted LGBT people, challenged the people who profited from excluding them, and ultimately put them on the path from presence to power.

The newspapers eventually felt that power. Editors and publishers changed the rules that many people thought could not be changed: They began publishing same-sex wedding announcements (though in a different part of the paper from the straight couple announcements), even though same-sex marriages were not legal in the state.

As the media environment overall began to change, so did the unwritten rules in politics: In 2006, Alabama got its first out state legislator, a woman named Patricia Todd. In 2007, Howard Bayless ran and won an election, taking his seat on the Birmingham Board of Education—the state's first openly gay man elected to public office.

There would still be anti-gay legislation circulating in those chambers (as there is even today), but the opposition was growing visible. Gay and lesbian people were becoming heroes in the story of Alabama, and the power to change at least some rules was in sight. Many LGBT Alabamans began seeing more of their own community members in the news in ways that were celebratory and made people believe they could win—and so did all Alabamans. That helped the movement grow so that eventually there would be more written and unwritten rules for protecting LGBT people than for attacking them.

First, the people involved in the movement saw themselves as change agents, then as culture-changers, then as rule-changers. Though I hadn't planned for it, I learned that the most important first step in the process of change is building a culture of belief among the people who are the best and only people to lead a fight. A culture of belief is a foundation for a culture of winning.

We can all become far too content sitting outside of power, assuming the role of the permanent minority. That is the most dangerous place to remain. We don't ever want to wind up playing a role like the one played by Alan Colmes, the liberal whose existence on the nightly Fox News show *Hannity & Colmes,* which ran from 1996 to 2008, served no other purpose than to make Sean Hannity the hero. Colmes never won. Hannity emerged victorious in every one of their nightly debates. And once Hannity no longer even needed the pretense of having a liberal foil in order to rant and rave against liberals, Hannity took the show solo. Colmes played the role of the permanent minority voice so well that he made himself irrelevant.

This is what Republicans are trying to do in many state legislatures: paint Democrats as so much of a permanent minority that they can start ejecting them from participation in lawmaking in any meaningful way and thereby consolidate power even more. Once you have been characterized as someone who cannot contribute to winning, your contributions overall seem less and less necessary. And you cease to even believe in yourself. They are trying to create rules to make the kind of structural changes that will produce and reproduce this outcome, for example, in Texas and other states, creating voting districts for seats in Congress that make voters who support Democrats a permanent minority, never able to win a seat.

Winning must be at the center of social justice movements. There's little value in being right but never winning. When working toward social change, it is essential to deeply internalize the belief that we can win—not just someday far, far away, but in the here and now. Even if we can't win everything now, winning a step forward demonstrates that we can win more and motivates people to keep going. That's how power begins.

FIND YOUR POWER

Increasing Your Belief

This activity is meant to provide you with one way to think about your belief in your power as an agent of social change, as well as guidance for how you can increase that belief.

It's not easy to keep believing that change is possible, or that your individual contributions are helpful, especially in the face of setbacks. Seeing your own personal power, and seeing how you can use it in service of change, is a critical first step. You don't have to be a professional activist to contribute something important: a meeting space, a meal, a clever way of saying things, some key relationships.

These are three important questions to ask.

1. What useful assets do I have?

What do I have (or have access to) that is valuable for a social change effort?

- Time
- Resources (money, tools, property, materials, memberships, etc.)
- The ability to support others' activism (childcare, travel, moral support, etc.)
- Skills and talents (the ability to bring people together, speaking persuasively, creating content, etc.)
- Access to information, people, places, or resources
- Historical insights or other perspectives (if you're an

elder who lived through another movement or an immigrant familiar with a relevant example in another country)
- The courage to stand out and speak up
- The ability to model new behaviors and norms

How can my specific assets be used to help a social change effort win?

- What does a social change organization or campaign need that I can offer them?
- How can I connect people working on change to people or resources that would help them take their work to the next level?
- How could I use my assets to start something new that increases pressure on decision-makers or makes people working toward change stronger?
- What is the contribution I've made to help people achieve something that made me feel proudest? How could I do that again for a social cause?

Think about things you do every day (reading or watching the news, talking to people in person or online, making things, organizing recreational activities, etc.) that you may not have considered assets before. Those may be some of your greatest strengths.

2. Who listens to me?

Without a doubt, there are people who listen to you: at home, online, at work, in friend circles, or in other social environments. Whether it's a lot of people or just a few, your listeners are a source of power and a way you can contribute to social change. Ask yourself: How many people will do different things I ask them to do?

- Donate money, show up at an event, or re-post something online
- Make introductions I ask them to make or get others involved in an activity
- Change a behavior (start doing something or stop doing something)

Now ask yourself: How many people look to me for guidance when making decisions?

- Asking me who they should vote for or donate to
- Asking me how they should handle difficult situations

You have an audience, even if it's just a few people. Are you taking stock of who listens to you, and asking those people to do things that can make a difference for a cause? And are you also listening to them? If your friends are passionate about an issue, do you support them?

It's not always comfortable or easy. But people listen to you for a reason, and though you never want to be manipulative or take advantage of those people, you can probably do more with those relationships than you have been doing. You may have created an unwritten rule for yourself about not asking people to do things related to social issues. But given the times we're living in, it's worth reconsidering that rule. If we want things to change, we all need to maximize the power we have and put it to good use.

You surely don't want to do anything that would undermine your relationships or turn people away from listening to you. But you don't have to cross that line to do more. What can you ask people to do that would strengthen a cause devoted to social change? How can you respectfully invite them to be a part of something that they might also believe in? Like you, they may find inspiration, purpose, and connection from getting involved.

3. What am I willing to do?

You can always start with something small: You don't need to give away all your assets, or ask people to go out and get arrested at a protest, to make a serious contribution.

Map out your assets, and the usefulness of different assets for different social change efforts: elections, protests, confronting decision-makers and pressuring them to change, changing policies at a school, a company, or another organization you're part of.

Map out the people you are able to influence and the boundaries of how far that influence goes (i.e., when they do and don't listen to you). Connect the things you are able to ask people to do with the most useful actions to support a social change effort.

See your power and make a plan: the intersection of what you are able to do and what you are willing to do. Try it out and see the kind of impact you can make. It's not always a direct impact, or immediately obvious, but see how you feel and begin tracking your contributions.

8

Building the Infrastructure of Power

DEFINITION: The *infrastructure* of a social movement is anything that enables its leaders, organizations, and communities to manufacture greater power. It consists of technologies, relationship networks, financial systems, research capabilities, training programs, means of content production and distribution, and any other assets that allow groups of people to produce success in the political or social realm: changing laws, winning elections, redefining norms of behavior, forcing corporations to end practices that hurt people, and so on.

CHALLENGE: It is easy to think that major social-change wins are the result of bursts in popular momentum for causes that took off on their own. The reality is that, behind every win, there is an entire infrastructure that made it possible. If we fail to understand either the infrastructure we're up against or the infrastructure we need to win—and fail to invent new infrastructure to meet our needs for gaining power in new ways as conditions change—we will find ourselves winning less and less rather than more and more.

The Engine of Power

Infrastructure is a tricky word. It brings to mind images of machinery, systems, scaffolding. It's hard to define, but it's essential to understand. It helps us focus on the behind-the-scenes resources, relationships, and technologies that enable us to accomplish our goals.

Infrastructure is an essential tool of power, which means the best way to understand it is not by defining what it *is,* but rather by defining what it *does*—or allows us to do. Infrastructure creates possibilities. In the context of understanding how to build power, infrastructure is anything that reliably makes it possible to become more powerful.

In chapter 2, I described how Mike Pence and the Heritage Foundation crew were able to move so effectively from ideas to action. Lots of people sit in offices, bars, and living rooms in Washington, DC, late at night, dreaming up ways to take over the world. But few of them wake up early the next morning and get started.

Think of how far Pence and the crew would have gotten after Katrina, or how far the Heritage Foundation coalition that wrote Project 2025 would have gotten, if they hadn't had the infrastructure required to bring the right people, resources, and systems together to implement the plan they'd dreamed up. They had the organizational ability to coordinate the people they'd brought together. They had funding channels that would support the continuation of their work, no matter how radical. They had staffers experienced at writing legislation, lawyers who could find loophole opportunities in the existing laws, and researchers who could produce and promote reports that made their ideas look reasonable (rather than criminally corrupt).

If the difference between a dream and an achievable goal is having a plan, then the difference between the hope of making change and having an actual chance at winning it is infrastructure.

The scale of change doesn't matter. Infrastructure is essential at every level of building and using power to get something done. Think of how well you would do as an individual parent going up against an unfair school policy affecting your child, as opposed to standing firmly on the foundation of a preestablished parent group that speaks with one voice, has mapped out its plan of action, and has the means for communicating, collaborating, and advocating that helps you amplify your leverage and win something that matters for your child. Alone, it might not seem worth trying. But by utilizing the infrastructure that a group provides, the chance of making change gets a lot better. Even if you decided to go it alone, you would need the infrastructure of social media, crowdfunding, or other means of amplifying your voice and leverage in ways that make change possible.

The measure of a good strategy is the extent to which people can implement it—that is, the extent to which it will actually work in practice. And the measure of whether it will actually work in practice is the extent to which we have put the right infrastructure in place to make implementation possible. Infrastructure is just as important as ideas. Power requires both. Not just the right message but also the right channels and messengers to communicate it. Not just the right target, but the right means to do what it takes to put that target under real pressure. Not just the right plan of action, but the right means of motivating and mobilizing people to participate in it at the scale required to win.

Infrastructure and Possibility

Before I get into the specific role infrastructure plays in building power, let me first explain how infrastructure, in general, can shape what is and isn't possible for us.

The New York City subway system, one of the oldest and longest interconnected set of underground tracks in the world, is a massive piece of public infrastructure. It makes certain aspects of life possible for everyone who lives in, works in, or visits the city. Even people who don't take the subway—because they cycle, drive, ride the bus, take a taxi, or use a ride app—benefit from it by not having two million subway riders competing with them for space on the roads. It's hard to imagine what people's lives would look like without the subway, or how New York would have developed as a city without it. It's an incredible resource that makes it possible to affordably participate in so much of what New York has to offer outside of people's own neighborhoods.

But while it makes it possible for us to do some things, it makes it hard to do other things. It's nearly impossible to get from Brooklyn to Queens quickly on the subway because every major line (save one) runs through Manhattan. Brooklyn and Queens are part of the same island, while Manhattan is a different island across the water from both of them. But the subway forces people to go into Manhattan to go from Brooklyn to Queens. And once the infrastructure was set down in that way, it was very difficult to undo it and redo it another way. Even the will of eight or nine million residents of New York City could not overturn the influence of that infrastructure. Whatever effect it did or didn't have on people's pathways through the city—and through life—that was it, for good.

So it became something of an unwritten rule: If you want to have anything to do with the Jackson Heights neighborhood in Queens, you definitely don't take up residence in the Crown Heights neighborhood of Brooklyn. I personally made decisions about dating based on what type of travel paths seemed reasonable, opening up some opportunities and closing off others. (Even if I liked him, it wasn't enough to overcome the fact that he lived off the wrong line.) To be clear, the New York City subway system wasn't designed in ways that just happened to make direct travel between Brooklyn and Queens difficult, as if by accident or coincidence. It was the result of conscious decisions made by people with specific agendas over the period of its development—decisions that locked in those structures and the cascade of written and unwritten rules that stemmed from them.

Decades later, the New York official Robert Moses designed many aspects of the transportation system for New York City to serve decidedly unjust ends: making it difficult for poor people and people of color to access certain parts of the city or suburbs that he wanted to restrict to white and middle-class people. For instance, he created bridges over roads that made it easy for cars to travel to certain places but impossible for public buses to do so. That cut off access to Jones Beach for people who didn't have cars and made it something of a private enclave for people who did. The fact that Jones Beach became a "white beach" was no accident: Not only was it designed to exclude nonwhite people, but it received investments that other beaches didn't, from art deco buildings to the white sand they used to make it such a privilege to be there.

In this way, Robert Moses built physical infrastructure in order to create social realities. Building infrastructure was part of the way he gained the power to control the rules for how New York City worked—rules that millions of people would be forced to follow for generations, in service of his rather unjust vision for society. (For an example of how people built their own infrastructure in response, to make possible what the city's infrastructure wouldn't, see the online Appendix at rashadrobinson.com/book.)

It doesn't get more "structural injustice" than that: infrastructure specifically designed to make ways of living possible for "desirable" white people while making those same ways of living impossible (or harder) for everyone else. And once that infrastructure was built it was (and remains) difficult to undo those possibilities and impossibilities.

That is one example of the unwritten rules that infrastructure affects: how it makes it possible or impossible to live a certain way, what it makes easier and what it makes difficult, the opportunities it gives us or denies us. Naturally, the way that we design infrastructure affects what we're able to do with it.

That is also true when it comes to building power: Infrastructure makes certain actions possible. It seems obvious, and yet many efforts at social change fail or remain limited because they do not develop the infrastructure they need to make their strategy possible or do not know how to maximize the possibilities of the infrastructure they already have.

Bayard Rustin: Infrastructure Hero

When I was living in Washington, DC, in 2002, I hadn't come out as gay quite yet, but I was becoming clear about who I was. With increasing frequency, I tried to get myself to the kind of events where the chance of meeting a cute, politically aware guy was especially high. One of those events was a gay pride event at All Souls Church.

The stage caught my attention when one of the speakers started talking about someone named Bayard Rustin. He emphasized over and over how Rustin's contributions weren't given the proper respect. There are people you may hear about a lot. And then there's that moment when you truly learn about them. It's the moment when that person's contributions come alive, when you suddenly realize that many things you care about and talk about can trace back to their work. It's the moment you realize you have a hero.

Bayard Rustin was a brilliant Black gay man who not only mentored Martin Luther King Jr. but also greatly influenced the direction and strategy of organizations that defined the Civil Rights Era, such as the Congress of Racial Equality (CORE) and the Southern Christian Leadership Conference (SCLC). Rustin's understanding of the infrastructure it took to build both presence and power was indispensable to the rule-changing achievements won during that time. (I made it a point to keep learning about him.)[1]

A Quaker from Pennsylvania, Rustin was born in 1912 and raised in a home steeped in politics and activism. After stints at two historically Black colleges, and a training program for activism with the American Friends Service Committee, he was drawn to Harlem in New York City, where his talents as a singer, an orator, and an organizer turned him into a coveted member of the many emerging political organizations at the time.

Rustin's eventual connection with A. Philip Randolph, the president of the Brotherhood of Sleeping Car Porters, led him to focus on organized labor and to hone his sense of strategy—for both disrupting the dominant powers controlling people's lives and for building the kind of Black power that could transform all of our lives. His understanding of infrastructure was exceeded by none. He saw new kinds of organizations, for example, as infrastructure that would be needed to change the rules that limited Black people's freedom. He understood what it would take to become truly unignorable.

Organizations are like roads that new ideas can travel on: They provide routes for ideas to go places they can't otherwise go. In 1956, some organizations brought Black elites together, while others brought everyday Black people together. But there were no organizations of scale and ambition that brought Black organizations themselves together.

I always think of Rustin as someone who asked the big strategic questions that could open up new paths to power. Looking back at that time, I would frame one of his most important strategic interventions as having posed this question: *What if activism could become a religious calling and Black churches became the vehicle for people to hear and believe in that calling, and take action to further it? What if religious institutions could somehow be connected through an alliance among their leaders, which would enable those leaders to reach, motivate, and activate the many thousands of people who constituted their memberships, at a level of coordination never seen before—to exert pressure on local leaders and institutions and create a level of both local and national leverage never seen before?*

The answers to these questions may seem obvious now—and we're all familiar with the ways in which the right wing has made churches a keystone of their own infrastructure over the last fifty years. But at the time, this represented a big innovation in infrastructure.

Rustin's idea was one that needed a road to travel on. And so he determined to pave it by helping to build the SCLC. He approached King with an idea for this new infrastructure. It would allow southern Black leaders to become more than the sum of their individual parts: a group of ministers who each had "ties to masses of people so that their action projects are backed by broad participation of people who gain experience and knowledge in the course of the struggles."[2] Rustin helped the nascent group gather and coalesce effectively, with

King as its first president and organizer Ella Baker as its first staff member.

The SCLC was critical infrastructure: It made a new level of Black power possible. Its Crusade for Citizenship in 1957, the first broad-based voter education and registration campaign to be run in the South, focused on ensuring that Black voters could make a difference in the 1958 and 1960 elections. The SCLC also led the successful campaign to take on discrimination by local businesses in Birmingham, Alabama.

Following those successes and others, with Rustin in the lead, the SCLC organized the 1963 March on Washington for Jobs and Freedom, which led to the 1964 Civil Rights Act—eliminating racial discrimination nationwide, at least in the form of written rules on paper. The SCLC then led the protests for voting rights in Selma, Alabama, which led to the 1965 Voting Rights Act—guaranteeing voting rights to everyone equally (again, on paper) nationwide.

But the SCLC also invested in another kind of infrastructure beyond direct mass mobilizations. In 1961, it integrated the Citizenship Schools program, founded by Esau Jenkins and Septima Clark, into its organization. This fusion of two important kinds of infrastructure—bottom-up popular education and bottom-up political action—created a new kind of power related to building cultures of belief and changing perceptions of what was possible. The program organized almost sixty-nine thousand teachers—including the civil rights powerhouse Fannie Lou Hamer—to teach principles of political power and the tactics of political protest across the South, while registering more than 700,000 Black voters by 1968. Ten years after the first voter registration drive across the South, the SCLC was still innovating, finding new ways to get to even bigger results.

(For more examples of Black innovations in infrastructure that increased power for Black communities, see the online Appendix at rashadrobinson.com/book.)

But it was the march on the National Mall in Washington, DC, in 1963 that took the Civil Rights Movement to another level, with Rustin playing a key role in making it what it was. Rustin organized the buses that brought hundreds of thousands of people to the march, which turned into the largest march that had yet taken place in American history. He drummed up volunteers to make eighty thousand bagged lunches: cheese sandwiches, apples, and marble cake to feed more than 260,000 people who showed up to march from across the country. He got the mimeograph machines needed to print flyers at the scale needed to hand them out to all those people.[3] He also made sure that cleanup crews picked up the trash left after the march. He anticipated there being a racist double standard, and he prepared for it. The movement's enemies wouldn't be able to play that blame card, claiming that Black people had made a mess and sullied the National Mall.[4]

Bayard Rustin was the architect and the contractor. To get it right, you had to be both. Strategy and logistics, both. The people power and the political power, both. He understood the dynamics necessary to make people in power nervous. As he famously said, "The only weapon we have is our bodies, and we need to tuck them in places so . . . wheels don't turn."[5] He combined that analysis with a profound sense of the kind of infrastructure that could make new wheels turn, including the ability for those without power to see their potential and their assets, and gain power over time.

Rustin was the lead strategist and organizer behind that game-changing day. He knew that he faced the dual challenge of amassing a historic crowd that would make the demands of the Civil Rights Movement unignorable, while also ensuring the safety of those involved, who would certainly come under attack for challenging the status quo.

At the March on Washington, Rustin spoke right after King, reading the list of demands the march was organized to achieve. But behind the scenes he played an even bigger role: working quietly beside A. Philip Randolph to turn the march from a dream into a reality, and to make it an effective accelerator for change. It was essential that the presence of so many people translated into the power required to change the rules for Black participation in society and in the political process.

For me, learning that a Black gay man was essential to the organization of one of the most important political events in American history was an inspiration. Over time, understanding Rustin's specific contributions to the strategy behind its success became equally important to my life as a leader.

Hearing the Message on Infrastructure

Bayard Rustin's far-reaching legacy really hit me when I found myself in the middle of one of the unlikeliest places for a young Black American activist to be: Serbia.

Serbia's bid to enter the European Union, which was submitted in 2009 and is still pending, is partially contingent on the country's progress toward ensuring freedom of speech and assembly. In 2010, after having been attacked during many previous attempts to stage a pride demonstration, Serbia's LGBT community thought they had found their moment to break through—they had the leverage of holding in their hands the verdict on Serbia's progress related to freedom of assembly.

As head of programs at GLAAD, I was tapped that year to participate in a U.S. State Department program that sent experts to support pro-democracy leaders in other countries. I was sent to Serbia for a short trip to support LGBT leaders who were planning a new round of pride events. The Serbian organizers were happy to have international representatives with them, people whose safety the authorities might be more concerned with protecting. Neo-Nazis were threatening to kill gay and lesbian people on sight, while the Orthodox Church had also made its opposition known. The people leading and participating in the march were risking a lot.

Shortly after I landed, I went to dinner with Boris Milićević, the president of Serbia's Gay Straight Alliance, the main queer advocacy organization in Serbia at the time. A burly guy in his forties, gay men everywhere would call him a bear. But I sensed that he and the other Serbian organizers were somehow disappointed to see me. When I started walking through a paper version of GLAAD's forty-slide presentation showcasing our media strategies, I could tell something was off. "This is all interesting, but we're not really interested in stories from the gay movement," he said. I stared blankly, more confused than ever. "We're actually very interested in the Black Civil Rights Movement as a model for how we do our work."

It turned out that Boris and his crew had been reading about Bayard Rustin, Ella Baker, and Fannie Lou Hamer, as well as many of our unsung civil rights heroes. The issue wasn't that I was Black, it was that I was not 1960s Black. Boris explained that he had studied the American Civil Rights Movement to understand how it was built and how its infrastructure resulted in the successes it achieved. He wanted to learn more about how the leaders knew exactly when and where to apply pressure to force change. He would also tell me, "We're interested in whether or not we have the right sound system or enough bathrooms. We're interested if we have the right sort of political and cultural ask. That's what we've been studying."

I could see how Rustin's thinking had influenced people on the ground in Serbia as they planned for their pride events: equal concern for the strategy and the logistics, a desire to organize people power in the exact right way to translate it into political power, and a belief in the need to make sure that their group's morale and motivation would survive whatever might happen.

Boris learned from Rustin that the greatest risk was not doing everything possible to make thousands of people's sacrifices mean something. People were going to risk their lives to participate in the pride events in Serbia. And whether those risks served a purpose everyone could believe in came down to infrastructure.

The Prize of Public Infrastructure

While building *movement* infrastructure is essential for social change, shaping *public* infrastructure is equally important for gaining power and changing how society works. Just as Robert Moses used infrastructure to create rules enforcing racial hierarchies, winning or losing fights over public infrastructure can have far-reaching consequences.

Liberals have often used education infrastructure to convey moral values and lessons related to equality and progress in society, moving us toward a more perfect union. But the right wing has long tried to take over that infrastructure, achieving much success at both the college and secondary-school levels in the last few years. They use their increasing control of the education system to rewrite history—erasing the story of Rosa Parks and countless others, for example, while peddling their own propaganda—as part of strengthening their movement and recruiting more people to it. They have also purged people from the ranks of education who were essential to advancing progressive values in society. It's a key part of their ability to control public perception related to what this country should be and what its biggest problems are—and aren't.

We are also in continuing fights right now over the design and resourcing of our infrastructure for public safety. What new mechanisms do we build? What have we inherited that we should dismantle? How do we define the role of law enforcement officers in our lives, what tools and authority should we give them or deny them, and what should they focus on? Who and what are the greatest threats to safety? Should we channel billions of our dollars to corrupt contractors and technology corporations so they can build new prisons to hold another eighty thousand nonviolent, hard-working immigrants who are vital to their communities, whom Trump's bloated ICE agency has often illegally targeted and abused?[6] Or should we turn the massive apparatus of law enforcement toward preventing cybercrime, investigating corporate fraud and tax dodgers, stopping polluters, and taking on other major crimes that actually harm people?

These fights over the power of government are really fights over public infrastructure, which determines what is possible or impossible in people's lives. Some of the biggest fights we take on are those related to our healthcare, education, transportation, and financial systems, as well as our environment and our natural resources. In addition to the obvious elements of these systems—such as the subway lines crisscrossing a city—there is also a vast, behind-the-scenes infrastructure made up of the people, resources, and logistics that make them work. Shaping public infrastructure means shaping all of those parts of it. Attacking the people who keep our infrastructure working for our benefit—for instance, by firing them in droves or gutting their pay and benefits, as Trump has—is a good sign that attacking that infrastructure itself will come next. And shutting down those systems shuts down so many opportunities, freedoms, and aspects of well-being in our lives.

Fights over public infrastructure require strong movement infrastructure. Historically, labor unions have been one of the most effective examples of movement infrastructure for battling back and balancing both corporate power and right-wing government power. They are one of the only forces built up to effectively restrict corporate power from taking over our lives and forcing us to live completely on their terms instead of our own.

Unions have also proved to be one of the only forces capable of going to bat against a right-wing government takeover of public infrastructure: Teachers' unions have been indispensable to preventing a right-wing takeover of many school systems, working with parents and students to hold the line—preventing regressive and destructive rule changes that could not be prevented otherwise.[7] And other public-sector unions protected government workers (and the infrastructure of public services and protections they keep functional) who were illegally and indiscriminately attacked by Elon Musk and Trump in the first months of his new term. It's not just about political fights. It's about what unions can bring about, not just what they can prevent. There is no other infrastructure, outside of the government itself, that can almost single-handedly lift entire communities out of poverty and provide fairness and economic security to millions of people.

In all these ways, unions demonstrate the incredible power of movement infrastructure: a mechanism for making everyday people socially, economically, and legally powerful enough to win changes that transform their lives, especially when it comes to protecting the public infrastructure our lives depend on. That is the reason the right wing has always tried to dismantle the laws that enable unions to exist and fight for justice, which they made more progress doing in the first year of Trump's second term than in decades.[8]

Outside of unions, nonprofit activist organizations are some of the most important examples of movement infrastructure run directly by movements themselves. Rustin knew this: If movements are driven by people power, then successful movements will always require innovative ways of organizing people. We are living in an age when individuals can become just as powerful as organizations—or more so. Both are essential to think about (and support) as essential infrastructure for any movement's success.

Whether we are operating today inside or outside a specific organization, it takes movement infrastructure to shape how any part of public infrastructure works. The following components, for example, are part of gaining power in a school system: winning school board elections; launching lawsuits; rewriting state standards and establishing oversight; mobilizing people to influence principals, teachers, and even textbook publishers; winning the contest over who represents the voice of parents and who represents what's best for students.

What does it take to be able to lead all these efforts? To take on the fights in education that matter and make sure schools are working as best they can to support students, their families, and our country at large, we need unions with leverage over the rules of a system; nonprofit organizations that know how to create popular, legal, and other pressure to effect rule changes and challenge corporate and political influence; volunteer networks of constituents whose demands officials and politicians must take seriously; and savvy individual influencers who can rally people in ways those above cannot. All working together in concert.

The right infrastructure makes a big difference. In the case of winning school board elections, some political parties and advocacy organizations working at the local level have built up a highly developed system for identifying, recruiting, training, and running candidates for school board—and some don't. It may seem that certain candidates come out of nowhere and launch themselves into office. But that's not how leadership usually works. Often enough, there's an entire operation working behind the scenes to develop leaders, align them with a set of clear movement goals, and facilitate their rise to power.

When we see schools and school boards being taken over by people with agendas we think are dangerous, we have to ask ourselves how much we're investing—individually and collectively—in building the infrastructure required to compete against them. Sometimes the competition is over before it begins because we are so outmatched. But that can be turned around, if we understand the path from building infrastructure to gaining power.

Case in Point: The Supreme Court

One of our most important pieces of public infrastructure is our court system. Just like the apparatus of law enforcement or our system for elections, the court system affects all of our lives by determining the fundamentals of whose voices and complaints get heard, which problems are recognized and addressed, what is and isn't acceptable behavior in society, and which rule changes across society will remain or get rolled back. The Supreme Court itself is a case in point for illustrating the grave distance between public infrastructure and movement infrastructure, not to mention the role of magical thinking in movement strategy.

It may be hard to believe, but in the span of just six short years, there were seven highly consequential fights over the character and role of the Supreme Court, all of which liberals lost.

1. In the year prior to Trump taking over the presidency in 2017, Democrats failed to convince Ruth Bader Ginsburg to retire in order to ensure she would be replaced by a liberal justice; she died just before the 2020 election, which put extreme conservative Amy Coney Barrett on the court.

2. In 2016, Republicans in the Senate blocked President Obama's appointment of moderate Merrick Garland to the Supreme Court, and would have likely successfully blocked Obama's effort to add Garland to the court by means of a recess appointment (a move that would have also required Obama to break a set of unwritten rules, which he was unlikely to do).
3. In 2017, Senate Republicans made a rule change that allowed Supreme Court confirmations to proceed by a simple majority vote instead of a sixty-vote supermajority, which immediately enabled Trump and his Republicans to put extreme conservative Neil Gorsuch on the court.
4. In 2018, Republicans convinced Justice Anthony Kennedy to retire early in order to be replaced by his former law clerk, conservative Brett Kavanaugh. Democrats had no influence in getting Kennedy to remain on the court so he could protect the few freedoms he valued in line with liberals, such as the right to access abortion and other reproductive care.
5. Later in 2018, Democrats failed to block the confirmation of Kavanaugh, Trump's second appointment to the court, based on accusations about his personal character and his alleged past sexual violence against several women—the type of accusations that had also failed to block the appointment of Clarence Thomas in 1993.
6. In 2020, during the last months of the first Trump presidency, Senate Democrats failed to block the confirmation process of extreme conservative Amy Coney Barrett on the same grounds that Senate Republicans had used to block Merrick Garland's appointment, enabling Trump to make his third appointment to the court and establish a 6–3 majority of radical right-wing justices.
7. In 2021, when Democrats held both the White House and a majority in Congress, progressive Democrats failed to convince President Biden to use his presidential powers to "pack the court" (that is, to add more justices to the court) or implement other structural reforms that could restore ideological

balance to the court and neutralize the effect of Trump establishing a right-wing majority.

Liberals lost every single one of these seven fights. And yet, as most of them played out, I would often hear confident declarations not only about our ability to win but, in some cases, about the inevitability of our success. As if we had not learned anything from each previous loss.

This reflected a larger pattern of either not taking the process of mapping power dynamics seriously or not being able to do it accurately—or both. Notably, as part of being caught up in this dangerous level of magical thinking, no one could point to any infrastructure that we had built on our side that could generate the power we needed to outmaneuver our right-wing opposition and win. This was belief but without a basis in anything real.

Our progressive movement infrastructure was not built to take on the fight over this important piece of public infrastructure. Right-wing Republicans, on the other hand, had invested in multiple forms of infrastructure, over decades, that made it possible for them to do just that. They made Supreme Court justice appointments a salient and urgent issue for their voters and for the media outlets that influence those voters, including establishing organizations dedicated to the cause. They created the relationships necessary to persuade the right people, such as Justice Kennedy, to do what they needed them to do. They invested in understanding how to manipulate Senate rules, as well as the media environment, in order to both facilitate and justify their power grab. They also invested in the internal alignment necessary to make sure they would be able to advance the careers of ideological extremists and ultimately appoint them without facing any opposition within their own ranks—even when it required breaking unwritten rules of politics.

These wins by the right wing led to a complete takeover and radicalization of the Supreme Court in a short time, resulting in the overturning of many essential legal rights and principles, as well as enabling increasingly authoritarian presidential rule by Trump. They won this prize. And it's paying off for them every day.

New Infrastructure, New Power: The Jena Six

Learning about Bayard Rustin made me a student of infrastructure. As a result, some big questions have preoccupied me all through my journey as a leader: What will our generation contribute? What new infrastructure for social change is needed for the twenty-first century? How can I be part of that? These are the questions all of us should ask ourselves—the answers will help us learn to innovate and build something new.

I was attracted to the idea of leading Color Of Change in 2011, only a handful of years after it had been founded, because I saw it as a new form of infrastructure built to ensure that Black people could utilize the internet for advocacy and activism—a means of building power that would clearly be relevant in a new century. The case of the Jena Six dramatized that potential, years before I arrived at Color Of Change myself.

The Jena Six are six Black kids who were in high school together in Jena, Louisiana, in 2006. They got into a physical confrontation with a white student, who was then sent to the emergency room and released the same day. Racial tensions in Jena—nooses hung on trees, arguments boiling over into fights—had been building for weeks before they boiled over in this particular fight.

But though the actions of white students had been ignored, the local prosecutor focused attention on this single fight and charged the six Black students with major felonies—five of them with attempted murder. Given the reality of the fight that took place, the charges were outrageous, harking back to the false or exaggerated charges trumped up against Black people that had defined the Jim Crow era in states like Louisiana. Many people saw them as an example of how white adults in positions of authority felt society's rules allowed them to own the fate of Black kids, without any consequences. The six students were incarcerated and punished in myriad ways throughout the ordeal, which played out from December 2006 until June 2009.

Initially, there was an outcry from the local community, but the school and town authorities were ready for that. They shifted blame, pitching themselves as martyrs holding back the stereotypical "angry Black mob" that was trying to defend indefensible Black youth and prevent the authorities from doing their rightful job to protect the truly innocent—in this case, a white student. In their world, among the people they cared about, the school administrators and the prosecutors would be heroes—rewarded, not punished.

Local protests were not enough to overcome the officials' power, any more than my Long Island community's outcry over Black students being sent off to be used as props in a police lineup led to any change in the people or policies that had made that injustice possible.

Yet Color Of Change brought something new to the table: leveraging the power of its online model of activism and bringing national attention to a local cause. The authorities in Jena were taken by surprise when a significant number of people from outside the state got involved in protesting the case.

The team at Color Of Change made sure that people who were outraged by the story but lived far away could participate in ways they otherwise wouldn't have been able to. They also helped put pressure on local decision-makers by raising awareness about the case in the national press, which would demand answers from local officials who weren't used to that level of attention and scrutiny. Calls were issued to pool together funding quickly so that the Jena Six could get legal representation skilled enough to go up against a legal system stacked against them—and people across the country answered that call, raising nearly $300,000 almost overnight. (This was not at all common back in 2006.) People banding together online helped swell the number of protesters at rallies and directly pressured the targets of campaigns demanding accountability and justice. Local officials had not been nervous about disappointing Black people before because they had never faced consequences for doing so. Now they were overwhelmed and on the defensive. They were beatable.

In the end, the charges against the Jena Six were reduced to battery, and none of the students served any additional jail or prison time. But without the national response, the controversy over their case might have ended very quickly without any social, political, or legal challenge—and resulted in the complete loss of freedom, justice, and humanity for all six students.

This was a strong example of achieving presence and then driving beyond presence to achieve power: gaining leverage over decision-makers by moving the fight to a field they were not prepared to play on. The novel infrastructure that enabled Color Of Change to activate online communities and networks of people ready to leap into the fight as needs rapidly emerged led to new powers that in turn led to different results for the Jena Six. The rules for how Jena, Louisiana, worked weren't completely rewritten, but they were seriously revised.

Like many other types of infrastructure that racial justice movements had leveraged before, the internet wasn't created with justice in mind. But innovative people figured out how to use it to make themselves more powerful. And that is always the continuing challenge. (For another example of innovation—figuring out how to use existing communications infrastructure to support Black activism during the Civil Rights Era in a game-changing way—see the online Appendix at rashadrobinson.com/book.)

FIND YOUR POWER

Infrastructure for Personal Power

This activity is meant to help you see the infrastructure that has supported your own involvement in social issues and the ways in which you can improve that infrastructure to help others get involved.

If you're reading this book, you care about social change—making the world a better place for all of us. And if you care about social change, someone probably helped you become aware of social issues and get involved in a cause at some point along the way.

Whether you or someone you know has been affected by an injustice, or whether you identify more broadly with others facing injustice, a lot went into your transition from understanding a given experience as unjust to taking action to do something about it.

Think about the following:

- How you got informed and got active
- How you discovered what you can offer and what you like about taking part in making change
- How you got connected to social cause organizations or social change efforts
- What you rely on to stay involved, both emotionally and practically
- What would happen if any of that infrastructure were not there for you

For me, public access cable television was public infrastructure that I was able to leverage early on in my activism. Before the internet, there were few ways for a high school kid to build an audience and get their views heard: becoming a child movie star, publishing a zine, or producing a show on local public access cable television. I chose the latter. I not only used that infrastructure to develop my voice and learn how to make persuasive arguments in a live setting, but I also used it to get things done: Through my TV show, I helped rally both students and adults to persuade our community to vote yes on the annual school budget that had failed before, which caused cuts in school programs.

Another example of infrastructure that was critical to my journey: Early on in my career, the game-changing activist Heather Booth, someone who has been consequential to social change struggles from the 1960s right up to this day, organized a series of meetings between older activists and younger, up-and-coming activists. That was a major platform for relationship-building for me: I still collaborate with people today whom I first met through Heather more than two decades ago, and I remember the powerful lessons from some of the elders who were there, many of whom are now ancestors.

Write down the specific infrastructure that made the following possible for you:

- Learning and becoming passionate about an issue
- Making your voice heard, including participating in demonstrations, signing petitions, making phone calls, arguing about the issue with others, and so on
- Building relationships and developing trust with like-minded people with whom you take action on different issues
- Supporting people, organizations, and causes that make a difference

Now answer the following questions:

- What forms of infrastructure supported you in different ways?
- What role did they play for you? What role does each still play?
- Which are no longer helpful for you?
- Is there something missing—something that you wish existed to support you (or others) in being more engaged and effective?
- What is the infrastructure that exists to engage people that you think could be stronger, or used better by movements?

Maybe the infrastructure you are thinking about is a radio station that informs people but doesn't really tell them what they can do about everything they just learned. Maybe it's a club or network you're part of that "stays out of politics" but could become an important space for conversation, maybe even collective action. Maybe it's the comment thread of your favorite cultural influencer connecting the content (exercise, cooking, etc.) to the issue or moment you're trying to elevate.

Now think about what your role could be in building, adding to, or somehow taking advantage of that infrastructure in order to advance a cause.

How could you demand more from that radio station, or start to organize people within that club or network? How could you help your friends or family make use of any of the infrastructure that's been important to getting you involved? How could you use your own assets—even something as simple as carpooling—to help people get involved in taking action to make change?

9

Building Winning Narratives

DEFINITION: Narrative power is the ability to influence the stories that drive people's behavior. Narrative is most useful as a tool in the process of social change when it's focused on the behaviors that lead to rule changes: either motivating people to take action in ways that influence decision-makers, or motivating decision-makers to change the decisions they make because they believe there are consequences for them.

CHALLENGE: It is easy to confuse narrative change with social change, a classic trap of magical thinking. We might hope that changing the way certain people think and talk about an issue will someday lead to a major rule change—but that doesn't always happen. Especially in today's world, it is easy to confuse narrative presence (making ideas visible and viral) with narrative power (turning ideas into drivers of change). The challenge is understanding both the uses and limits of narrative as a tool for change, and never getting caught up in the idea that narrative change is the goal in itself.

The Story of Narrative

The power of direct control is ordering your kid to go to their room. The power of narrative is making your kid think their stuffed animals are lonely and waiting for them to come home, so they choose to go to their room on their own.

Narrative is about motivation. The idea is simple, but the practice of narrative is hard. Authoritarian governments use narrative with great skill to get as many people as possible to go along with them without having to exert explicit force or coercion, saving that for the people they know they can never convince. That is why building an effective narrative infrastructure—the ability to counteract influence at scale—is so important in the fight against authoritarianism. It is also why the consolidation of corporate technology and broadcast media in our country, and its alignment with Trump, is so scary.

Although I have been deeply involved in narrative change efforts that proved instrumental in winning big rule changes—in areas from LGBT rights to criminal justice reform to tech policy—I have faced more struggles than successes. Getting outplayed in a high-stakes narrative contest at the White House that I should have won, but didn't, was one of those humbling moments (and a story I tell at the end of this chapter).

Using narrative as an effective tool is hard work, and we can never pretend it's easy. The lesson I carry with me: If I'm not constantly questioning how to do it right, I'm probably getting it wrong.

But what is narrative? In all my years of working in the realm of social change, never have I seen people get more obsessively distracted in an unproductive way than when debating the meaning of the word *narrative*. We get caught up in magical thinking about it, as if we would win the fight if we could just land the right definition. (I even wrote a paper in 2018 titled "Changing Our Narrative About Narrative," in an attempt to break up a conversation that I knew wasn't serving the progressive sector well.)[1]

As with the term *infrastructure*, it's far less helpful to debate what narrative *is* and far more helpful to understand *what it does. Narrative* refers to the stories we use to change people's behaviors and decisions in ways that lead to big rule changes—both written and unwritten. *Narrative power* is having the ability to do that. If our focus on *narrative change* isn't helping us get there, and either giving us false hope or stalling us out, then it's either the wrong strategy or not really a strategy at all.

Stories are powerful. They fill our minds with ideas strong enough to influence every decision we make and every action we take. They can drive us to take great risks without fear, or to fear situations that pose no risk at all. They can make us passionately reject evidence staring us right in the face or easily embrace lies that should be impossible to believe. The stories we carry in our mind influence our deepest assumptions and instincts—our very sense of what is true and false, right and wrong, good and bad, ally or enemy, helpful or harmful. More important, they influence whether we see our decisions as being in step or out of step with the people and principles we care about most—or with our own best interests.

If the written and unwritten rules define the range of behavior that's possible, and infrastructure is what makes power possible, then narrative is often the bridge between the two: Narrative makes it possible to motivate people to believe that new rules are necessary, and that they can and should play a role in changing them.

Recall from chapter 3 the story I told executives at Coca-Cola and at several other corporations about the way ALEC was hurting people with regard to Stand Your Ground and voter suppression laws and what would happen if they continued to fund it. That story not only incentivized those corporations to leave ALEC but also led to a domino effect that created a (temporary) rule change: Corporations that want Black people to believe they care about them cannot be members of ALEC. A persuasive story turned into a behavioral reality.

The stories Mike Pence and the Heritage Foundation crew told about New Orleans needing white, conservative leadership in their game-changing moment of rebuilding from the crisis of Katrina was also highly motivating: Far too many people saw an opportunity to profit from going along with that story rather than standing up against it.

But one of the biggest mistakes we can make is confusing stories that drive behavior change with stories that don't. For instance, **in all the resistance to Trump, there is great confusion between the narratives that merely express dissent and those that truly drive disruption.** While dissent is necessary (and can motivate people to become active participants in change), it is not the same as disrupting the ability of the Trump administration to do what they do. We can remain permanently out of power as dissenters, but disruption is what allows us to gain power and turn the country around.

For example, while placing the blame for numerous instances of wrongdoing (through the impeachment and other means) expressed dissent against Trump's decisions but didn't fundamentally impede his ability to stage a political comeback after 2021, being able to place the blame for COVID deaths on Trump truly undermined his authority during the 2020 election year. By making enough voters want someone new to take charge and making certain influential people not want to be associated with the mess the administration had caused, it was truly disruptive.

Telling ourselves the wrong story about what we need to do can lead us to miss opportunities for gaining real power. Many of us want someone to stop Trump from lying. But the real issue isn't that Trump is lying, it's that people believe him. More to the point, not only do people believe him, they believe *in* him. That is the true challenge. If Trump didn't know that the right type and number of people would believe in him—or at least act as if they do—his pathological habit of telling outrageous lies would not have been an effective strategy for gaining and maintaining political control of our country. That is what needs to be disrupted; calling out his lies may be necessary, but it is not sufficient to do that.[2]

That is what distinguishes Trump: He built a greater audience for lies than most people can build for the truth. Long before he was in politics, banks listened to him and made decisions to give him huge loans and credit based on his lies. So did church leaders, other business leaders, and, eventually, voters and the politicians who wanted those same votes. He's effective not because of what he says, but because people do as he says. That's what real narrative power looks like.

Words are important, but narrative power is often not about the words. It's about building an audience for whom a given set of words is meaningful. During the 2016 race for president, for example, many people ridiculed or disregarded Trumpian phrases like "Build the wall" and "Lock her up."[3] But the Trump campaign knew that the newly emerging force of MAGA voters would internalize them deeply and find them meaningful and motivating enough to vote him into office, and also persuade others to do the same. Meanwhile, some of Trump's Democratic challengers, whose words were chosen by out-of-touch consultants and outdated polling methods, neither of which were grounded in a deep understanding of narrative power, failed to get the results they needed.

Trump may not understand what a vaccine is, or what bleach is, but he has understood, perhaps more than anyone else in modern American history, how to use narrative to his advantage: making certain actions possible that once seemed impossible, while making other actions impossible that had defined the normal course of business for decades. Whether it was leading a personality-first social media strategy that could not be neutralized, finding the perfect insult to call someone that they could never seem to shake, or so brashly telling lies about immigrants, elections results, and his own accomplishments that people thought they must be true, his instinct for understanding how to use narrative to put himself in a position of strength and control over other people's behavior was unmatched.

His narrative power is one of his most effective strategies for rewriting the rules—often in real time. If using ultraviolet light "inside the body" or using disinfectant to make an "injection inside or almost a cleaning" to treat COVID-19 was off the table in any set of science-based rules for healthcare ever created, Trump put it on the table.[4] The bigger rule he put in place in that moment: An unqualified politician can invent and promote bogus solutions contrary to all available evidence and dominate the conversation rather than being dismissed from it. And the list of new rules born of his narrative power goes on.

Until Trump's supporters face more consequences than rewards for abiding by his lies, we will not disrupt his influence. Disruption will require building a wider audience for our own stories, driving people to action while changing the incentives for those who follow Trump's stories. But building an audience means building a system of meaning around a set of ideas. That meaning will derive from who is promoting which ideas, how they're doing it, and what channels are used to expose people to those ideas in ways that influence them. Chuck Schumer, for example, is not building an audience and feeding them meaning. Even if the quality of his words went from embarrassing to savvy, it wouldn't make them any more effective.

The Nature of Narrative

It is no surprise that people trying to influence how society works would spend a lot of time trying to influence the specific stories that motivate the decisions we make. Those with serious narrative power can affect both our conscious choices and our unconscious instincts. Whether ethically or not, they try very hard to embed these stories within us, while also making it as difficult as they can for anyone else to change those stories.

Narratives can make us feel attraction or aversion with regard to people we trust, activities we join, and identities we embrace. Three types of narrative are most important to use well in the context of social change—not just individually but all at once, in coordination:

- *Brand narratives* are stories we tell about individuals and institutions that influence the relationship we choose to have with them—including the products we buy and the people and ideas we buy into.
- *World narratives* are stories we tell about how the world works (or should work) that influence us to support different issues

and causes and to make choices about how we live—both big and small.

- *Personal narratives* are stories we tell about ourselves that can shape the impact we believe we can have in the world and therefore the roles we choose to play in it.

To be successful, a weight-loss brand, for example, must (1) embed in its target consumers a story about how its product, versus all other products, allows them to lose weight when they have not otherwise been able to do so (a world narrative); (2) tap into and intensify its target consumers' feelings about needing to lose weight and feeling that who they "really" are is not who they are now (a personal narrative); and (3) make its target consumers believe that signing on with its brand will be one of the most fruitful and reliable relationships they can maintain for turning their lives around (a brand narrative).

Politicians, essentially, need to do the same thing. As do churches and anyone else who wants to secure our commitment to doing what they want us to do. **Controlling the answers to our deepest questions makes people powerful influencers of our behavior.**

Corporations don't spend hundreds of millions of dollars on storytelling (branding, advertising, public relations, social content) because they don't know what else to do with their money. They tell stories because their business model depends on people believing the narrative that says a particular product or service can solve their problems. That often includes defining what those problems are in the first place. When we spend money to solve a problem that a corporation has convinced us exists, whether or not it does, the corporation wins. A huge part of its revenue is the sum total of our belief in their stories.

As much as corporations spend on marketing, all that money is still far less costly than any other way of getting people to purchase their products. Creating a monopoly is one way to ensure sales, but that is out of reach for most corporations. Creating products and services that actually make people's lives better is another way to ensure sales, but quality and effectiveness are often too costly—it takes more money to actually make products safe and good than it does to simply *convince* people they are.

That is why narrative power is an indispensable tool in the hands of corporations, governments, and anyone else trying to get people to do what they want them to do without having to spend too much effort doing it. Unlike the raw power of having direct authority or physical control over someone's behavior, narrative power is a tool for getting people to do things in a way that makes sense to them. Ironically, rather than widening the conflict between those in power and those who are subject to their power, a savvy narrative strategy can strengthen bonds of trust between them.

When people use narrative power to establish patterns of behavior that are reliable, widespread, and unquestioned, they can create highly influential unwritten rules and are often well on their way to codifying them as written rules with real force behind them. The narrative that a certain rule is based on "nature" is always their go-to. It gets easier to establish a rule by saying, "Hey, this isn't *our* rule, we may not even like it fully ourselves, but this is just *the* rule for how the world works. It may be unfortunate, but it's certainly not unjust or unnatural." Both the right and left can play that game, but recently, the right has generally been able to do so with greater effect.

We all have a deeply internalized story about gravity. Whether it's explicit in our minds or not, it's an idea about how the world works that affects the decisions we make—including our instinct to step away from the edge of a roof lest we fall or even come close to falling. We don't think of gravity as a story, however; we simply think of it as the way the world works—the truth. That understanding guides our behavior every moment. Once we've internalized it to the point of believing it's a rule of nature, we never doubt it or argue about it. We just follow that rule. It becomes part of our own nature to do so. And it gets harder for people to get us to come near a ledge. Of course, while gravity is actually real, many stories that people deeply internalize about how the world works—and take action on, like storming the U.S. Capitol on January 6, 2021—are not.

Someone can trick you into going to the gym one day, or give you a reward—say, cash back from your health insurance corporation—that keeps you going to the gym a little longer. Sometimes that's enough to trigger a longer-term shift. But not often. Because neither of those interventions compares to someone engaging you in a way that completely reorients your understanding about health, your feelings about exercise, and your practical ability to get to the gym. Those deeper changes result in you integrating the behavior of going to the gym into your daily routine. **That's what makes it a new norm—when you feel a greater threat of loss and pain from not doing it than doing it.**

We have all been "normed" at some point. A person, a group, or even the culture at large motivated you to do something, in some way clearing the barriers that prevented you from doing it (perhaps by getting you to no longer experience those barriers as barriers). By changing your motivation and removing the barriers that you couldn't overcome on your own, they've changed the very rules you live by: what actions feel acceptable or unacceptable to you, what you value at the deepest level, and therefore what decisions you make every day.

They've somehow tied that behavior to your very sense of self, or at least to your sense of survival and success. Now your very identity would be threatened if you didn't do it. Once it's embedded at the core of your belief system, and part of your identity, not doing it would feel like going against your own nature (even though it's really theirs).

As I've emphasized in earlier chapters, making something feel "natural" grants immense power to those who want to control how society works. In the United States, there are many deeply internalized stories about how the world works with respect to race, gender, and religion—stories that people feel they are obliged to follow because they are deeply rooted in the eternal truths and rules of nature. We demonstrate the power of those stories through our behavioral norms—for instance, many people's instincts to "step away" from Black people, LGBT people, Muslim and Latino immigrants, and others not only literally (as in an elevator or walking on the street) but also metaphorically (in a thousand different ways).

Narratives of blame and fear are strategies in an effort to achieve one goal: control. When leaders convince us of who or what will hurt us, and whom or what we can blame for the pain we're in, we tend to follow their directions for what to do next. That's why those who think we can counter the authoritarian control of someone like Trump without uprooting the deeply race-rooted stories of blame that give him and his allies so much power are telling themselves their own fictional story. It's magical thinking.

One painful example: Leading pro-immigration advocates tried to step away from Black people by coming up with their own term for jailing immigrants. Instead of the inclusive term *mass incarceration,* they chose to use the word *detention* because, at some level, they believed the former was too entwined with Black people. They wanted their own word to create their own cause that wasn't linked to Black people. It wasn't just a word game, either, or a distinction rooted in the technicalities of the system. When I challenged immigration leaders about this, some conceded the point but others emphasized that the fight for immigration reform was different from the fight for racial equality. The underlying narrative of their argument was clear: Immigrants aren't criminals the way Black people are. They felt they represented a different group.

Running away from race in that way has only come back to haunt pro-immigration advocates in a time when Trump has racialized immigration and built an entire infrastructure and policy agenda based on the anti-Black "slave catcher" model. As a result of the narrative choices they made, not enough people see themselves in each other's causes now, and we are not able to unite at the scale necessary to stop what's happening. Meanwhile, the right wing has become more and more united behind their general justification for attacking immigrants of all kinds, not just undocumented immigrants, even if not entirely united behind all the specific tactics they are using.

Narratives That Stop Change

As human beings, we're full of conflicting thoughts, assumptions, beliefs, allegiances, and desires. Which one wins when push comes to shove? Which one determines the changes we actually support versus the status quo we accept? Usually it's the belief or desire rooted in a narrative we have deeply internalized—an idea contained in a story that may trigger us at any given time.

As an example, criminal justice reform is often difficult to win because of the narratives that surround it. The injustices of the system are clear to many people, and the need for reforms to end those injustices feels urgent. But many of those same people are easily activated to oppose reform by stories that trigger much more deeply ingrained ideas they have about crime and race. And those ideas always feel more relevant and urgent whenever those stories are in play. The old refrain that a white conservative is just a white liberal who got mugged has some truth to it. People know that criminal justice reform is right, but if they feel scared because someone has tapped into ideas embedded over decades and centuries that Black people or outsiders are dangerous, or if they feel nervous because someone has tapped into deeply embedded ideas about rotten people never being able to change, then it becomes difficult for them to sign on to those reforms.

Profiteers who benefit from the status quo of the current legal system know how to manipulate people in this way. For decades, police unions have miseducated people about the fundamentals of crime and punishment, embedding narratives within us that have nothing to do with the truth and everything to do with their own power and profit. Police unions and police departments—and those aligned with them in politics, in news and entertainment, and in the tech and weapons industries—realize that people have more defenses up today when it comes to explicit racism and excessive cheerleading for violence. But scientific-sounding arguments embedded within emotionally effective storytelling can slide through those defenses and successfully influence people to deeply internalize false narratives about crime.

That was true about the "broken windows" theory of policing made famous by Rudolph Giuliani when he was mayor of New York City in the 1990s.[5] Many residents didn't necessarily feel it was a good idea to expand the authority of police to be able to violently patrol nearly every aspect of public behavior, as the approach required, knowing who would bear the burden of police abuse: women, kids,

LGBT people, nonwhite immigrants, and most certainly Black people. But the combination of "This is what the science says" and preexisting ideas about who causes crime and who in society needs to be controlled and disciplined made it feel like the only workable solution—an unfortunate but natural one. Of course, the approach has since been debunked, along with other pseudoscience that has been instrumental to perpetuating the injustices of the system for decades. But there's another hard truth about narrative in this example: Those approaches being debunked doesn't stop people from believing they work, as long as they believe in the people promoting them.

People pushing highly self-interested policies related to crime tap into deeply regressive, fear- and blame-inducing narratives that have been ingrained in us and reinforced in our culture, in some cases over centuries. Not to mention truisms about human behavior that are not actually true at all but are constantly reinforced in people's lives, from church to children's rhymes. When we go up against their rhetoric, we are going up against the long-running momentum those ideas have had and the way they have shaped people's deepest instincts.

When people's sympathies get swayed by an overwhelming degree of pro-reform stories during events like the Black Lives Matter protests in 2014 or 2020, it's not long before police unions begin exploiting people's more long-standing commitments—their deepest beliefs and assumptions—to sway them back and even motivate them to passionately fight reforms. That makes it harder for any major structural changes in the justice system to hold. It is no accident: Those who hold power rely on a wide array of narrative infrastructure—which gives them the ability to influence the media people consume and the public figures people trust—to help them pull it off.

The Role of Reinforcement: Bail Reform

Bail reform is a telling example of backsliding. In 2008, local prosecutors and judges kept a national total of more than 785,000 people in jail every night—many of whom had not even been convicted of a crime but simply could not afford to pay bail. Prosecutors often demand unattainable bail amounts that they know will result in people going to jail, and judges happily oblige, knowing the same. It's hard to believe, but people sit in jail for weeks, months, or even years simply because they don't have the money to pay the bail required to get out. Their detainment has nothing to do with the severity of their alleged crime, the risk that they will flee before trial, or any other legal reason. When judges and prosecutors collude to set bail that is out of reach for defendants and their families, they thereby sentence those who are arrested to serve time whether or not they're guilty.

According to the written rules of the law, they are to be presumed innocent. Yet they are still trapped in jail, victims of the unwritten rules that treat poor people differently from those who can afford to post bail. It has been one of the biggest drivers of mass incarceration. Part and parcel of that reality is the unjust targeting of Black people by police and prosecutors for no other reason than being Black. I've heard the civil rights attorney and founder of the Equal Justice Initiative, Bryan Stevenson, distill the reality of our criminal justice system in a very clear and simple way that has always stuck with me: *You are better off being rich and guilty than poor and innocent.*

Following several years of focused community activism during the 2010s, states across the country finally took action to limit the demand for cash bail as part of a larger effort to reduce mass incarceration, with wins in New York, New Jersey, Illinois, and more. It took a long time to put the right people in place as prosecutors and legislators, and to mobilize enough people convinced of the injustice of bail, to win those rule changes. Some places eliminated mandatory cash bail for certain offenses, while others introduced alternatives to ensure someone's return to trial that did not involve incarceration. Many different types of bail reform were implemented across the country, some by law and some by prosecutor practice.

Big changes took place in dozens of cities, including Los Angeles, Denver, Houston, New York, and Atlanta. Where it did, thousands of people without money to pay bail were freed to rejoin their families and neighborhoods, awaiting their trials in the same way that people with money do. By 2025, the number of people sitting in jail on any given night had declined to 562,000—a major reduction. It was a huge victory.

But in some ways, those of us who took part in the bail reform movement left it there and moved on. We didn't put the energy and resources into proving the value of the win. We did not communicate about all the people returning home, nor did we convey the restoration their return represented for everyone whose lives they touched. We didn't tell the story of how the elimination of cash bail made everyone safer. We did not adequately reinforce the narrative that bail reform was not only just but also effective. Study after study found no relationship between advancing bail reform and increasing crime rates, but that didn't prevent people from claiming there was one.[6]

When politicians latched on to the perception of rising crime as a hot issue during the pandemic years, they used bail reform as a scapegoat, as did those who profited either monetarily or politically from filling jails. A total misdirection, but a persuasive one that even sympathetic politicians felt boxed them into a rhetorical corner, making it difficult for them to defend the recently won reforms. The right wing then used its narrative power to change behavior—even among people who had become highly supportive of police reform in the wake of the 2020 protests set off by the murder of George Floyd. Suddenly, many of those people actively supported reversing bail reform. The narrative those of us advocates had advanced to win reform wasn't present enough in the conversation or powerful enough in its influence to defend those wins.

One long-standing narrative is that whenever there's a spike in crime, it's because we've become too "soft" on it—or, more specifically, we've become too soft on Black people and other marginalized groups, like undocumented immigrants, who need to be much more aggressively controlled. The story is that we need to rein in reformers rather than changing anything having to do with how the system works. That's a classic profiteering narrative. All we need to do is look at who benefits from it. That story leads to more police, more equipment, more technology, more money, more authority—and less accountability—for law enforcement. These are the solutions that make sense when profiteers introduce their wrong but persuasive narrative about the problem.

In many places, bail reform efforts ceased to move forward, while existing wins in other places were reversed. We had used narrative as a very effective tool—motivating people to demand change in ways that forced politicians to do the right thing. But then we lost the narrative battle that came next: the backlash, the blame game, the profiteering posing as concern for public safety, the need to show that advocates of reform actually cared more about people's concern for safety than anyone else.

As soon as we won the first bail reform in a state legislature or prosecutor's office, we should have launched a campaign twice as big as the campaign we ran to get that win, telling people over and over about the value of it. We should have had billboards posted everywhere with the faces and families of people returning home. We should have had people talking about it on podcasts and on YouTube pre-roll ads. We should have blitzed the media environment and shown up to community gatherings far and wide, to make sure people understood what was happening, knew how to interpret it, and felt committed to bail reform as a new rule that should never be overturned. But we didn't. We didn't have the funding to pay for it or own the infrastructure to do it on our own, but we also didn't make it a priority.

Because we hadn't embedded a story about its benefits for everyone, and a competing story about how crime worked, it was easy for pro-incarceration people to successfully lie about it. Their arguments about bail reform being a driver of crime felt intuitive to people. *Crime is going up,* they said, *because people who should be in jail are going free.* That narrative was consistent with long-standing (if completely misinformed) stories about crime in general. They didn't have to work too hard at it, because people already had those underlying beliefs. All they had to do was scratch the surface to activate those beliefs and agitate people against reform.

We should have done the narrative work to ensure that no one would advocate for turning back the clock on bail policies because a single person out on bail committed a crime, any more than someone would advocate for completely banning cars in response to a single car accident. The story would not have been that the one instance is representative of a larger problem. But we acted as though the facts would speak for themselves. They didn't.

The evidence was on our side, but the story wasn't. And by the time we tried to tell our story, defending against the attacks on reform, we were on the defensive—and we sounded like it. We sounded like we were begging for charity rather than telling the truth about safety and justice, and under the threat of increasing crime, no one felt charitable.

I'm proud of all the progress we *have* achieved on bail reform, but this is one of my biggest regrets: We didn't defend what we won. It was magical thinking to presume we didn't need to do so—that we had won people over and we could never lose them because we were right. Part of that is due to the donors who fund policy campaigns having the habit of moving on after a win (or loss), and not understanding the fundamental mechanism of narrative: investing in reinforcement. Constant reinforcement. But those of us who led these campaigns share greatly in this loss. We knew that no win is permanent, and yet we were eager to build on our success and move on to the next, more ambitious rule change.

It was not easy to let go of our own story about bail reform to anticipate what would likely happen if we didn't reinforce the narrative. I couldn't blame people who were being told that bail reform was dangerous: They were holding on to a story that wasn't true, but I had done the same thing in other situations. We all do that. It is easy to blame people for thinking a certain way. It's harder to do the work required to help them let it go.

Not recognizing the critical importance of narrative reinforcement is a classic trap of magical thinking. When he's on air, the news anchor Anderson Cooper looks at us through the camera before he breaks for a commercial and says, "You're watching CNN." Why? Does he think we don't know what channel we're watching? No. He knows we do. But part of his job is to reinforce our conscious awareness of that fact, in order to strengthen our commitment to continue watching. He is reinforcing the idea that CNN is responsible for whatever informative or entertaining moment we just experienced. It's part of building the brand narrative that makes us want to come back to CNN and, perhaps, makes us feel it's the only news worth watching. It may seem like overkill, but that is only because we don't know what it's like to live in a world in which a news anchor does not do that. By constantly telling us what we're watching, Anderson Cooper is reinforcing the story we tell ourselves about our experience. A powerful brand never takes a "one and done" approach to narrative. Its leaders know that if they are not constantly working to hold their place in people's hearts, they will quickly fall out of them.

It's helpful to think about effective narrative work as focusing on achieving four different outcomes, including reinforcement. The challenge is to achieve those four outcomes all at the same time, with equal force, in highly coordinated ways, in service of a clear rule-changing goal. Those outcomes are:

- **Reinforcement.** Strengthening the preexisting narratives that support a behavioral goal, which always requires more work than we want it to.
- **Destabilization.** Weakening the preexisting narratives that undermine our goal so that people no longer experience those narratives as the unwavering truth.
- **Replacement.** Embedding new narratives as the prevailing truths about how things work that shape people's intuitions, instincts, and decisions.
- **Activation.** Tapping into established narratives—new or old—in ways that motivate people to take specific actions and make specific decisions—that is, not assuming people will act because they hold certain beliefs, without being intentionally and effectively activated.

Any successful social change effort has the infrastructure and determination to achieve all four at once. But even when you're arguing with a family member or trying to get your friends to join you in an effort to take on problems you see at school or work, it's important to keep these four objectives in mind. You will see how much further you can get if you do.

Losing the Narrative on Policing at the White House

The fight over the rules governing how policing works in our country is another, even bigger social change struggle that escalated in the 2010s, also focused on criminal justice. For a long time, the main strategy of police and police unions was to deny the very existence of systemic racial bias in policing, despite all the evidence to the contrary. Talking about defining and controlling what's possible: If the problem does not even exist, then big changes are not needed.

This is exactly why instilling doubt in people is the biggest narrative goal for anyone trying to defend the status quo. Police unions are expert at the "destabilization" track of narrative work. I came face-to-face with this narrative strategy during a White House meeting in 2016. After the police killings of two Black men in July that year—Alton Sterling in Louisiana and Philando Castile in Minnesota—followed by the retaliatory killing of five police officers in Texas and three in Louisiana, both by Black gunmen (both military veterans), President Obama called together a meeting of people he thought could advance the national conversation on policing.

We met in the Eisenhower Executive Office Building, across the street from the White House, in an enormous room with an elegant parquet floor. The president had invited more than thirty people, from police chiefs and activists to mayors and Fraternal Order of Police (FOP) representatives. (The FOP is the largest single membership association of police officers in the United States, functioning as an official union in many localities and a highly influential political and legal organization everywhere else.)

I arrived planning to sit next to my friend Judith Browne Dianis from Advancement Project, a legal and policy organization supporting grassroots racial justice efforts. Instead, I was directed to an assigned seat between Mayor Tom Tait of Anaheim, California, on one side, and Pittsburgh's police chief, Cameron McLay, on the other. The seating was intended to be uncomfortable, with activists and academics seated next to police chiefs, officer association leaders, and elected officials. We all sat in a square formation with Obama at the front of the room, sleeves rolled up to his elbows. He was ready to make something happen.

The meeting lasted four hours. It was exhausting, but not because of the length. When it was my turn to speak, I shared my own scary experience with stop-and-frisk by officers who profiled me in Central Park in New York City. "Stop-and-frisk terrorizes Black communities," I told the group. Very soon after me, it was Jim Pasco's turn. He was (and still is) the executive director of the national FOP. He addressed his comments partly to me. I remember him saying something like this: *I gotta say, all this talk of racial profiling, well, this is the first I've heard of it. This is all news to me.* There was a gasp in the room. I interrupted him right there, breaking the expected etiquette of the scene and potentially starting a fierce debate, but Obama stepped in to keep the conversation moving around the room. Other people referenced Pasco's comments later on, but he had already won.

Pasco was well trained in narrative, understanding not only how to deliver a message but also how that message would work within the narrative environment of a given situation to get him the outcomes he wanted. Obama created the space for us to establish common ground, a consensus about the national problem of police violence. But Pasco knew that if he could prevent that from happening during the meeting, and prevent news stories about the meeting from being able to report that a consensus had been reached, then he could close down the possibility of advancing any real change anytime soon. He wasn't wrong.

The idea that the head of the FOP would be the authority on whether or not I experienced racial discrimination from police is absurd. Imagine a sexist needing to admit they are sexist in order to be labeled a sexist. Imagine a patient needing to admit they have COVID-19 in order to be diagnosed as having COVID-19. None of that makes sense. But it's not about making sense. When it comes to policing, the logic people hold doesn't have to make sense. It just has to be held deeply.

A great many people across the country believe a preexisting narrative about policing. That narrative includes the idea that police officers are fundamentally good people and so policing itself must be fundamentally good—and also the idea that if the police don't see there's a problem, and they aren't in favor of change, then change should not go forward or society will pay a high price. Similar to the banks being brought in to solve an economic crisis they created, or any tech corporation being allowed to regulate itself, the narrative insists that police are the only experts on policing worth trusting. **Maintaining authority over solving a problem—and even defining the terms of the problem—is a major achievement of power: creating unwritten (and sometimes written) rules about who can and can't be in charge of implementing solutions.**

In the narratives about policing that run deepest, police are ultimately the only experts on policing, not the communities who pay them and not the communities who pay the price for what they do. And within all of that is the idea that activists, reformers, and especially Black community leaders are not trustworthy. We are somehow biased, no matter how much impartial evidence we present, while police are somehow neutral and not self-interested, no matter how biased and dishonest many of them actually are—or how many corporate and political profiteers are clearly in on the lies along with them. That race-rooted double standard, which we have inherited across centuries in this country, remains an active narrative tool for people like Jim Pasco.

Pasco's claim about never having heard of racial profiling was laughable to me, but it worked to upend the meeting because it activated a deep and powerful narrative. It was as if he'd quoted the lyrics to a song everyone already had in their mind: He drew on the full power of that song without even having to sing it. **Being effective at narrative isn't about coming up with a new story. It's about tapping into a story people already know—one they already believe in—and using it to your advantage.** It's rare that we need to invent entirely new stories in order to motivate people. Much more often, the challenge is figuring out which stories they already carry with them that we can tap into to motivate them—and how best to do that.

It wasn't Pasco's narrative of doubt and denial that was the winning narrative overall. That was just his message for the day. He knew that if the group had reached a consensus, demands for changing the rules would flow and momentum would build. To prevent that, he couldn't just disagree with the point I had made; rather, he needed to negate it and disrupt the trajectory of the whole conversation. All he needed to do was to introduce a fundamental sense of doubt—confusion about what the problem was, and if there was any problem at all, as well as confusion about what the best solutions for that problem would be.

Today, the insurance corporations that work with police departments are having a conversation with them about the high cost of all their payouts related to lawsuits for police brutality. Perhaps those corporations will have the leverage to force the police to change, in ways that the narrative games of people like Pasco will not be able to neutralize.[7] It's unlikely they will use that leverage to push for the changes that matter most, yet the conversation about money might work at the level of incentives that can lead to major rule changes governing police behavior. Either way, we still need to find ways to win the narrative contests with players like the FOP, in service of making any rule change last.

During the meeting, I had spoken the truth—and I was more well-spoken than Jim Pasco—but I didn't have the power to control the story, which meant I didn't have the power to make that meeting a turning point against the status quo. If, *before the meeting*, I had seeded the idea among the other participants and the press that the FOP never owns up to anything or admits even the most obvious wrongdoing, then I might have been able to neutralize Pasco instead of the other way around. When he pulled his move, I would have been able to say: *There he goes again, proving my point.* With that, I could have turned his statements from being an asset into being a liability for him. I could have also engaged reporters beforehand to influence the questions they asked after this closed-door meeting let out, and therefore the story they would tell. I would have had to prime them to inquire about how Pasco was playing the game corruptly, rather than going to them afterward to complain, hoping they would referee. That, of course, would have taken time, infrastructure, and intention. Unfortunately, I was focused on other needs as I prepared for the meeting, and so I missed my chance.

There were more people in the room who wanted to see real change than didn't, but still the police narrative won and the status quo prevailed. That's power.

What happened in that room with the elegant parquet floor was a miniature version of what is happening in the larger room of public debate all the time. It may seem like most of us have reached consensus about what makes sense, and what the rules should be, and yet the majority opinion does not automatically dictate the rules. Far too often, those of us who are fighting for a cause we believe in are trying to win a debate in conversations that are set up for us to lose.

In my case, it wasn't about having the right argument to debate Pasco. It was about needing to have undermined his authority before he even walked in the room so that his interventions in the conversation would not have carried any weight. Part of the challenge of gaining narrative power is learning how to work at the level that truly changes power dynamics, decision-making, and people's deepest beliefs. Before even taking on the challenge of how to frame an issue in the most logical or most truthful way, it's about changing who is listened to, what is credible, and what stories drive action.

(For a deeper dive on the reinforcing relationship between narratives about policing and the culture of policing, and what that has to do with changing the rules of policing, see the online Appendix at rashadrobinson.com/book.)

FIND YOUR POWER

Being the Messenger

This activity is meant to help you see your role in narrative change, even when you do not have a major platform to broadcast your views or the ability to create viral content.

It can often feel difficult to take part in narrative change. If you don't have a video channel with a large following, a billboard you can rent, a pulpit with hundreds or thousands of people listening, or a business making political ads for a living, then how can you reach people? How can you influence the way people talk about an election or an issue?

Effective activism begins with understanding the reach you already have, and making sure you're seeing and seizing all the opportunities to use those spaces and places to your advantage. At a time when traditional media outlets are less trusted than ever, a single individual can often carry a message a lot further and a lot better than a TV ad can.

With the power of the internet, people can now take the place of media channels. Don't discount your influence, or the impact you can have just by speaking up and adding your views to the mix.

Think of yourself as a mail carrier with an important message to deliver. How many places can you deliver your message to? What is your route? How many people do you have contact with along the way? Sometimes, you may be the only person with your message who makes it down a given street. How do you use that opportunity?

1. Write down all the spaces where you go to interact with other people.

- Comment sections on news sites or online chat forums
- A community club, a church, or some other spiritual space
- A radio station that allows people to call in
- A newspaper or newsletter that publishes commentary from its readers
- Family or social gatherings
- School board meetings, city council meetings, or other venues for registering your opinion
- A professional network or committee you participate in

How can you carry your message to the places you go? Can you introduce something to the community that gets them thinking and feeling differently about an issue? Where and how can you make your views known? Can you provide opportunities for others to be part of the social change efforts you believe in?

2. Write down the ways you could engage in those spaces effectively.
There are at least two different roles you can play:

- Challenging people who may be promoting a false or harmful narrative or promoting attitudes and actions you disagree with strongly
- Sharing perspectives, stories, information, and action steps that people may want to hear but would not be able to learn about without your help

Try it. Try being the messenger in a space in which you've never offered your opinion before. Offer a way to take action on an issue you know everyone cares about. Or help people see an issue from a different perspective—reframing the conversation.

How are you received? What is the response? How can you work to gain those people's trust over time? How can you show them that you are willing to really listen to them? How can you be even more effective in engaging with them next time?

10

Changing Roles to Change the Rules

DEFINITION: A *role change* is a change in the public "job description" for a position of authority in government, business, or another system. A *role* is our shared story about what people in power are expected to do in their jobs and what happens if they don't. A role can change only if the people capable of enforcing those expectations believe in the new story and are motivated to hold leaders accountable.

CHALLENGES: It is often not possible to change rules without first changing roles. Even when it's possible, it is much easier to win big rule changes after winning big role changes. The challenge is knowing how to change the public definition of a role in ways that truly define the range of action for the people in that role—raising the floor for what's acceptable and raising the ceiling for what's possible.

Chuck Schumer Was Dead Wrong

"Orrin Hatch is an institutionalist. There are others, too. There are not enough votes to get rid of the filibuster for Supreme Court justices. It's safe," Senator Chuck Schumer told me immediately after Donald Trump was deemed the winner of the electoral college in the fall of 2016. It doesn't get more magical thinking than that.

A small number of national social justice leaders were meeting with Schumer in the hopes of defining some common ground for strategy. The result of the election was alarming. No one knew what would happen next. People were scared and standing on shaky new ground. We were all eager to fortify our defenses against the likely attacks we were about to face, targeting hard-won progress like voting freedom, reproductive freedom, and national programs like Obamacare and Social Security.

It was clear that a well-organized opposition would be critical for preventing the worst from taking place under a right-wing and largely incompetent presidency. Political leaders and community leaders, often in deep disagreement about policies such as raising the minimum wage and regulating Big Tech and Big Oil, would need to work together.

It turned out that agreement over strategy would prove far more important than agreement over policy. Under Obama, the centrists and the progressives struggled constantly over policy. But none of us would do well if the right wing consolidated more power under Trump, so we would need to work together to mount an effective challenge that did not depend on everyone agreeing on policy.

Even so, we were each starting from very different places when it came to strategy because we were starting from different sets of assumptions. Whether it was an outgoing Obama official, a long-term fixture in politics like Chuck Schumer, or even "expert" career advocates and politicos who had lived their entire professional lives in DC, there was a distinct break between those of us recognizing the seismic change Trump represented and those treating the incoming administration as part of the business-as-usual, we-win-some-we-lose-some cycle of politics—as if the Trump administration were merely going to be George W. Bush round two.

When Schumer called Utah Senator Orrin Hatch, then the longest-serving Republican senator in U.S. history, by the name "institutionalist," he was referring to how he believed Hatch played the role of senator: using all the written and unwritten rules of the Senate to get what he wanted, while protecting the Senate's historic processes and traditional ways of doing business. That is, playing by the rules, not changing them. Schumer was assessing the range of actions Hatch would take by using a fixed definition for what an institutionalist does and doesn't do.

(In that same meeting, Schumer emphasized how he had long been a gym buddy of Jeff Sessions, the incoming attorney general—they worked out together all the time. He told me he'd be able to work with Sessions and keep things reasonable. This Jewish Brooklynite was telling me, a Black country boy from Long Island, that I shouldn't worry about an old-time white politician from Alabama who was about to take control of the largest law enforcement agency in the country. I'd like to think that Schumer, after everything that played out over the next decade, would not make that particular mistake now.)

Schumer's 2016 assessment of Orrin Hatch was very wrong. He did not understand that the definition of the role of senator was about to shift for Hatch and other seemingly traditional Republicans. **Trump was issuing a new job description for every Republican politician, and most would accept the new set of expectations (whether they agreed with them or not).**

Schumer knew that, historically, the role of "conservative" could involve advocating for the rights of individual states to make their own laws when a Democratic president was in power, and then advocating for top-down presidential authority when a Republican president is in power. That was just the self-serving dynamics of politics. He had probably called out that hypocrisy many times. But he did not recognize that the Senate's "institutionalists" would be much more concerned with staying loyal to Trump and the new roles he had laid out for them than with staying loyal to their traditional role (even, for some of them, their lifelong commitments) in upholding the institution of the Senate. It became career-ending to betray Trump and the opportunities for conservative dominance he represented.

Whoever could wrest control of redefining the role of senator, and thus redefining the actions that could take place under the banner of that title, would ultimately gain power. By doing so, Trump quickly secured control of a major part of the infrastructure of government decision-making—a major piece of the infrastructure of power. We had already seen him successfully redefine an even bigger role: In 2015, the preexisting definition of "Republican nominee for president" had seemed like it would prevent Donald Trump from ever becoming one. But Trump—with his lack of experience, insults against Republican Party policies and past presidents, obvious lies, vulgarity, demagoguery, theatrics, and offensive rhetoric—redefined that role quickly.

Schumer *overestimated* the power Democrats had to keep the preexisting definition of the role of "institutionalist" in place, and therefore keep Orrin Hatch and other similarly oriented Republicans in check. He also *underestimated* the cultural and political power that Trump had quickly built to be able to radically redefine roles and, by doing so, open up the range of possibilities for all the rule changes he could then drive forward. There was no longer room for the role of "institutionalist" in the definition of Republican politician, no matter their tenure.

Needless to say, Hatch did not play the role Schumer wanted him to. He played the role Trump wanted him to—the role Trump had redefined for him. Schumer thought that there would be enough institutionalist Republicans to block any effort to end the sixty-vote minimum threshold for confirming Supreme Court justices. Up until that point, it was possible to filibuster (i.e., endlessly delay) Supreme Court confirmation votes unless there were sixty votes in place to stop the filibuster, usually requiring at least some members of the minority party to participate. All the signs were there: Using procedural tricks, Mitch McConnell, the Republican Senate leader in 2016, had denied President Obama his appointment of a Supreme Court justice at the end of his term, rewriting the unwritten rules of the Senate in quick order. But Schumer was fully locked in magical thinking mode.

Of course, the Senate threw out the filibuster rule immediately. It happened just two months after Schumer assured me it wouldn't—not only that it wouldn't, but that it *couldn't*. In his mind, Orrin Hatch was constrained by a narrow, fixed definition of his role. Schumer didn't see what was possible for big rule changes because he didn't recognize how many big role changes were underway, rewriting the job description for people like Hatch. We got the ultraconservative ideologues Neil Gorsuch, Brett Kavanaugh, and Amy Coney Barrett on the Supreme Court as a result—confirmed with votes of 54 (three of whom were Democrats), 50 (one Dem) and 52 (zero Dems), respectively. (In 2025, continuing the pattern, Schumer was outplayed yet again when Republican Majority Leader John Thune erased another long-standing rule of the Senate, accelerating the confirmation of previously blocked Trump political appointees across the government.)

In turn, the three justices Trump appointed further enabled a newly empowered six-to-three majority right-wing court to change the definition of the role of a Supreme Court justice. In one decision after the next, the court erased the long-standing unwritten rule of abiding by the decisions of prior Supreme Courts, rewriting the law in line with their ideology about how America should work—not only defying precedent but also defying any credible reasoning for interpreting our Constitution. They no longer even needed to pretend they cared about it. That role change has shifted the rules for how our country works, eliminating, for example, affirmative action, protections against religious discrimination, the constitutional right to an abortion, much of our ability to regulate corporations, and our ability to hold a president accountable for clearly criminal violations of the law.

This is how changing roles proves to be vital in the process of changing rules, and why the power to change roles is critical to gaining and holding power.

The Three Rs of Social Change

There's a secret for understanding how major change happens in society: Every major *rule* change is preceded by a major *role* change. It's part of the three Rs of social change: roles, rules, and results.

It's hard to get big results without changing the rules for how things work, and changing the rules often requires being able to change the roles of the people who make them.

A *role* is the set of prescribed functions for any person who plays an important part in the story of our lives and in the life of our country. Parent. Pastor. CEO. Influencer. Teacher. All of these roles have definitions that determine what we expect from them and how we evaluate them. For instance, there was a time when being openly gay was not part of the definition of teacher, which prevented students from benefiting from all that those potential teachers had to offer. We needed to change the definition of what a teacher was—our shared public job description—before we could change the rules for who gets to take on that role. (In some places, we still need to do that.)

We must always change the public expectations of any role that is perceived to be an authority before we can change the rules of the institutions they command—institutions that determine the type of country we live in and what is or isn't possible in our lives, communities, and culture.

For example, before we could prevent police officers with a long history of lying and abuse from continuing to give false testimony in court, and unjustly send more people to prison, we needed to redefine the role of the local prosecutor. Only a prosecutor who sees their role as pursuing justice—rather than pursuing convictions at all costs, with justice being a remote, secondary concern—would have the motivation and resolve to set a rule in place that bans police officers with a history of lying on the stand from testifying any longer. (And it was a lot easier to do that than to change the public definition of *police officer* to exclude people who lie on the stand.) Once we redefined who a prosecutor should be, how they should behave, and what standards and which people they should be accountable to, we got a new kind of prosecutor in offices across the country—and we started to get the rule changes we needed to reduce mass incarceration, decrease discriminatory prosecutions, wind down the biased drug war, and increase police accountability.

Understanding the importance of role changes helps us get out of the trap of magical thinking in which we act as if we will win all the changes we want to win by going after one policy change at a time. When someone embraces kindness or generosity as part of their identity—that is, as part of their definition of who they are—it leads to a whole new set of behavioral changes, far beyond the slow pace of changing one behavior at a time. Similarly, winning big role changes in society makes a huge number of cascading policy and practice changes possible—both written and unwritten rule changes—that would not be possible even to fight for, let alone win, going one by one. The new policies and practices flow from the role change, all at once. (In chapter 14, I share the story of a nationally coordinated effort to redefine the role of local prosecutors, and detail all the positive changes that stemmed from successfully doing so—as well as the backlash.)

Donald Trump is often seen as a rule-changer. But first he was a role-changer. The Republican Party, motivated to capitalize on Trump's popularity, ultimately allowed him to redefine the role of the presidency. There was some resistance at first, but then everyone saw the profiteering potential of getting on the bandwagon instead of trying to derail it. As a result, Republicans got a whole lot of rule changes that simply would not have been possible under any previous Republican president. By redefining the role of president to include Trump, they set themselves up to win policy changes they had struggled to win for decades. Trump then helped them change many other roles, which led to even bigger changes. (Even before Trump, other changes had to take place. The definition of the news media had already been changed to include the explicitly right-wing, agenda-driven, and truth-optional Fox News—thus including *Republican propaganda arm* in that definition—which opened up many possibilities for winning enough power to change rules.)

In 2020, however, the right wing proved to be too late to change the role of chief election official—usually the secretary of state, the person who oversees election procedures—in each state. Had they been successful a bit earlier, they might have had in place all the rules they needed to convert their attempted coup into a real one and keep Trump in office for a consecutive term. They did not win that particular role change in time, but they are working on it now.

Trump did push on many other role redefinitions in his first term—for instance, appointing someone to lead the Environmental Protection Agency who didn't believe in protecting the environment. But his second term is operating at a whole other level. The list of role changes the right wing won for itself, through Trump, in just one month between January 20 and February 20, 2025, is a long one. Never before have we seen a Republican Senate majority deem more unqualified, incompetent, and ideologically driven people to be appropriate for cabinet positions. Trump's power to redefine roles has proved extremely dangerous: Robert F. Kennedy Jr. as secretary of Health and Human Services, Pam Bondi as attorney general, Kristi Noem as secretary of Homeland Security, Kash Patel as FBI director, Pete Hegseth as secretary of defense (now styled as secretary of war). The people in those roles have done things that were simply not possible for people in those positions to do before. And they represent just a sampling of how Trump is redefining the entire role of government by redefining the roles of people who run the government. They, in addition to countless lower level appointees across the government who control vital information and other systems we depend on, now serve the personal interests of Trump with little allegiance to the actual law. Whatever their responsibilities used to be are now subservient to Trump's whims.

With respect to judges, the right wing was already way ahead of the game by 2016. The Heritage Foundation and the Federalist Society put time, money, focus, and passion into redefining the role of a Supreme Court justice, and the role of federal judges in general. For instance, they changed the definition not just to *include* ideological extremism but to fully *require* it. They did it, in part, by making conservative voters feel invested as a group in that role change and, most important, personally invested in all the rule changes that would result from that role change. They motivated people to organize, donate money, vote, and take other actions in service of achieving this role change—clarifying and building a culture of belief around the upside of doing so. When they finally got Trump in office, there was a full slate of judges ready to be appointed to the bench and assume their new role and run with it. The results are clear.

After Trump's first term, liberals also set about changing the idea of what a qualified Supreme Court justice looks like. Justice Ketanji Brown Jackson has changed expectations for what a liberal justice should be. She set a precedent: Though educated as a law student in the Ivy League, like almost every other justice, she had a public defender background and had worked on a different side of the justice system than most of the lawyers who had risen to the court in the past, almost all of whom had worked at the nation's most prominent private law firms or as lawyers representing the government. (Thurgood Marshall forged his path to the judiciary by working at legal advocacy organization the NAACP, while Ruth Bader Ginsburg worked at the ACLU for several years.)

If we want the role change implemented by liberals to be truly influential, however, we will need to promote and defend it in subsequent nominations over many, many years, in the very ways the right wing has done for the standards they have set for their nominees. If we are able to define the role of Supreme Court justice to include a demonstrated commitment to those who are usually in the crosshairs of the legal system rather than its beneficiaries, we might see many rule changes as a result. But only if we focus on making this role change a goal.

Lina Khan is a less enduring but still important example. In 2021, Biden appointed her to lead the Federal Trade Commission, and she redefined the mandate of that office to focus it on highly aggressive anti-monopoly enforcement, which was not a role the federal government had played in generations. She modeled corporate accountability at a new level by taking on Big Tech, the most powerful corporations currently operating in America. That role change led to efforts at rule changes in the form of lawsuits and other actions that could change the way corporations in America do (and don't do) business.

Right now, we are in a major battle over redefining the role of corporations in our society, from Big Tech to the Big Banks and more. As one example, Big Tech corporations like Meta and Google want their role to be seen as impartial communications platforms, just like a telecom corporation that cannot be held responsible for what people say when they talk on their phone lines. But this definition is self-serving. Telecom corporations don't profit from what people actually say on the phone, whereas Meta and Google do profit from the ad revenue that appears next to the content that people create and publish on their platforms. They are highly partial publishers and not impartial platforms. The telecom corporations don't interrupt your phone call with your grandma to play an advertisement, let alone an ad triggered by whatever story you just told her (which they had been "listening" to). But Big Tech corporations place and play ads wherever they possibly can while you're interacting with the content and people on their platforms. If advocates for social change win this battle, properly defining the role of many of the Big Tech corporations as publishers rather than mere channels, then a whole new set of rules for holding them liable for the content they publish will become possible. And those rules can help create a safer, fairer, and less profiteering internet for everyone.

Many corporate executives have also tried to have it both ways when it comes to defining their public role: changing the rhetoric surrounding the role, but none of the actions they take as part of playing that role. They try to have us believe that their role is to do right by their workforce or to champion diversity, only to spend their days doing the exact opposite. They do whatever they can to maximize their profits and share prices, while trying to convince us through their public image and public relations campaigns that their role is something else. And then when the political winds change, and it works to their advantage to eliminate DEI programs or other efforts they once touted, they take on the role of helpless victim—as if they had no choice.

Just as we must remember that presence is not power, we must also remember that winning the rhetoric of a role change is not the same as winning an actual role change. And confusing the two is dangerous. The telltale sign: If corporations are not changing their rules, then they probably haven't actually changed their role.

Roles Are Infrastructure

Each of us has a lot more names attached to us than the names printed on our birth certificate and the names we use on our social media accounts. World's Best Mom. Customer Service Representative. Executive Director. The peacemaker of the family. Winner. Loser. That neighbor down the block who can fix anything. BFF. Class clown. Becky with the good hair.

Many of the names we give to other people (or to ourselves) tell a story. They tell a story about what we mean to people, and the range of action they can expect from us. When I say that Bayard Rustin was a builder, I'm giving him one of these names. *Builder* says more than *activist* or even *civil rights hero* does. It describes a range of actions that Rustin performed and a range of contributions he made. Roles that tell a story are part of the infrastructure of power. When someone plays a certain role in a certain way, they can become an instrumental part of manufacturing power. How do we define the role of *politician* or *corporate executive*? What is someone expected (or allowed) to do as part of having that name and being in that role?

If *die-hard liberal* can mean reading and talking about an endless stream of articles reporting on everything that's going wrong, but never taking any action to make it right, then the overall infrastructure for increasing liberal power becomes weak. If it refers to someone who takes actions every day that express their feelings but are not part of a larger strategy, that also limits the infrastructure of our movements and therefore limits the power we can attain.

In chapter 8, I talked about the critical importance of infrastructure: the mechanisms that any successful movement are built on. People are the most important type of infrastructure when it comes to social change because of the roles they play. When people play roles in ways that work to change the rules in favor of justice, we need to encourage and defend them—and also expand the number of people playing those roles. When people take over roles and play them in ways that work against us—that is, in ways that prevent positive change or even make conditions worse—we need to either change the people playing those roles or change the definition of what is expected from them.

11

Avoiding the Traps of Magical Thinking

DEFINITION: *Magical thinking* is when we fool ourselves into thinking that what we want to be true is the actual truth, ignoring all the evidence to the contrary.

CHALLENGE: If we don't catch ourselves before we fall into the traps of magical thinking, we will never be able to see the path to real change. We will be stuck on paths that do not and cannot lead where we want to go.

I Knew I Had to Write this Book When . . .

I was at the White House after the 2016 election as the Obama administration was closing down and getting ready for the transition to the incoming Trump presidency. Loretta Lynch, the attorney general for two more months, was part of a fireside chat with Valerie Jarrett, longtime adviser to President Obama, detailing all the progress they were proud to have made on criminal justice reform during the Obama years.

There was a decent amount to highlight. The administration had changed rules for federal employment to discourage discrimination against people with criminal records, and greatly reduced the sentencing disparity between offenses related to powder and crack cocaine, both of which were major drivers of racial inequality in the system. Lynch hit all the highlights, including educational programs for people incarcerated in federal prisons. Most of us in the room had been involved in pushing for the policies they were celebrating. But joining in the victory lap was not what was at the top of my mind.

When the mic came to me, the last person to ask a question before the session closed, I pushed: "Could you say more to the room about your confidence in these policies moving forward beyond the life of this administration, both in terms of funding and enforcement? Could you say more about the vigilance, the organizing, the activism, the work that's going to be required from the people in this room in order to keep in place the things that we've achieved?" I hoped they could show everyone a credible path forward.

The attorney general looked at me and thanked me for the question. My questions during events like these were never on script, and though the administration's leaders kept inviting me into the room, I knew there were times they wished they didn't have to.

"These initiatives will live on after us because the structure has been set in place," Lynch said, specifically referring to the prison programs. "We're confident that the Bureau of Prisons leadership will continue these initiatives because they're effective initiatives. You know, educational programs also improve safety in correctional institutions for the inmates and for the correctional officers. That's in everyone's interest."

She went on to say, in an effort to calm the anxieties steadily increasing across the room, that leaders like us knew how to make progress on criminal justice reform even when we were not in power. Advocates for reform knew how to make their voices heard. Bipartisanship was possible because reforms were sensible. The message was clear: The pace of change might slow, but we were not going backward.

It was all very reasonable. Yet it seemed totally delusional to me. Magical thinking.

This was also the attitude promoted by many establishment Democrats and liberal organizations rooted in Washington, DC. Somehow, seeing how unprepared we were to stop Trump during the 2016 election didn't prompt them to consider that we might also be unprepared to stop him from doing terrible things once he was in office, including a whole range of things that weren't "sensible" or "in everyone's interest" at all.

Loretta Lynch wasn't alone. I heard many such declarations in those last days of 2016, and I've heard more in the years since: *If we just get his popularity numbers down, he won't be able to get anything done. If we just expose the harm he's doing, and the lies he's telling, he'll become weak enough to stop.* Obama officials, in particular, seemed to believe they had set America on a fundamentally new course. They didn't see the movement behind MAGA and how forceful, game-changing, and enduring it would be.

Like Chuck Schumer, Loretta Lynch was very wrong. Private prison stock prices shot up a week before Trump took office, and Trump's first year resulted in record profits for the industry. The administration prohibited federal investigations of police abuse. His new attorney general, Jeff Sessions, fired the person leading the prison education programs and rolled back pretty much all the gains of the Obama administration.[1] At the end of his seemingly endless term, Trump rushed through thirteen executions of federal prisoners, blowing past the unwritten (but previously honored) ban on federal executions that had lasted seventeen years. Seven of the people put to death were Black men, some with plenty of questions surrounding their cases.

To be fair, Trump's legacy with regard to criminal justice was not solely punitive. Prodded by his son-in-law Jared Kushner (not to mention media personality Kim Kardashian), he championed the

First Step Act. Across the federal system, the act limited the use of mandatory minimums for particular drug offenses, expanded incarcerated people's eligibility for compassionate release, and granted funding for more prison programming like addiction treatment, job training, and literacy education.

Yet, when returning to office in 2025, Trump seemingly abandoned criminal justice reform. On her first day, Attorney General Pam Bondi issued one memo that lifted the moratorium on the death penalty, which Biden had reestablished, and another that instructed federal prosecutors to exercise no leniency in charging people—in other words, the mandate was to be as tough on crime as possible. Trump's numerous executive orders included calls to increase prison capacity and to "strengthen and expand legal protections for law enforcement officers"[2]—which, according to Sam Raim of the Vera Institute of Justice, was "an attempt to remove guardrails on police when they abuse their power or break the law." Overall, Raim wrote, the administration signaled as strongly as possible that "meaningful criminal justice reform is not coming under a second Trump presidency."[3]

It was clear from the first days of the first Trump presidency in 2017 that we were definitely going backward. After getting the yellow light for a bit, racism got the green light again. And Team Trump would open additional lanes for exploiting working-class people for profit, taking advantage of people with mental illness and disabilities, putting LGBT people in danger, hurting women in the system, and traumatizing children. Within the first year of Trump's first presidency, most of the incremental criminal justice gains and reforms made under Obama were undone with the glide of a pen. And we had no way of getting them back anytime soon. Loretta Lynch's belief that "the structure has been set in place" crumbled in the face of reality.

To a bank robber, the newest model of a safe is simply the next challenge to conquer. To a right-wing administration that came into office insulting everyone and everything associated with the status quo, there was no policy that couldn't be broken. It was obvious to some of us that Trump wasn't merely a "change" candidate, as Obama had been. He was a "change the rules" candidate, prepared to turn everything about the way politics worked upside down. It wasn't as much about the specific outcomes he promised to change as it was about changing how the entire system worked—and making sure it worked for him and people he favored.

It was clear to me that the old tools we had for preventing rollbacks to progress were not going to work, no matter how smartly we used them. We would need new tools and new approaches. Politics as usual was not up to the challenge of taking on a billionaire reality TV star with authoritarian aspirations, millions of die-hard adherents, and a long line of people ready to profit from everything he did.

Why was this not obvious to more people by the end of 2016? Often, when I raised this issue in the political circles I traveled, I received blank stares in return. There was a barrier in the way, blocking our collective vision about what was happening and what we needed to do about it. No one on our side wanted right-wing extremists to control our lives and the fate of the country, but there was little understanding of how they were doing it and how we could prevent it from happening or, later on, undo it.

Then, as now, too many people who ran unions, think tanks, advocacy groups, grassroots organizations, political networks, and other liberal organizations—all of whom passionately wanted the values of fairness, justice, and freedom to shape our country—were focused on playing by the rules of politics and policy, the rules of precedent and progress. It was the set of rules with which they were familiar and comfortable. That was clearly not going to work.

They didn't understand that social change is—and has always been—about playing by the rules of power. That's because power means having the ability to change all the other rules.

The right wing has embraced that. We can, too. But only if we first reject magical thinking—the kind of thinking that clouds our assessment about what is happening and what we're up against, and clouds our judgment about what to do. Some people were genuinely caught up in that thinking. Others knew they benefited from it. They were incentivized not to break the pattern of magical thinking because their consulting contracts and their authority in the ecosystem depended on those myths.

Magical thinking explains a lot about the transition from Obama to Trump, and from Biden to Trump, and also why those transitions happened in the first place: how Trump became president twice. But it also explains a lot about why we hit a wall in trying to bring about change, even in small, everyday contexts.

The Biggest Trap: Magical Thinking

Crossing the line from hoping things will be different to pretending they are is a very normal thing to do. The question is whether we can pull ourselves back in time to avoid the trap of magical thinking and make decisions based on a more honest view of what's happening around us, instead of assumptions that are wrong and take us off course.

As I noted before, my father is a tile artisan and a residential builder. I learned from him that wishful thinking doesn't get you very far in the nuts-and-bolts reality of home construction. Merely hoping that a column on the first floor will hold up the second floor is not the way you go about building a house that can protect a family over the long term. I realized early on that I wanted to build things that last. My dad helped build countless homes, including our own, with its tin-roof "juke joint" lounge on the second floor of the old potato barn that served as his workshop. He helped create spaces in which people could live great lives. I wanted to do that, too, but instead of houses, my contribution would be trying to build better social systems. I wanted to contribute to changing our criminal justice system, our economic system, our media ecosystem, and any other system that profoundly affects people's lives—and the fate of entire communities. These are the systems that define what's possible in our society and who gets to thrive within it.

What is the difference between building a system that forces some people to be subservient to others and building one that enables all people to be free enough to thrive? I have realized that building anything requires being bold and being real at the same time. Bold enough to envision something that doesn't yet exist and to believe you can bring it into existence. Real enough to actually execute your vision and not get lost in a fantasy. Being a builder means understanding when cutting corners will cut you down, and understanding when not bringing the right tools for the job can stall it.

That's what happened back in 2016. The system that people in the realms of Democratic politics and liberal policy had confidently built to win the presidential election and continue Obama's legacy completely collapsed. It collapsed under the weight of Trump and everything the visionaries on the right wing, both bold and real, had been building to replace politics as we knew it. And then it happened again in 2024: More people in the liberal political ecosystem, focused on how Biden had been reinventing government, were so busy hailing the type of massive social spending, public investment, and progressive regulation we hadn't seen since Franklin Delano Roosevelt was president that they missed the more tangible-seeming problems and solutions that were being sold to voters by Trump.

During the Biden years, I spoke to people in the White House ahead of more than one State of the Union address. Each time, I stressed the need to be real with people about where they were in the cycle from vision to execution. In his moment of widest reach, I argued, Biden must explain to people why things are not changing—aside from Republicans, he must name and blame the corporations and other forces that are standing in the way of change. He must give people something to rally around, pivoting from the question of stalled progress and pointing to the profiteers who are stalling it. He must tell a different kind of story: Instead of touting what's going well (when people clearly don't feel it in their lives), explain what's going wrong—and who's to blame. Help people make sense of it all, and then enlist the entire party infrastructure in reinforcing that story for the country.

Biden had promised to increase the minimum wage, revive police reform, invest in communities in tangible ways, make sure everyone could vote, and make sure their votes counted. Major corporate brands, from McDonald's to General Mills, were members of the National Restaurant Association, which was doing everything it could to block minimum wage increases at the federal and state level. In fact, corporations were involved in blocking all the progress promised. Biden, I urged, would need to call out corporations and rally people against them. That would be the foundation of his success in moving popular ideas forward and also winning reelection. In the midterm elections of 2022, Democrats held the Senate but narrowly lost the House. Historically, that was not a bad outcome, but it only helped Democrats and their allies hide from deeper problems that were emerging.

Trump, who announced his bid for a second term a week after the midterms, was not worried. He didn't see a lot holding him back from rising to the presidency a second time by insulting, blaming, and vilifying everyone he could think to blurt out in his speeches and online rants. He had "the swamp" and "waste, fraud, and abuse." He had "illegal immigrants," trans people, "the radical left," and "fraudulent voters." He had countless villains (partly to distract from his own crimes). Who were Biden's villains? In today's age, if you don't tell people whom to blame, they are going to blame you. There are no blameless realities. You need to point the way for people to direct their righteous anger, or else that anger will be up for grabs to anyone who does. It was magical thinking to believe Biden could be successful without telling a strong story about villains, and without the popular movement that kind of story feeds.

Biden was going to need a movement with a lot of energy to change any rules: People on the outside—whether protesters on the street, supporters in the media, politicians at every level, or advocates and evangelists operating in alignment across all walks of society—are indispensable partners for creating the environment for people on the inside to advance progress. (Democrats too often ignore this fact when in power at the federal level.) And people on the outside are motivated by hearing about who is profiting from denying them the progress they deserve. Without that, too many voters would simply conclude that Biden was weak and ineffective. Investing in that movement would be critical. The occasional light criticism of the pharmaceutical industry was not going to do it.

But the response I got before each State of the Union address was the same every time: *That's not Biden's way.* Biden's way was to talk about the good stuff. He wanted to tell a story about the heroes doing good things across his administration, while pretending it wasn't necessary to name villains (or even build an effective coalition that could talk about villains for him). It was magical thinking to pretend he could win today's fights with yesterday's traditions. And so, as the 2024 election drew near, Biden had not established any specific corporate villains—or any motivating villains at all. Naming abstract principles like racial discrimination, or general plagues on society like climate change or inequality, was not going to work. At the same time, he was facing an opponent who was more adept at blaming people—falsely but loudly and persistently—than anyone in politics ever.

If we don't recognize and understand the power we're up against, it's unlikely we'll be able to effectively compete against it and win. Both the 2016 and 2024 elections proved it. Almost the entire 2016 election effort on the Democratic side was run on assumptions about power that were deeply wrong. Of course, what happened in 2016 cannot be reduced to a single factor. Malicious Russian state influence was enabled by a permissive, profit-at-all-costs culture led by Mark Zuckerberg and Big Tech corporations, who also flooded the country with a steady stream of misinformation that rivaled even Rupert Murdoch and Fox News.[4] Increasingly targeted laws aiming to prevent Democratic-leaning voters from voting, led by Republican state legislatures, may have even cost Hillary Clinton the election just by sabotaging voters in Wisconsin alone.[5]

But there was something else going on. The people charged with running the Hillary Clinton campaign, as well as many of the most influential people who supported it, did not understand the new kind of political power they were facing in Donald Trump. They didn't want to accept that racism could still play a determinative role after Obama. They didn't want to accept that the Trump brand was highly motivating to people, and the way he leveraged any and all types of media would motivate people to participate in the election, even without the centralized ground game they thought was necessary for any candidate to win. On the one hand, they ignored how some of the old ways of politics were making a comeback, like racial pandering. On the other hand, they refused to let go of some of the other old ways of thinking about and doing politics, even as new ways were being invented and used against them in real time. (For a deeper dive on how people kept missing the power of Trump to manipulate the media and win people over, see the last section of this chapter.)

In our everyday lives, we all exhibit a certain degree of magical thinking. We tell ourselves that we'll be fine and fit even if we don't exercise. Or that we have the energy to do five things in one day when we can barely get it together to do two of them. Or that it will only take us a few minutes to get somewhere that takes an hour to get to. It's all too easy to hope that something that we want to buy won't hurt our budget too much, or that someone who is usually difficult to deal with will be nice to us the next time we see them. It's wishful thinking. It can even be delusional thinking.

In the realm of social change, however, magical thinking is dangerous. Whenever we don't win, it's usually a big part of why. If we pretend our strategies work when they actually don't, or that our opponents are less powerful than they are, we lose fights over changing conditions that affect hundreds, thousands, or millions of people—including ourselves.

Starting with Ourselves

The hardest work of achieving any goal is always the internal work. It is the time we spend honestly looking at ourselves in the mirror and understanding the truth of what we want, what it takes to get it, what we're willing to do, and whether what we do will be enough. It's hard to admit, afterward, when it wasn't enough.

No one has a perfect record of pulling back from magical thinking before it's too late. It's easy for me to write about the instances of people succumbing to it in different ways across progressive movements, but I myself went through a very tough period in 2023 when my own magical thinking caught up with me in a big way.

When I was leading Color Of Change, I knew that philanthropic foundations, the source of most of our funding, would often focus on certain issues only to deprioritize them later in favor of something else—sometimes with good reason. We'd always had ups and downs but had a steady track record of overall growth. I assumed we wouldn't be hit that hard—that the supercharged interest in racial justice sparked during the 2020 Black Lives Matter uprisings might lessen but not drop off dramatically. I figured that the belief in criminal justice reform as a way of driving more people to participate in social change, which had been widening in adoption across the philanthropic landscape, would prevent the bottom from dropping out. I was wrong about that.

We had blazed new paths for aggregating Black power and winning real change. We'd won in the areas of bail reform, progressive prosecutors, challenges to Big Tech, the big Wall Street banks, and more—and now it was time to invest in both defending those wins and working toward new ones. So I thought. But, for many reasons, that's not where the funding trajectory was headed. I wrongly assumed I didn't need to make a big case for continuing this work, not nearly as big as the case I had needed to make to start it. I was also wrapped up in the growth I had created for the organization, believing I could keep increasing our budget as our presence and achievements grew. But those two factors are not always linked.

Many funders and partners with whom I spoke emphasized the moral imperative of our work. But of course, all of social justice work is a moral imperative, and no one issue area can remain central forever. When foundations and individual philanthropists moved away from funding criminal justice reform, and from racial justice work more broadly, we hit a funding cliff that I should have seen coming—but didn't. We had layoffs for the first time, which hurt a lot of people who relied on me to provide a way for them to continue doing their work.

The budget issues came quickly and required immediate action, but in reality, I should have prepared the organization for it better than I did. Being overconfident about our ability to continue growing greatly narrowed my options when everything got real. I let down the communities we represented in our fights, and I also let down the people who had joined the organization expecting (and deserving) more.

I had convinced myself that the external victories we'd achieved would make up for unresolved tensions running through the organization itself. But when our internal systems and morale could no longer support the work we were doing, I realized that the substance of the work itself wasn't enough to keep us together. I hadn't invested enough in building a stronger internal culture, which made going through a crisis even harder for all of us. I lost the faith of many of the staff. I had hoped we were aligned and united by the work we were doing in the world, but I hadn't done enough work to ensure that we were. Such work, which involves listening to people and involving them in the process of building systems, requires an enormous amount of time and attention—always more than many leaders believe it does, including myself.

Looking back, the budget crisis and layoffs at Color Of Change unfolded during a period of staff unionization, amid the broader layoffs that many movement organizations were facing at the time. The first wave of COVID-19, which led to office closures and an immediate breakdown of personal connection, as well as the demands of the around-the-clock urgency and dramatic growth faced by racial justice organizations in the wake of the 2020 uprisings, only added to the internal challenges we already faced.

Decisions—made by me, the board, and senior leadership, and guided by legal experts—were extraordinarily difficult, and they ultimately led to an unfavorable ruling from the National Labor Relations Board that the organization appealed. I don't revisit that period to justify every choice, but to be honest about what I learned and where I fell short, and how I should have leaned into the union process a lot more.

One of my biggest lessons is that I should have slowed—perhaps even paused—organizational growth as soon as unionization began. That development, which was happening across the movement, called for a shift in posture. Sacrificing some short-term wins in favor of stability, clarity, and stronger internal structures would likely have put the organization on firmer footing. I also recognize that while I sought advice from many experienced people—often being encouraged to delegate labor relations and keep my time focused on our work—I should have spent more time directly engaging in that process myself. Ultimately, the decisions I made did not take us in the right direction. A strong Color Of Change internally was not separate from movement work; it was central to it. And internal weaknesses within organizations successfully challenging power always invite outside attacks.

Facing attacks on me and the organization from the outside taught me a lot about the costs of a publicized crisis and also what it takes to lead through it. In many ways, the crisis only further incentivized more magical thinking: Just to get through the day, I would hope and wish that things were going to resolve quickly and without drama. But that only kept me stuck in the crisis longer. I had to break that cycle of thinking, accepting failure and the lesser of many bad options, in order to find a credible way to get to the other side of it.

When I started with Color Of Change in 2011, I never imagined that I would serve as its president for more than thirteen years. Looking in the mirror as the crisis unfolded, I realized that both the organization and I myself needed something new. I announced my departure in September, seeing through the election year in January 2025.

With regard to power, the worst form of magical thinking is the idea that feeling powerful is the same thing as being powerful. And I learned that the hard way. It is often easy to fall into the various traps of magical thinking because we hear people repeat unquestioned truisms over and over—or we repeat them to ourselves over and over. It is hard to pull ourselves out of that trap, but there is so much to lose when we don't. The stories I tell in the next section of the book demonstrate both how hard and how important that practice is.

The Pop Culture Election of 2016: Different Rules for Different Brands

By the middle of 2016, most of the liberals and establishment Democrats I was talking to assumed that Hillary Clinton would be the next president. Yet they were all still angry: They could not find a line of attack that would definitively sink Trump and make him go away, even as the news media seemed to be hounding Clinton. No matter how many times it seemed that Trump had crossed the point of no return, he returned. No matter how many times Clinton seemed to position her win as inevitable, it remained a question.

It was clear that people all around me were not seeing what I was seeing: It made perfect sense that Trump and Clinton were being held to different standards, given the rules of the world they had stepped into. There was much talk about how our sexist culture encouraged people to lift Trump up and take Clinton down. Of course, that was a factor. But the talk about culture ended there. I realized that many people in politics simply did not understand how culture actually works, how the world of made-up symbols and stories impacts the world of real people's behavior.

They were looking at all of Trump's lies and all of Clinton's truths, and holding them both to the same standard, as if each candidate had to meet a legal burden of proof. In a court of law, which arguments would be accepted and which would be thrown out? Many liberal leaders were still confounded as to how Trump had a case. That made sense to me, because many of them were lawyers.

As a Black person, I didn't have the same level of faith in the system that they did. I knew that legal standards were always shifting. I could never rely on the culture of American law. The law, historically, had rarely provided Black people any security. And in the rare cases when the rules of the justice system did not subordinate, control, or exploit us, someone would simply change those rules to make sure they did. Of course, women were also highly attuned to double standards. And there we were: Hillary was essentially being prosecuted by the press according to the highest standard, while Trump was getting away with everything.

Black people are forgiving, and motivated, so there wasn't a question about whether we would do our part. We never cease to show up to take part in systems that were designed to lock us out and oppress us. Throughout American history, an extraordinary number of laws related to voting were specifically written to prevent us from voting. Yet we show up and vote. The more we know someone is trying to cancel our votes, the more Black voters show up to be counted. We show up to play on unfair grounds, everywhere, even though we have been given endless reasons to give up and go home. (That's not to say that a well-orchestrated suppression campaign doesn't have an effect.)[6] That experience has taught us to have high hopes but low expectations. Nothing surprises us about American culture. In 2016, we knew that legal and political culture was organized around making sure that the odds were in favor of Donald Trump. We were very used to living in that culture, even as we were used to building our own independent cultures that could compete with it, or at least provide shelter from it. And we were used to the rules of that culture constantly changing in ways that kept us down. But many white liberals weren't used to having the rules changed on them. They pressed on, wondering why the rules that used to apply no longer applied. Shouldn't the news media follow the highest standard of proof to evaluate truth? Weren't candidates essentially under oath during their campaigns? Wouldn't perjury disqualify them? Didn't *The New York Times* standard of printing only "the news that's fit to print" still apply? Weren't there any rules?

All of these questions assumed that there was a referee who would eventually come in and blow the whistle, that the rules Donald Trump and Hillary Clinton were accountable to were the rules of a culture organized around our laws and the political and journalistic standards that should fortify them. Many liberals in the political ecosystem couldn't believe that voters were clearly being influenced by a system of double standards that was deeply unfair and dangerous, which is what often happens when people who grow up in privilege encounter unfairness (and general bad behavior) in the world: They find it hard to accept that the world works that way. The world working against them, and against the ways things are supposed to work, is an exception to their norm. Their disbelief in the face of Trump's mounting success also exposed their deeply flawed beliefs about the past. They were imagining a fictional era—the "good old days"—when journalists were fair and accurate, when they had standards, when they never failed to call out racists and liars. But that past never existed.

When, at a campaign stop, Donald Trump said he could get away with anything—specifically, "I could stand in the middle of Fifth Avenue and shoot somebody, and I wouldn't lose any voters, OK?"[7]—many Black people knew that was the one time he wasn't lying. Because that was the truth of America. For every white person in shock, there was a Black person giving them side-eye.

Few white people I interacted with in politics during that year could understand why breaking the rules did not come with consequences for Trump. It was clear that he had committed many crimes in the past, was doing so during his campaign, or both. If Trump could break the rules without consequence, were there any rules left at all? They thought about rules in a legalistic way, missing the point: This wasn't about legal culture, it was about popular culture.

In fact, Trump operated in a highly rule-governed system. It was just a system that differed from the one people were used to: the system of popular culture, which has very different standards for enabling and evaluating behavior. It also has very different standards of truth.

Ironically, the very people who helped Barack Obama develop a level of cultural momentum in 2008 that Democrats hadn't seen in a long while were, just eight years later, refusing to recognize how politics was being subsumed by popular culture. A great public yearning for politicians that operated outside of traditional politics elevated Trump. Many people wanted a different kind of show. Everyone seemed to get that except for the leaders of the big organizations, including the Democratic Party, working to elect Clinton. They were waiting for the referee to come back from their extended break and call a penalty, waiting for the judge to come back to the bench and rule in their favor. Meanwhile, nearly everyone else—voters, news media, community leaders, celebrities—was thinking about the match between Trump and Clinton in different terms.

For millions of people, Trump was like a big-budget action movie. In an action movie, nothing is supposed to be taken at face value. It's all about blowing things up (Trump's specialty). It's all a fantasy. It's all a lie. But as people say about fiction, it's the lie that tells the truth. The implausible but highly engaging antics of a big action movie can reveal a deep truth about relationships, life, and society that can be very meaningful. And it's fun, too. Obviously, you don't cry "Liar!" and storm out of the theater during a movie in which people battle one another by means of shooting lasers, using dubious technology, pulling off impossible stunts, or flying across the sky at super speed to save the day. You sit back and enjoy it. And you take away the deeper truths the movie is offering about heroes and villains, winners and losers, right and wrong. When people looked at Trump, they weren't looking to count up all the lies. They were looking for the few truths that meant something real to them.

The fact that everything else was exaggerated, or even made up, was beside the point. That's what you want in an action movie. You definitely do not want to walk out of the theater and spend the rest of the night debating whether or not it got the facts right. If there is a debate at the bar, or on the ride home, it's about which fictions—which ridiculous moments of dialogue, which unbelievable plot twists, which fantastical ways everything lined up—were the best.

Let's also not forget that while watching an action movie, you sometimes root for the bad guy even more than the good guy. Democrats thought making Trump a bad guy would sink his chances of winning. But for many people, seeing Trump as the bad guy only made him a stronger character in the story, and in some ways a more enviable and attractive one. Trump would not be held accountable for turning politics into a joke. He would only be held accountable if his followers no longer thought the joke was funny. **Those are the rules of popular culture: If you fail to be entertaining, people will leave**

you behind. But if you keep them engaged, you earn quite a bit of loyalty.

Clinton was definitely not an action movie. She was a documentary. Proudly. But there are different standards for a documentary. If a documentary is exposed as fabricating information, or if there is even a widely validated suspicion that the documentary is not telling the whole story, critics and viewers alike will completely sink it.

The Clinton campaign was protesting about a double standard. In reality, Clinton was merely being held to the standard of the role she had chosen to play in people's lives—the character she had chosen to play in the story of politics. And she was seen as violating her own rules: failing to be honest. For a documentary, that's a deal-breaker with many audiences. It wasn't fair, but it was very consistent with how the rules of brand work. She wasn't being judged against Trump, she was being judged against her own perceived promises to her audiences. (And so was he.) Though it was blown out of proportion in deeply unfair ways, a betrayal by journalists of the role they should have been playing for the sake of the country, the Hillary Clinton email "scandal" became a symbol of everything she might be hiding.[8]

Think about what a bad review can do to a documentary, especially if it questions the integrity of the director. Now think about an action movie that scores 50 percent on Rotten Tomatoes but fifty million people go see anyway. People saw Trump and Clinton as representing different brand archetypes—characters with which they were already familiar, stories they already knew. Different rules applied to those different archetypes, especially when it came to standards of truth. There was nothing surprising about it. It was a perfectly ordered cultural system. The opinion of critics didn't matter. The effective engagement of key audiences did. Pretending the game worked differently was magical thinking at its worst.

Hillary still won the popular vote in 2016, of course. And we should never forget how many forces corrupted that election, not the least of which was a new level of highly effective disinformation and voter suppression that favored Trump. But the misreading of the power of brand narratives, how they were functioning, and how people in key states were responding to them, enabled Trump to edge his way into the White House. Magical thinking held us back.

It should be instructive as we continue figuring out how to stop the right wing from using brand power to capture political power. And the lesson about brand narratives is also instructive for anyone trying to make change at any level: Outside of a court of law, rarely is there a referee in high-stakes battles over social change who will step in to declare one party the liar and another the truth teller. People respond to the character type we claim and project, and while there are no rules for the character types we choose, there are rules for maintaining their efficacy.

FIND YOUR POWER

Seeing and Stopping Magical Thinking

This activity is meant to help you identify the classic traps of magical thinking so that you can prevent them from influencing the decisions you make and the attitudes you embrace.

Read through the following examples of magical thinking, and write down your answers to the prompts after each one:

- **Ignoring the rules of rule-making.** In what ways have you developed an understanding of how systems of power work, and how could you learn about the power dynamics that are most relevant to the particular situation you are facing?
- **Misreading trends.** Where can you go to learn more about current trends in how people are thinking about and responding to both the issues you are concerned with and gain critical perspective on the ways you go about advocating for them?
- **Believing the arc of history inevitably bends toward justice.** Are you acting as if you believe progress is inevitable? In what ways might you have gotten complacent? How can you act to defend your wins against a backlash, and are you actively planning for it?
- **Believing that brands build themselves (or aren't important).** How have you worked to build your brand power or help causes and organizations you believe in build their brand power?

- **Thinking a given fact, law, or program will be a silver bullet.** Do you believe that, for change to happen, all you need is to get some smart researchers to create a report? Or that once a lawyer goes into the courtroom and wins a case that everything is done? That if someone gets behind a computer and creates the right code, everything that's wrong will magically change? In each of those scenarios, what can you do to get beyond silver-bullet thinking?
- **Overauthorizing thinkers instead of doers.** How does your organization or social cause group work with consultants, lawyers, academics, and journalists? Who are the doers, versus the thinkers? Are there people with more experience whom you could listen to, to gain more useful insight?
- **Not tailoring strategy to your specific context.** To what extent are you copycatting another community's strategy without understanding why it worked for them, whether it applies to your community, or what you'd need to tweak to make it work?
- **Trusting facts to speak for themselves.** Have you found yourself believing that if you just get more people to know the facts, it'll change how they act and give you leverage? How can you use those facts instead as a tool to build power and leverage?
- **Misjudging opponents.** Do you believe that your opponents will play by the rules? How might you account for the fact that they will keep fighting against you in ways that may catch you off guard?
- **Believing that a single victory can force enduring, systemic change.** Have you ever found yourself going after one player, aiming for changing one thing rather than the whole structure? How could you take a more systemic approach, using one win to create a cascade of others?

- **Being placated by gifts and attention.** In what ways might you have been mistaking attention, flattery, gifts, or proximity to power for actual power? Are you accepting agreements and promises that are likely to fall apart? How can you be less influenced by them?
- **Believing your analysis is right and complete.** How might you avoid misreading people's motivations? What facts might your opponents have that you aren't accounting for? Other more reliable or expansive sources of information you can consult, even if they don't tell you only what you want to hear?
- **Believing you can win without aligning strategy with infrastructure.** How can you make sure that your strategy includes a plan to gain the resources, expertise, talent, and other needs to execute it?
- **Believing that publicly visible work is the only work.** What steps can you take to elevate behind-the-scenes work in your organization or in your approach to change?
- **Believing you can vote your way to progress.** How can you build power beyond the voting booth? How can you stay active and productive in years when elections are not taking place?
- **Believing you can make transformative change without much disruption.** How will change create disruption? How can you help people become comfortable with disruptive change?
- **Believing progress is easy.** Have you lowered the bar to entry so as not to scare people away from getting involved? How might you balance providing an easy on-ramp for people with getting them to understand that systems change is not always easy, and may eventually require more commitment?

PART III

The Practice of Power

Stories and lessons from two decades of working to end profiteering and change society's rules in favor of justice

12

Corporations and the Landscape of Power

In the first two parts of this book, I outlined some of the core concepts for understanding, gaining, and using power in service of social change. In this part of the book, I use personal stories from the front lines of several fights to illustrate specific lessons about how to win. My goal in sharing these stories—both the successes and setbacks—is to offer you a behind-the-scenes look at what I've learned in two decades of working for justice from Washington, DC, to municipal buildings across the country to Hollywood and Silicon Valley. They offer important insights about navigating the landscape of power, both the power we can gain and the power we're up against.

Developing a strong sense of the landscape of power means seeing how different forces work together—like different machines in a factory—to manufacture either justice or injustice. There's rarely just one thing we need to do to achieve our goals within that landscape. It almost always requires fighting on several fronts at once, while also adapting as conditions shift.

As I have emphasized, the way we perceive a problem determines the solutions we see for solving it. Corporate power plays a role in every injustice we experience. But if we do not recognize the role of corporate power then we will not see taking it on as a necessity for achieving social change. But it is. We can't win big rule changes without taking on corporate power. That is the challenge of our time.

The role that corporations play in our society is one of the most important roles we need to redefine to make changing the rules that affect our lives possible. Corporations should serve a purpose that benefits society at large, and be held accountable to doing more good than harm, rather than merely serving as profit engines for billionaires.

When I use the word *corporation,* I'm referring to businesses that are structured in a certain way. They have boards of directors that are responsible for appointing and managing their CEOs, as well as for making some of the biggest decisions about the company and its policies (including when to sell it off). A corporation is owned by shareholders who can make money by buying its stock and later selling it at a higher price, by receiving a share of the profits it generates (dividends), and by receiving a share of the proceeds when the company is sold or merged with another corporation. In many cases, the dominant shareholders who control corporations are their founders, the descendants of their founders, or, increasingly, private equity firms (networks of investors) that buy up a significant number of shares. Most importantly, the board members, executives, employees, and shareholders of a corporation are legally and financially shielded from liability for most of the actions the corporation takes.

Corporations can be big businesses that dominate their industries and employ tens of thousands of employees (Walmart, Amazon, UnitedHealth, Apple, ExxonMobil) or small but influential companies that can play a major role in the fields of technology, construction, communications, government contracting, media, or any other area, despite their relatively small size.

Not everything corporations do is bad, and not every corporation does bad things. Our goal is to set the right norms and force every corporation to move a lot closer to them. That is becoming more difficult, however, as the consolidation of political power under Trump is intertwined with the increasing consolidation of corporate power and consolidated control over media, technology, and other industries. **The two are related, which makes every political challenge a corporate challenge, and makes every corporate challenge a political challenge.**

The next chapters share four in-depth cases of making change, and the lessons that go with them. As an introduction to them, I want to offer some context about corporate power, which cuts across all of them.

The Story We Tell Ourselves About Corporations

A while back, I was in a conversation with someone a bit older than me who had just bought a new car. They were saying how impressed they were with how much safer cars are today, compared to when they were growing up, as a result of all the cool safety mechanisms that car manufacturers have invented over the years.

I was pretty sure that while car-related fatalities had declined over time, as a percent of the population, there were still a lot of people dying every year in car accidents. (As it turns out, it's about forty thousand per year, the second biggest cause of unintentional deaths.) I imagined this person would perceive those deaths as an unfortunate but acceptable reality, not an unjust one. They would probably think it's inevitable for there to be a certain amount of deaths with so many cars on the road, and that if anyone has limited those deaths as much as possible, it's the car manufacturers.

Thinking about their enthusiasm for the car industry put a smile on my face. They felt safe in the hands of carmakers. They were clearly proud of our collective progress as a society. And no doubt, they were proud of their shiny new car. I was witnessing the results of decades of marketing dollars at work. In this view, corporations set their own rules, and those rules lead to benefits that we all enjoy. Corporations improve because they choose to do good and strive to improve (or perhaps because they feel pressure from competing corporations to do so), and not because anyone forces them to.

I paused, and then asked, "Do you think it's the car manufacturers that got us to this better place? Or was it the regulations the government forced them to adhere to, as a result of people affected by car accidents organizing to demand greater protections? Do you think they made cars safer out of goodwill, or that they made cars safer because the government forced them to take some responsibility for all the ways they were putting lives at risk, and gave rewards to car manufacturers that prioritized changes that made people safer? And didn't it also have to do with rules mandating safer roads and driving conditions, effective speed limits, and more serious inspections for car owners?"

I was still smiling. They were thinking it through. I was talking about who made the rules we now live by: a responsive government that regulates corporations in order to change the outcomes for all of us who are affected by their products. I was asking this person to see their new car as a product of a powerful movement—albeit a movement that doesn't have a multimillion-dollar marketing department pumping out positive stories about itself—and not the product of a benevolent corporation.[1]

Long after our conversation, this person would send me links to articles about unregulated corporations gone wild, and would hit "like" on information I posted about corporate campaigns. Seeing corporate power everywhere can be discouraging, but understanding how powerful ordinary people can be is motivating.

When I speak with people in Silicon Valley, they talk as if it's a fact that regulations and social justice movements inherently stifle innovation. And then they get in their electric cars and drive away. Of course, government regulation and investment, as well as the social movements that forced the federal government to proactively help reduce gas emissions in the first place, were essential to normalizing electric vehicles and incentivizing car manufacturers to create them. Many of the car manufacturers fought it every step of the way. Now there are more than four million on the road.

The shift toward producing electric vehicles was not about corporate self-interest; rather, it was about the public interest. We shouldn't have to say the obvious: Favoring what's in the public interest helps the public a whole lot more than siding with corporations and their self-interest, hoping it pans out for the rest of us.

Regulation can open up possibilities. With regard to food safety, for example, people built power and voiced their demand, rules got changed, and industries got better. Ingredient labels, inspections, standards for what's organic, and other changes originated with people power, not with corporate power. Conservative or liberal, everyone now benefits when they get in a safer car or eat safer foods.

In order to believe we can change our country for the better, we must believe we can change the way corporations do business—and we can't wait around for anyone to do it for us. Knowing how many times people have beaten corporations in the past is critical to building the culture of belief that can motivate millions of people to take part in doing so now.

Taking On Corporate Power Is Key for Taking On Political Power

Corporate influence within our political system has always been strong. In the 2000s, George W. Bush and Dick Cheney invited the fossil fuel industry into the White House to write the very regulations (and often choose the regulators) that would oversee them. Bush and Cheney also let major arms manufacturers and military contractors essentially dictate the strategy for the war in Iraq and Afghanistan, especially the spending strategy. Corporations were uniformly aligned with getting tax breaks from Republicans, and Republicans were uniformly aligned with granting them.

That still happens, but the Trump administration took things to a different level, especially in his second term. To get rewards from Trump, corporations are being asked to betray even their anemic commitments to values like fairness, freedom, and a democratic society—as well as to their employees, customers, communities, and constituencies (including women, LGBT people, and people of color). Trump is asking them to do his political bidding in exchange for the privileges they seek. And they are complying.

Trump has given corporations nearly everything they might want, from bloated contracts and subsidies with no oversight, to control of government agencies (through diligent proxies like former CEOs and investors), to the kind of self-regulation that amounts to no regulation at all, to access to public land and resources, to something approaching a tax-free environment. It's far more than what Bush offered. But it has a higher price. Corporations could always get politicians to do what they wanted, but with Trump and the rise of MAGA, politicians can now get corporations to do what they want—making corporations political in new ways.

That is why almost every major tech CEO took their place by Trump's side at his second inauguration, like altar boys. And it's why corporations have increasingly canceled diversity, equity, and inclusion programs; censored media content not aligned with Trump; and contributed millions to his personal causes (and personal bank accounts). Even if they dislike him, or dislike many of his policies, they fear him. And at the same time, they love how they profit from him.

It's up to us to make it harder for them to do so. It is critical to understand that almost every political fight is really a fight with corporations that advance unjust policies and profit from them, all while supporting politicians who do the most terrible things.

Everything we want Trump to stop doing requires going after the corporations and billionaires that allow him to do it. That is the main takeaway from looking at our landscape today. Trump is helping corporations to get stronger (through tax giveaways, a siphon into federal funds, and approved mergers) and to expand their control over our lives (through massive deregulation). Corporations are helping Trump consolidate his rule across government (by funding extremist politicians and by giving in to his every request) and thereby consolidate his own political control over our lives. We must go after corporations in order to succeed in going after the right wing.

To win with ALEC, Color Of Change had to go after ALEC's policies, politicians, corporate donors, and its own reputation—all at once.

And even then, we cut off corporate funding only briefly. The drop in funding did not overturn Stand Your Ground or voter suppression laws in states where ALEC had a strong foothold. Nor did it prevent ALEC from ratcheting up attacks on our freedoms and safety once those corporations rejoined and helped them build back up. Letting up on corporations let ALEC back into power.

While the federal government of Trump's second term is playing from the Heritage Foundation's relatively new Project 2025 playbook, right-wing control at the state level is still heavily guided by the think tank's cousin ALEC. Still going today, ALEC is passing laws that weaken worker and consumer protections, increase environmental destruction, wreck our education system, and more.

Corporations may pretend to play neutral and stay out of partisan politics, but their behind-the-scenes partnership with groups like ALEC or the Trump administration puts them right in the middle of it. They need that quiet political access to keep profiting, and they have found ways to evade any accountability for all the bad things that happen to people as a result of their political funding. In fact, they fund groups like ALEC, trade associations, and political campaigns specifically so they can have someone else do their dirty work for them.

Both corporations and the people they turn into billionaires persistently aim to undermine people in favor of profits. Fighting injustice almost always puts us up against corporate forces that will employ a seemingly endless amount of money to prevent us from changing the rules they're forced to play by. But that investment amounts to little compared to what they rake in from the profiteering it enables—and therefore what they'll lose if we change the way they do business.

Knowing the Business Model: The "Business Case" Versus the "Justice Case"

Certain fights are easier to win than others. Most media corporations can adapt to eliminating anti-LGBT content without going out of business, for example. It's a small part of their business model. And so there's a relatively clear path to getting them to change. In contrast, most fossil fuel corporations cannot adapt to losing their ability to profit by destroying the environment without having to pay for the damage they cause. That's at the core of their business model. Like an organized crime family, they have no clean way to do business. And so it's a lot harder to force them to change their practices.

People often tell me that I'd be a lot more effective in getting corporations to change if I made the "business case" for what I want them to do—telling them how they'll benefit financially in some way. Some people who work on environmental issues love to lecture people about this. They'll say, "Make the business case: The manufacturer will save money if its factories are more energy efficient." It is absolutely important to do that when making the business case can lead to changes that actually end profiteering. Impact on the environment is one of those cases when a social change goal and a business goal sometimes align. The goal of ending discriminatory hiring practices at corporations has also been helped along by making the business case: Corporations will lose out when they narrow the available talent pool, and they will gain a great deal if they widen it. The business case can thus include the carrot (the positive rewards the corporation will get if it changes) and the stick (the negative consequences it faces if it doesn't).

But what if there is no business case? What if the only business case we can make is the threat of public blowback we can cause if they do the wrong thing, and we don't have anything to "sell them" on why doing the right thing will grant them a big reward? **It is magical thinking to believe that a corporation can always make a change for social good that also furthers its own interests.** What if, as in the case of a cigarette manufacturer, what it's doing has no redeeming social value—it's just wrong? If profiting from other people's suffering is what a business is all about, then there is no point in trying to get what's good for society and what's good for the business to align.

And even if there is a business case, it is still magical thinking to believe that we can win change with good arguments instead of real power. Corporate power depends on us believing the business case is the only way in. But when we make the business case, we're surrendering to the corporation's terms. And we surrender our power.

Why don't corporations have to make the "justice case" to us? Before they are allowed to bring a new product or service to market, or conduct business in a new way, why don't they have to make the case that it will not hurt anyone? That would be moving the conversation to our terms instead of playing by theirs. That's what being able to rein in corporate power is ultimately all about.

Maybe that day will come. Until then, it's up to us to make the justice case by showing that causing injustice will create consequences that ultimately affect a corporation and its executives more adversely than if they were to make the changes we need them to make.

But it's not always easy to understand how a corporate business model works and therefore how to create consequences that actually matter to them—enough to change their practices. And when that model changes over time, strategies must be updated to match.

For example, there was a time when Fox News was more vulnerable to advertiser pressure: a strategy of creating consequences for brands that bought airtime on a network, in an effort to get them to pull their ad dollars until the network took action to address their problematic content. In the late 2000s, advertising made up close to half of Fox News's revenue, according to a range of available estimates. That meant that organizing sustained advertiser boycotts could directly affect the network's bottom line—or at least the bottom line for a given show on the network—and therefore the decisions it made about programming.

Following Fox host Glenn Beck's repeated inflammatory and racist statements, which heated up after Obama took office in 2009, Color Of Change and others initiated an advertiser pressure campaign that, by 2011, led to an estimated three hundred national advertisers (such as Procter & Gamble, GEICO, Verizon, and Progressive) pulling their ads from his program or declining to run commercials. Fox News did not cancel the show immediately, but the advertiser exodus significantly reduced its ad revenue and made the program increasingly costly to maintain. Beck ultimately left Fox News in 2011, demonstrating the leverage advertisers held with the network at the time—as well as activists' leverage with those advertisers.

But over the last decade, the Fox News business model has shifted away from advertising toward cable subscription fees and other sources. Today, an increasing share of Fox News's revenue comes from affiliate fees paid by cable and satellite providers, money collected automatically from millions of households regardless of whether they watch or not. Fox News is now one of the highest-paid cable channels per subscriber. According to a 2023 estimate, the channel charges cable providers roughly $2 per month per household, generating well over $1.5 billion annually in subscription revenue alone.

It's a testament to its brand and following: Cable providers know they need to offer it to their customers, so they pay a high fee to do so. This shift in the underlying revenue model has fundamentally changed Fox News's vulnerability profile. Advertiser boycotts that once posed a real financial threat have become incredibly difficult to pull off, as the network's core revenue stream remains largely insulated from public pressure. As a result, efforts to change Fox News's behavior require a different strategy, targeting what could make injustice costly for them today, not a decade ago.

Corporations, just like Donald Trump and right-wing political leaders, are not invincible. They may sometimes seem as if they are, but that's just a story that benefits them. They want us to think that. But throughout history, people—whether organized in the form of labor unions, consumer activist lawsuits, or gender and racial justice organizations—have always been able to find ways to win against them. We need to build on those legacies now. And we need to believe we can win—because we can.

Corporations at Work in an Integrated World

Sometimes corporate power towers over the landscape like the tallest tree, while at other times it's hidden like a root system networking unseen underneath the entire landscape, allowing politicians, church leaders, media figures, and others to remain the visible targets (even as many of them are backed by corporations). Either way, corporations are there, part of the landscape. Knowing the role they play helps us understand how to engage them.

People who care about criminal justice would often ask me about Color Of Change's Hollywood work: "Why are you spending so much time on all of this cultural stuff instead of hard policy?" I would answer that even though the nonprofit sector is organized by issue silos, people live in a world that's integrated. All of the injustices in their lives are interrelated, and our strategies for social change need to take that into account. Seeing those connections is an essential first step.

Racist policing requires racist corporate media to survive—not only crime dramas on CBS and NBC but also segments on local TV news stations that show Black people's mugshots more often than anyone else's, even if Black people don't commit more crimes than anyone else. That's one corporate force shaping public attitudes and the political climate, and therefore the unwritten rules that give police officers the incentive to harass Black people disproportionately, and that give schools the incentive to punish Black students more than non-Black students for the same behavior.

But racist policing is also a response to economic incentives. One example involves the written laws in some cities enabling hefty fines for minor traffic violations and other slight infractions. Such laws give police departments the financial incentive to constantly target Black and Brown neighborhoods, knowing they couldn't get away with targeting wealthier white neighborhoods in the same way. Corporations also profit when police departments spend endless amounts of money on equipment, surveillance technology, and militarized weaponry. Of course, when police departments have all that stuff, they are incentivized to use it—justly or not.

There are always corporations at work making injustices possible, even if we don't see them doing it. Whether they profit from injustice directly or simply profit by enabling politicians and others to do terrible things in exchange for some reward, they play a role that we need to redefine.

Systemic Corporate Accountability

There are many definitions of *corporate accountability,* including definitions designed to create a very low bar for corporations to meet in order to claim they are "good." In activism, the term *corporate accountability* means something more: It is the act of forcing a corporation to reckon in a tangible and proportionate way with a harm it has unjustly caused—making it pay for what it's done, perhaps even forcing it to make those it's harmed whole again.

But accountability is not always the same thing as systemic change. *Systemic corporate accountability* forces corporations to change the way they do business: eliminating the specific patterns of behavior and practices that produce injustice and cause harm—that is, not merely making up for what they've done in the past but making a serious commitment not do it again.

The first thing to get right in any systemic corporate accountability effort is setting the right goal. Sometimes, individual instances of corporate accountability can be stepping-stones to achieving systemic corporate accountability. Other times, they may allow us to fool ourselves into thinking we have won systemic change when we haven't, a case of magical thinking.

Systemic corporate accountability requires being able to change the rules both inside a corporation (its culture and policies) and outside a corporation (our laws and regulations) in a way that changes how it does business overall. (In chapter 15, I give the example of how we shifted our Hollywood strategy at Color Of Change after winning a lot of instances of accountability without winning enough systemic changes.)

It is easy to get distracted from the systemic goal. Punishing a corporation for doing something bad, for instance, is not always a step toward achieving systemic corporate accountability. It can feel very satisfying. But punishment in itself cannot be the goal, because it may take us off course. If the punishment addresses past actions but not present and future actions, it will likely not lead to systemic change. In fact, it could be an intentional distraction.

We cannot think that punishing a corporation for doing some-

thing bad will teach its leaders a lesson without changing the incentive structures that determine how they work. That is magical thinking. Corporate executives who make mistakes do learn lessons (or sometimes pretend to, in press releases), but corporations that create injustice for profit—as part of their business model—do not. We need to force corporations to adopt new rules, not simply try to teach them lessons.

Donald Trump is a classic case. Whenever one of his businesses was sued, he would work to settle the case with all records sealed and confidential. He knew then that he would be off the hook: He wouldn't have to change a thing about how he worked. He counted those settlements as the cost of doing business, not as a mandate to change *how* he did business. It is the same with big corporations. A corporation would much rather pay off someone whom they got caught hurting, in exchange for their silence and an end to the headlines, than actually change the profitable practices that hurt others in the same way but without getting caught.

Corporations change when rules that constrain their actions are put in place and enforced against them consistently. That change may come in the form of any of the following:

- The passage of a law and the serious prosecution of that law.
- A new corporate policy and the serious enforcement of that policy.
- An unignorable force of people no longer tolerating their behavior, using their purchasing power, shareholder power, or other power to change the incentive structure for what the corporation can get away with doing.

The goal can be achieved in many ways, but the goal must be clear.

Making It Too Easy for Corporations

Outrage is real. And important. Advocates for social justice rarely get anywhere if no one is expressing outrage in the face of bad corporate behavior. Yet it is critical to distinguish when outrage drives corporate accountability from when it helps corporations evade it.

Corporations do not like being challenged. But when they do get challenged, they generally love when it comes in the form of outrage. It gives them the chance to apologize. It gives them the chance to be forgiven, often by taking symbolic actions rather than systemic actions. **In fact, one definition of the strength of a corporate brand is the extent to which it is forgiven when it does something wrong.** There are many business-oriented definitions of *brand equity.* But I believe brand equity is the ability of a corporation to remain highly profitable even when its actions are highly questionable. Corporations build extensive narrative infrastructure in order to manage their brand and ensure they remain forgivable.

When outrage leads to punishment becoming the goal, the story gets personal. When the story gets personal, the fight can too easily become a matter of addressing just one incident—or one person. One consumer or community member who's been hurt, who needs to be compensated. Or one executive or employee whose actions hurt the brand, who needs to be punished. An individual harm deserves its own restitution. And an individual story can be extremely important for motivating people to participate in a much larger fight if it draws attention to a series of systemic incidents, beyond a single person's harm, and if that larger pattern of behavior becomes the focus of change. But if that one story becomes the entire fight, and the fight ends there, then the personal becomes a way of covering up the systemic—turning momentum against movements trying to win changes that matter for millions of people. That makes apologizing an easy way for corporations to smooth over the situation and get everyone to move on.

Hidden in Plain Sight

When a corporation has made injustice profitable, and profiteering is running wild, the corporation's biggest weapon for continuing to get away with a harmful practice is convincing people that it is not even happening. Or, if it is happening and generates high profits, that it's good for the economy and there aren't many downsides—no one is really getting hurt. The corporation either hides the evidence or distracts people's attention from it.

Even when a moment of injustice is recognized on principle, a corporation's greatest trick is getting people to think the injustice stops there. Often, they get us to pretend that the people they've hurt do not have to live with the consequences of that injustice for the rest of their lives.

Think about a bank denying a loan to a Black-owned business, as many banks did as part of their role in the 2020 Paycheck Protection Program (PPP), which was launched to help offset the downturn businesses faced during the initial year of COVID-19. Racial discrimination was massive. In a pattern so obvious it had to be the result of the program's design, banks approved PPP loan applications from white-owned businesses at a much greater rate than applications from Black-owned businesses. It was its own pandemic. Color Of Change was a leading force in exposing this injustice. Banks acknowledged the disparity—*That was not right, let's do better next time*—but the conversation largely ended there. There was no remedy. Acknowledgment is not accountability.

There was also no conversation about how many Black businesses had to shut down because banks cut them out of their own government's aid program. There was no conversation about what those banks did to those people's careers, to their trajectory as entrepreneurs, to their families, to their employees, to the communities those businesses would have been part of and would have invested in. Such injustices can ruin the future of an entire community and force its people to live with that legacy for decades. Without that conversation being central to the way people and decision-makers saw the problem, the solution would never lead to any restitution or rule changes.

Going In Eyes Open

Who can challenge corporate power successfully in our time? It is no easy task. That is why many liberal and progressive organizations focus so much on government policy: They are more comfortable, better suited, and better resourced to compete over elections and to run campaigns focused on passing laws and changing policies than to take on corporations. Some, of course, think that *is* the best way to challenge corporations. But they miss the two-way nature of accountability: government affecting corporations and corporations affecting government.

In a time when systemic corporate accountability may be the most viable path for challenging government policies and politicians, at least at the federal level, we cannot turn away from it. We must expand our thinking and also our capabilities. We cannot default to what's most comfortable, especially if that means ignoring what's most needed.

If you're a professional organizer or advocate, I hope that some of what I'm offering is useful for developing your own strategies. If you're working to start or join an effort focused on changing something you care about, I believe some of these lessons will open up new possibilities for thinking about the role you play—and how. And if you're a person who shows up to rallies, donates to causes, engages your friends in group chats and dinner conversations, and amplifies content on social media in the hopes of moving our country forward, I hope these stories will give you insight into what it takes to make social change movements powerful and successful—everything corporations don't want you to know.

Corporations are deeply invested in preventing people from understanding how to challenge them and preventing us from seeing the difference between performative PR and meaningful change. In the stories and examples that follow, I share what I've learned through wins, losses, and mistakes I've made. My goal is to demonstrate that you don't have to be a billionaire to take on a billionaire CEO, but you do have to believe it's possible and understand how to get the upper hand.

FIND YOUR POWER
Corporate Accountability

This activity is meant to help you see opportunities for holding business profiteers accountable at the local level.

Corporate accountability is a lot easier to talk about than to achieve. But corporate accountability isn't only about thousands of people banding together across the country to go after the likes of McDonald's, Amazon, Walmart, or other corporate profiteers at the national and global level. Corporate accountability also involves holding smaller businesses (and their owners) accountable for the role they play in creating or exploiting injustice, and changing the rules to make it unprofitable for them to do so. There are often leverage points for getting them to make different decisions that don't exist with bigger corporations—such as their need to maintain a good profile in a given community.

The practices of small business owners and managers can have a huge impact in our lives. For example, small businesses still employ about half of all people working in the private sector in the United States, which means unchecked issues like hiring discrimination or cheating employees out of health insurance can have a major impact on large numbers of people. Raising the floor for what's acceptable at the local business level is critical.

And raising the ceiling for what's possible at the local business level can be equally influential: When local businesses decide to protect undocumented workers and their families from attacks by the government, or to be proactive about good environmental practices or collaborating with Black-owned and other suppliers traditionally shut out of the market, they help create momentum for changing the rules at larger corporations.

Your voice, whether your own individual voice or the voices of people across your community that you are able to organize, can make a big difference. But how do you know when a business is doing something wrong that must be changed?

There are many ways to bring local business practices into the light:

- You can find out if businesses or their owners are making contributions to politicians that hurt people and support right-wing policies through the nonpartisan, nonprofit research group Open Secrets (opensecrets.org). You can refuse to do business with them and rally others to do so.
- Some local businesses (like gyms or diners) are constantly playing Fox News, helping the right wing spread its lies. You can demand they stop doing that.
- Local businesses can be stealing wages in many different ways from their employees.[2] You can check with local unions, local government offices for labor and worker protections, and other news and advocacy sources that may have investigated them. Sometimes holding them accountable legally can take far longer than mounting a local public campaign capable of pressuring them to change.
- Local businesses can practice blatant discrimination against potential employees, current employees, or customers. (Think about the local pharmacies refusing to fill prescriptions for reproductive medicine or refusing to bake a cake for a same-sex wedding

ceremony.) You can refuse to do business with them and rally others to do the same.

- A corporation like Amazon owns all of its local distribution warehouses, but you can still support local efforts led by workers of those warehouses to unionize or fight for improvements in working conditions.
- In other cases, local franchises or business partners of larger corporations doing wrong may be susceptible to influence from local community members (e.g., local contractors building a private prison for GEO Group).

By looking at businesses proactively through these lenses (and others), you can connect the dots between the big social issues you care about and the practices of specific businesses in your area that you may be able to influence—or, at least, make sure to no longer support. The right wing plays this game very well, and there is no reason you can't do it, too.

When you identify a local business with practices you want to change, consider different ways you can help increase the pressure on them, with the aim of making what they're doing unprofitable:

- Drawing attention they can't avoid by putting it on the radar for local news media outlets and social media influencers with a big reach locally and a commitment to turn up the pressure.
- Raising money and rallying people to attend demonstrations in support of workers or others hurt by these businesses to fight back.
- Organizing people to stop shopping there or doing business with them, including getting any groups you are part of to stop doing business with them.

- Reporting them to local, state, or national government agencies that can open up investigations, fine them, or pressure them to change in other ways.

Businesses depend on people looking the other way. Refusing to play along can be more powerful than you think in forcing them to change.

13

Taking On Big Tech Profiteering

CHALLENGE: Big Tech corporations represent a dangerous mix of causing a lot of harm and evading accountability. Their leaders are very good at hiding the harms they cause. They have also built enough influence across government, and enough control of their businesses internally, to prevent change. Many of Big Tech's harms have been exposed—and we must never forget or excuse them—but exposure in itself is not enough.

OPPORTUNITY: To change the rules for how Big Tech does business, we need to be honest about what does and doesn't work, which means seeing new fronts in the fight, widening our capabilities, and building new infrastructure that will generate the right kind of power to challenge them. There are many lessons to learn from having successfully fought other industries that once seemed all-powerful.

REMINDER: *Profiteering* is about benefiting from injustice: creating, increasing, or exploiting an injustice for money, social status, professional advancement, or access to special privileges. People with power often change the rules to make profiteering easier to get away with—reducing the consequences for it and even encouraging it outright.

Rules of Engagement

Corporations may not always appreciate irony, but they certainly generate a lot of it.

Even if you don't know the name Meta, you certainly know some of the brands under its umbrella: Facebook, Instagram, WhatsApp, Meta Quest. Mark Zuckerberg founded Facebook in 2004, bought and integrated other platforms over the years, and rebranded the whole operation as Meta in 2021.

Meta's most popular products are generally free to use, but they come with another kind of cost. One of its lesser-known but most lucrative innovations is its ability to collect, organize, and analyze incredible amounts of its users' personal information—and profit from either selling it or helping advertisers use it to manipulate consumers on various Meta platforms.[1] The Meta surveillance system identifies and exploits its users' vulnerabilities. Violating users' privacy isn't a concern for them, it's their goal.

That's why I could only smile when I was asked to sign a nondisclosure agreement (NDA) just to walk in the door at Facebook headquarters in November 2019. My signature would have forced me to keep silent about anything I heard or saw during my time there. Facebook is deeply worried about its own privacy, of course, especially related to all its secret ways of profiting from violating everyone else's. Irony in full force.

Even a private conversation with Zuckerberg had rules that worked against the truth. An NDA can be used as a classic power move coming from people with something to hide. Donald Trump has long used NDAs to silence people in his life and neutralize whistleblowers at his businesses.[2] It's one way that profiteers of all kinds evade accountability for what they say and do in front of witnesses—it prevents those witnesses from telling the truth, even to authorities.[3]

I refused to sign it. This wasn't my first time on Facebook's sprawling campus, and it wasn't my first time refusing to sign the NDA. And so I knew what was coming: The badge they clipped on me read "No NDA." It was a written sign that I should be treated with caution because I was breaking an unwritten rule of Silicon Valley: refusing to play along with the idea that every conversation these tech leaders had should be on their terms alone. The rules of engagement were not subtle; the badge symbolized the imbalance of power we faced.

I was there that fall for a meeting with Mark Zuckerberg as part of a long-running effort Color Of Change was leading to change the rules for how Facebook did business, given the way it was giving new life to job discrimination, voter suppression, and other injustices that hurt Black people deeply. I was there along with two powerhouse civil rights leaders also involved in that fight: Sherrilyn Ifill, then the president of the NAACP Legal Defense Fund, and Vanita Gupta, then the president of the Leadership Conference on Civil and Human Rights (and later the third-highest official at the Justice Department under Biden). They didn't sign the NDA, either.

Because I didn't sign that NDA, I can now share this chapter's stories with you.

Big Tech corporations—which I define as including Meta, Alphabet (parent of Google and YouTube), Amazon, Apple, X (formerly Twitter), OpenAI, Microsoft, Nvidia, and TikTok—are perceived as a source of new and exciting technologies, but they have also created a devastating set of problems for all of us. This chapter is about taking on Big Tech in order to protect the people its products hurt. My struggles in fighting that fight over the last decade taught me important lessons, which I believe are relevant for anyone hoping to make change—in any context and at any scale. First among those lessons is understanding the opportunities and limits of directly engaging decision-makers.

Dialogue Is Not Negotiation

If you are able to cause enough trouble for profiteers, at some point you get invited to meetings with them. If they can no longer ignore you or undermine your momentum in some way, then they move to the next step: trying to "deal with" you.

Inevitably, they will try to convince you of one or more of the following:

- That they're good people.
- That they care about whoever you represent just as much as you do.
- That both you and they actually want the same thing.
- That they're not responsible for doing whatever bad thing you're saying they're doing.
- That they do far more good than harm, and you should learn more about it.
- That the thing you're saying they're doing is bad isn't really so bad.
- That you should work together to resolve your issues instead of getting into a big, nasty public fight about it.

That is, they will try to get you to give up. It always amazed me that they thought it would be easy to get us to back down and that they expected us to believe whatever *they* said when they were so busy denying everything *we* said. And yet these meetings can be important points of leverage.

Over time, I learned that I needed to keep two questions front and center whenever I was directly engaging with profiteers:

1. **Is this a dialogue or a negotiation?** The answer would largely depend on their assessment of their *own* power relative to their perception of *my* power.
2. **Are we talking about real solutions or fake solutions?** The

answer would largely depend on my own clarity about what and who I was fighting for.

The first question is a lot harder to answer than it might seem. Especially early on in my career, I often went into situations thinking that I was in a negotiation when it turned out I was merely in a dialogue. Had I seen it more clearly ahead of time, I could have made much more of the opportunity. I might have even skipped the meeting altogether, which, in some cases, would have given me much more leverage than if I showed up.

So what's the difference between the two? **If you're in a negotiation, you are in a genuine struggle to win something meaningful. If you're in a dialogue, the struggle is most likely already over.** Thinking you're in a negotiation when you're actually in a dialogue is a sure way to fail your cause. It's a classic trap of magical thinking.

In the context of corporate accountability, a *dialogue* is a conversation in which you do not have the leverage to force the other party to make a decision (whether a full rule change or some kind of concession or compromise). It's about listening and learning. It's about understanding and relationship-building—and gaining intelligence. Among everyday people, dialogue can lead to persuasion (changing people's minds) and persuasion can lead to different decisions (changing people's behavior). But that is rarely true for dialogue between change-makers and corporations, no matter how much "insider" access those change-makers think they have.

Dialogue does not lead corporate executives to change their behavior any more than an online petition signed by ten thousand leftist activists in California would change any of Senator Mitch McConnell's votes in Washington, DC. The senator from Kentucky is not accountable to a small group of people in California, let alone liberal activists. He would never abandon his goals for them. They could schedule meetings and sit with him all day long—dialoguing—but no change would come of it.

Engaging in dialogue with corporate executives with the aim of persuasion is not an effective strategy. Even when I did change the opinion executives had about an issue, I did not win unless I changed the incentives that governed the decisions they actually made—the rewards and punishments that defined the dynamics they operated within.

Using dialogue to educate influential employees could be part of a long-term strategy to cultivate the desire for change more broadly within a corporation, ultimately making it unprofitable for corporations to continue acting in ways their own employees did not like. But new knowledge, in itself, rarely translates directly into new decisions. When it comes to changing corporate behavior, knowledge is not power. Only power is power.

Negotiation, in contrast to dialogue, is a conversation in which compromise and concession are necessary and inevitable because you have real leverage. As a result of negotiation, corporate executives will do something they do not necessarily want to do, or had not considered doing before, but feel compelled to do because they conclude it is in their best interests. They may not even believe in doing it, or have not been rationally persuaded to do it, but they know they have to do it. They do not want to suffer the consequences of not doing it. Being able to convince people of the *consequences* of their decisions is far more important than being able to convince them of the *goodness* of their decisions.

Of course, dialogue can turn into negotiation if the stakes for the decision-makers are relatively low. Educating corporate executives about an emotionally engaging issue that does not implicate their own behavior, with the aim of getting them to donate to a charity focused on that issue, can lead to a favorable decision. That may begin as a dialogue but turn into a negotiation when the executive sees an opportunity or feels some kind of attachment to a cause.

When you're trying to change the rules that determine how (and how much) corporations can profit, however, friendly, informative dialogue rarely leads to any changes. Corporations tend to assess power pretty accurately. Executives who believe activists do not have the power to force them to do anything differently are happy to dialogue, sometimes endlessly. Being in a continuing dialogue makes them look good. They're listening. They're talking to people. *Look at them shaking hands with those Latino leaders—amazing.* They gain something valuable without having to give anything up, the opposite of negotiation.

Mark Zuckerberg Is Not Innocent

I already had history with Mark Zuckerberg when I arrived at his office in 2019.

Starting in 2015, we at Color Of Change began seeing how Facebook was helping to facilitate attacks on Black activists advocating for police reform, fighting discrimination against Black and Latino people looking for housing and jobs, and working to stop the general spread of hateful content aimed at warping perceptions of Black people. We urged our members to take action against Facebook through submitting petitions demanding specific changes, posting personal stories of harm, and getting their voices into the press. We wanted Facebook to change the practices that allowed its most malicious users to publish personal information about Black activists campaigning against white nationalists, which put those activists in danger.

We also worked to get Facebook to stop allowing real estate agents and hiring agencies to openly discriminate—excluding Black-identified people and several other groups from being able to see their listings. Black people had fought hard for decades to make this type of discrimination illegal in the traditional venues of real estate deals and job hiring, but it was now rampant online. Instead of building on the major gains we had won—setting up their rules to continue that legacy—Facebook was canceling them.

In 2016, we called for a civil rights audit at Facebook. Other groups joined in, and we finally won in 2018 after launching public campaigns, adding more outside pressure to the inside pressure we had created.[4] The goal was to systematically examine the impact that Facebook's platform and business practices had on racial discrimination. Conducted by Laura Murphy, a longtime civil rights advocate and civil liberties leader, the audit delivered a damning rebuke of Facebook's role in voter suppression, hate speech, and discrimination.[5]

We hoped that the conclusive results of the audit, along with our advocacy, could help force Zuckerberg into a negotiation rather than mere dialogue. Our hopes were not unfounded in the beginning, as the corporation's executives did agree to make some minor changes. As time went by, however, Facebook got worse, not better. In the heat of 2020—the year of COVID-19, #BlackLivesMatter, and the Biden-versus-Trump election—its amplification of hate speech became extreme, promoting so much anti-Black, anti-LGBT, and anti-Jewish content that most everyday users couldn't get away from it even if they wanted to.

I helped lead a coalition—along with groups like Free Press, the NAACP, and Common Sense Media—that targeted Facebook advertisers. Knowing that major brands wouldn't want their ads to appear next to white nationalist or other extremist content, we orchestrated the largest advertiser boycott in history. Advertisers far and wide withdrew all spending on Facebook for one month, signing on to our message that Facebook needed to make a serious change.

The boycott led to a significant (if temporary) loss of hundreds of millions of dollars in advertising revenue, resulting in a $7 billion loss in net worth for Zuckerberg due to the hit on the Facebook share price, as well as a huge embarrassment for him. Racism had been profitable for Zuckerberg, but we found a way to make it unprofitable—mostly in the form of employee disgruntlement and hits to Facebook's public brand. Company executives were not happy. But if they were going to keep us in dialogue mode, we were going to raise the stakes. That led them to agree to some of the recommendations in the civil rights audit they had been avoiding for years. We entered negotiation territory—for a while.

Also in 2020, Facebook broadcast that it had created tools to prevent harm ahead of that year's election, making sure its algorithm would stop recommending political groups to users. Yet Facebook's own internal documents later revealed that while it banned the primary Stop the Steal group (the group of Trump supporters promoting conspiracy theories about that year's election vote tallies and driving people to take extreme action as a result), it didn't stop other groups from using the same slogan and massively expanding their reach. That was to both the tools Facebook made available to those groups and its own bias for promoting sensationalist content in order to drive engagement. Facebook's decisions, along with those made by other platforms, increased the radicalization of Trump voters that contributed to the invasion of the U.S. Capitol on January 6, 2021.

Investigative reporting published after the fact by *The Washington Post* revealed what Facebook employees were seeing. "Not only do we not do something about combustible election misinformation in comments," wrote one employee in November 2020, "we amplify them and give them broader distribution."[6] According to an article posted in January 2022, an investigation conducted by ProPublica and *The Washington Post* presented "the clearest evidence yet that Facebook played a critical role in the spread of false narratives that fomented the violence of Jan. 6. Its efforts to police such content, the investigation also found, were ineffective and started too late to quell the surge of angry, hateful misinformation coursing through Facebook groups—some of it explicitly calling for violent confrontation with government officials, a theme that foreshadowed the storming of the Capitol that day amid clashes that left five people dead."[7]

Mark Zuckerberg clearly placed profit over any other concern. Facebook's choices were acts of injustice, not unfortunate coincidences or innocent mistakes. Rather than monitoring and dismantling dangerous groups on its platform, the company provided momentum for one of the most dangerous moments in recent U.S. history, an unprecedented assault aiming to murder people who represent us, in the very moment in which they were certifying the results of the votes we had cast. (Zuckerberg's record of undermining democracy in other countries isn't any better.)[8] For Black people and anyone else in the crosshairs of hate from white nationalists, the through line from the 2017 Unite the Right rally in Charlottesville, Virginia, to the January 6, 2021, mob violence in Washington, DC, was chilling.

During this same period, but before the truth came out, many journalists who were cozy with Silicon Valley, as well as people working in the industry itself, told me that I was overreacting. *You're being dramatic to gain attention,* they claimed. *It's not really as bad as you say it is. You don't understand what's really going on. Zuckerberg's heart is in the right place, and he has the best goals and plans in mind.* No one, though, could verify what those goals and plans were, exactly. Many people who spoke to me then have since built up their reputations as critics of Zuckerberg, Meta, and Silicon Valley overall. But when it really mattered, and they could have played a role in stopping what was happening, they played along instead. They were clearly not in touch with the history of corporations' role in society, nor were they personally connected to the decades of lies and abuse that corporate profiteers routinely visited on Black communities and others. They were the experts, they claimed, and I was just an activist who didn't know any better.

The immense power that Big Tech corporations like Meta hold, and their lack of transparency and any commitment to protect public safety and stop the dangerous spread of misinformation and disinformation on their platforms, has led to violence and real consequences for real people. Unchecked, it will continue to. January 6 was neither the first nor the last example. And the propaganda those corporations flood their users with, to quell any complaints and neutralize any significant pushback, is an important part of their power.

Big Tech, Out of Control

From designing products and services with rampant racial biases, to enabling and amplifying rampant misinformation and violent extremism, to knowingly hooking people on content that leads to bullying and crippling levels of anxiety and alienation, executives across the tech sector have continued to ignore or undermine practical and proven solutions that would address the systemic racism and many other harmful social effects that result from their products and platforms. Instead, they have favored business models that *depend* on injustice and profit from it.[9] All while so many different people all across our society pay the price.[10]

A very few Big Tech corporations maintain near-total control over three areas of online life in America: online commerce, online content, and online connection. Those are also Big Tech's three domains of profiteering from injustice. Their influence over how we live our lives is unmatched in modern society, and their control over the rules we live by has dire consequences for our social cohesion, political processes, environmental protection, economic well-being, and fairness in society when it comes to race, class, gender, and other hierarchies. Social media giants like Meta and YouTube have successfully monetized polarization and propaganda, and now depend on it for revenue. AI is only enabling and incentivizing them to do worse.

I presented this three-part framework to Congress during a hearing in December 2021. Alongside Facebook whistleblower Frances Haugen, I was testifying about the dangers of Big Tech continuing to receive legal immunity from being held accountable for its effects on society. Frances and I both emphasized that it was long past time for Congress to understand that serious regulation of the entire tech sector was necessary to protect our communities, our freedoms, and our political system. Although our testimony helped bolster support for legislation that was on the table—the Justice Against Malicious Algorithms Act, the SAFE TECH Act, and the Civil Rights Modernization Act—none of those laws ultimately passed. That same year, I also co-chaired the Aspen Institute's Commission on Information Disorder, whose final report detailed recommendations "to reinforce the integrity of our information ecosystem."[11] (For more on tech corporations' profiteering, and details on the three-part framework I presented to Congress, see the online Appendix at rashadrobinson.com/book.)

The implication for all of us is clear: The longer the sector evades regulation, the harder it will be to stop them from profiting from injustice—increasing the number and extent of the injustices they profit from. We should be reining in the corporations that have injustice at the core of their business model, not letting them loose on society.

Politicians on both sides of the aisle, many of whom received contributions and other perks from the tech sector—and still do—refused to do their jobs to protect us. There were other ways to win rule changes, however. As a result of strong social movements late in the 2010s, several key tech platforms had begun changing their approach with the aim of increasing safety, empowering new leaders to change policies and practices, and to respond to the demands of the communities they harm. At Color Of Change, we got Google to stop racially biased advertising that took us fifty years backward. We got Indiegogo and GoFundMe to stop hosting fundraisers for police officers who killed unarmed Black people. We got Airbnb to change many of its practices, a story I share later in this chapter. And other organizations had other similar modest successes, not yet changing the business model, but changing some of the rules for doing business.

Though it took far too long, with far too many casualties along the way, Twitter, which had been rife with trolls and others who caused outsized harm, was moving in the right direction and implementing changes to internal policies that would have had a meaningful positive effect. That was before Twitter board members sold out to Elon Musk, however, whom they let buy and entirely take over the corporation in 2022 in the midst of its biggest challenges related to the harms of misinformation the platform was causing.

One of the biggest problems with the laughable idea of voluntary self-regulation is that corporations can change the rules (and their rulers) whenever they want. Progress is easily overturned by transfers in ownership or financial pressures that lead executives to cave in to profit-over-people policies. Today, Big Tech remains united in forcefully undermining the type of meaningful internal and external oversight that would address systemic injustices.

Big Tech has grown to dominate ever greater portions of our economy, our culture, and our political landscape, to the point where it feels more powerful and more in control of society than industries decades older. A huge amount of power is concentrated among a small number of corporations, and decision-making in those corporations is concentrated in the hands of an even smaller number of large stake owners and executives. Those owners and their top executives collectively work as one on many fronts that keep their profit centers clear and free.

And who is there to stop them? We may hear a lot about Mark Zuckerberg, Elon Musk, Jeff Bezos, Tim Cook, and other tech leaders throwing their support behind Trump because they want favorable regulation, government contracts, and approval for mergers. But it doesn't help that Democratic officials and operatives have also worked with these corporations and helped them do all the bad things they do. Which is worse, corporate leaders aligning with Trump or Democrats aligning with corporate leaders after claiming their party defends people against them? And which gives those corporations more cover?

We need to change the incentives for all the people who enable these corporations to do wrong, so that eventually we change the incentives for the people who run them. But how do we help people understand the control these corporations have? How do we disrupt the impact their control has on our lives? How do we shift the belief system about serious regulation from being a question to being an answer—from an impossibility to an inevitability?

Disingenuous Dialogue

In June 2020, several years into our engagement with Facebook, I was on a Zoom call with Mark Zuckerberg, along with Sherrilyn Ifill and Vanita Gupta. It was the year Biden ran against Trump for the presidency, and this call was aimed at pressuring Zuckerberg to enforce his own policies related to ensuring the election would be fair and honest.

As president, Trump had posted wildly reckless misinformation about mail-in voting (questioning its legitimacy and reliability), as well as making a post inciting vigilante violence ("when the looting starts, the shooting starts"). Both posts violated even the fairly weak policies Facebook had implemented as a result of our movement's collective activism. But when it came time to enforce those policies,

Zuckerberg didn't do a thing. (Even his own employees blasted him for that.)[12] He didn't need to follow his own written rule because the bigger written rule was that since he owned the majority of the corporation he could do whatever he wanted at any time. And, of course, the unwritten rule for CEOs was not to aggravate Trump—the only rule Zuckerberg felt obliged to follow.

At one point during the call, Zuckerberg started arguing about mail-in voting with Sherrilyn and Vanita, two of the most prominent voting rights experts in the country. It was laughable. He clearly wasn't trying to understand the law, or understand the danger he was putting people (and the country) in. He was just trying to keep the conversation going to the point of exhaustion. I could imagine good people at Facebook getting stuck in these same conversations with him: presenting him with evidence and solutions for addressing real and urgent problems but getting only doublespeak and distraction in response. So that's when I stepped in to say, "What are we doing here? How are we supposed to stay in this conversation with you? I know when I am being listened to and when I am not. You're clearly putting your hand on the scale for the president." If he was going to be his own expert on civil rights—and everything else—what was our role?

We were not in a negotiation but in an endless dialogue, the purpose of which was clear: to let Zuckerberg test out arguments with us (and gauge our responses) so that he could develop a better strategy for going out to the public, people in Congress, regulators, and anyone else who might question him or try to hold him accountable but could be neutralized if he got to them in advance. He was just rehearsing with us to refine his act.

That's when I realized we needed to build more pressure in order to be taken seriously, and that's when it was clear to me that our coalition of partners should no longer hold off launching our boycott. We had to step back from the magical thinking that dialogue was going to have an effect.

I had a more positive relationship with Facebook's chief operating officer, Sheryl Sandberg. She seemed to genuinely care about racism and eventually came to see that Facebook was causing real problems in the world, especially for Black people. But she did not have the power to make the systemic changes we needed. Ultimately, there was no negotiation with her, either, because the path to change did not run through her. Zuckerberg was in charge, no matter what the organization chart looked like. And Sandberg was not going to risk trying to change that.

At one point earlier on in the process with Facebook, in 2019, we were organizing an event in Atlanta with community members passionate about racial justice. It was going to be something of a celebration for having won the commitment to conduct the racial justice audit. Sandberg brought her family to the event on a private jet. I felt she was proud to be part of it and wanted to engage with us productively.

But two days before the event, Facebook made public a new policy (which it claimed had already been in place for a year) exempting politicians from their independent, third-party fact-checking program. It would not moderate the content of political leaders for accuracy unless they were sharing a post that Facebook had already flagged as being debunked. It was a new rule clearly created to appease Trump and excuse all of the false content he was promoting. The entire tone of the event changed: from celebrating progress to reemphasizing Facebook's ongoing harmful impact. It was clear to me that Sandberg hadn't been in the loop.

Zuckerberg's strategy was simple: Deny that any of those problems outweighed the benefits of his great product, and that solving those problems would only cause worse problems, no matter how much was presented to him to demonstrate the contrary. Touted as an innovator, he seemed to have no imagination for problem-solving when it didn't help him dominate the tech sector. We were a distraction to him, a drag on his dreams, and he knew we had no laws or leverage on our side that could force his hand.

Even earlier, starting in 2018, after a few years of dealing with staff and executives at lower levels across the organization, I was part of a series of in-person and video meetings with Zuckerberg and Sandberg, as well as other senior leaders like Nick Clegg, vice president of global affairs and communication, which ultimately demonstrated that Zuckerberg's participation was nothing more than a performance.

It was November 2019 when I went to his office in Palo Alto with Sherrilyn and Vanita, and we all got the "No NDA" badges. The three of us met with him and his team in advance of a larger group dinner with civil rights leaders at his home (many of whom ran organizations taking money from Zuckerberg in one form or another). I had refused to go to the dinner, at first, until we secured a more serious meeting with just the three of us, to happen earlier that same day. Sandberg agreed to make that meeting happen; they didn't want my absence at the dinner to become a story the press latched onto, since I had been one of the most public voices criticizing them and my absence would be noted. That's the leverage I had.

At one point during the meeting, the three of us argued for changing Facebook's internal rules governing content amplification algorithms, since they allowed the spread of disinformation that would suppress certain people's participation in both the 2020 census and the presidential election. Zuckerberg told us about someone he met from East Palo Alto who had been brought to the U.S. as a child without official authorization, one of millions of young people often referred to as Dreamers in an effort to humanize their struggle and their quest for citizenship. He said her name was Gabrielle, and he claimed that she was afraid that answering the census might put her immigration status in danger. He said that our proposed changes would prevent her from safely voicing her questions and concerns about the census on Facebook because it could be flagged as misinformation and even lead to disciplinary action against her. It said a lot about him that he would use this person's story in such a self-interested and disingenuous way, aiming to distract from the issue at hand.

I responded that the policy changes we were asking for would not target everyday users like Gabrielle, who likely had a small number of Facebook friends. The changes we wanted Zuckerberg to make were instead aimed at reining in two Facebook practices related to users who influenced many thousands of friends, followers, and viewers of widely shared posts:

- Deliberately programming feeds to amplify sensational misinformation in order to increase user engagement, which kept people active on the Facebook app for longer and therefore helped the corporation's ad revenue.[13]
- Allowing right-wing political operatives, well-funded white nationalist leaders, and other bad actors to advertise and target users with the purpose of boosting clearly influential harmful misinformation.[14]

Zuckerberg was hiding behind Gabrielle. But if she wasn't paying to exponentially amplify her content, then her posts would not even reach the threshold to be flagged through the process we were recommending. Gabrielle wasn't the problem, and he knew it. He was playing dumb about how his own platform worked. Even for me, it was a bit surprising that he believed he could get away with such a deceitful distraction in the face of people who actually knew what they were talking about.

Vanita jumped in right after me. "Mark, we are not trying to prevent free speech," she said. "What we want to deal with is algorithmic amplification, and what the platform amplifies. This is about what type of ads can be run on the platform, which is very different from freedom of speech and things I may or may not dislike online." Sherrilyn didn't let his lies fly, either.

Zuckerberg finally retired that particular argument in favor of equally misleading and fallacious arguments, and the conversation went nowhere. I learned the hard way that Mark Zuckerberg didn't answer to anybody but himself. While he saw a benefit in having a relationship with us and keeping the dialogue going, he wasn't afraid of us, even after we created some degree of pain for his company. He and his team resisted every change we proposed, and eventually conceded on a very few minor changes, with the outcomes of those few changes still remaining unclear. It turns out, according to internal documents later revealed, they understood the harm they were causing even better than we did. But they also understood the limits of our power and the extent of their own.

At Facebook, the issue wasn't simply that most leaders didn't take racism seriously and that the few who did didn't have the power to do much about it. It was also that key leaders didn't have the range for understanding the issues or understanding the people whose lives were at stake in the decisions they made.

After a full day together, including the small sit-down with Mark and Sheryl and the larger group dinner, I boarded my flight back from San Francisco. Sandberg texted me to thank me for the meeting and to tell me that I was "the most articulate person in the room." I wasn't even offended by that comment and all its historical triggers in the way I might have been in my twenties. What hit me was something else: She clearly didn't have the people around her, or make space to include people around her, who could help her understand what she was stepping into—with that comment and everything else. She was the one tasked with dealing with the Black people, but she was far from understanding Black people.

Sheryl Sandberg had taken a strong position in defining what women's leadership in the corporate world should look like, in Big Tech and beyond. She knew something about gender equity and what white women had to do to succeed—and to be heard. She knew that men were constantly demonstrating how little they understood about the paths women take. Yet for her to think that sending that text was the best next step in our process demonstrated clearly that she could not see how the lessons about gender could apply to race.

Sheryl Sandberg couldn't see our shared fate, or what was shared in our experience. She was trying to manage a set of issues and people without putting in place the right support for doing so, recognizing the gaps she would need to bridge. If she had flown to Japan for a high-stakes business meeting, she might have had an entire team helping her figure out how to act and how to make those dealings successful. But when it came to meeting people a few neighborhoods over but still a world away, she did not take much responsibility at all for getting educated and getting ready for the negotiation.

Of course, it clearly wasn't a negotiation. But I realized in that moment that it ran two ways: We could not move our agenda with Facebook because we didn't have the power to do so. They could not move their agenda with us because they didn't even consider they needed to do anything differently in order to be effective with us, even if it would have been easy for them. Sandberg was one example of that, but Zuckerberg himself was far worse. And the situation would quickly transition from ignorance to aggression.

The Meta Playbook

Assessing corporate power can seem complex, but it boils down to a fairly simple two-part question: What are corporate executives willing and able to do in order to make money, and what are they willing and able to do in order to neutralize the barriers to making money?

I have learned a lot from trying to win systemic change in the Silicon Valley tech sector, especially in trying to reduce the massive negative impact of Facebook and Instagram. In addition to tangling with Mark Zuckerberg and other top Facebook executives, I worked with different internal departments, battled the corporation in the public realm, and made the case for change on Capitol Hill. Even so, and even as the ranks of people working to hold them accountable grow every year, we have not yet won the systemic changes that we need to win in order to end Meta's destructive effect on society.

But it is not surprising that we have not yet won major change, given the power they have built to prevent change. The source of Meta's power is threefold:

1. More than three billion people around the world use one or more of Meta's services every day and likely do not want to give them up.
2. In the United States, there is no meaningful government (or even independent) regulation of those services whatsoever.

"Self-regulation" still dominates the sector's ethos—and both the written and unwritten rules.

3. Even though Meta is a publicly traded corporation, Mark Zuckerberg owns the majority of it and has complete, unchallenged, unchecked control over every single decision.

Whenever they are challenged, Meta's leaders have a clear playbook. It both draws from the general corporate playbook we have seen develop over the past years, while also adding new plays that other corporations will draw from in the years to come.

- **They apologize, insincerely.** Mark Zuckerberg loves apologizing and pretending he cares. He once said in the company's early days that it's better "to, like, make things happen and then, like, apologize later."[15] He still seems to think that way. He's made empty apologies in front of Congress, even in the face of parents whose kids, digitally poisoned by Facebook/Instagram's content and harassment, experienced great harm, some even ending their lives. He apologized to civil rights leaders, including me, for the challenges Black people have faced on his platforms. He has made no-commitment apologies in posts online and other channels. He apologizes and apologizes, and then continues doing exactly what he was doing.
- **They lie.** Mark Zuckerberg and his executives have consistently denied any knowledge of the harms their products and platforms cause—let alone having intentionally designed them for profit while knowing what the effects on people would be. Yet the whistleblower Frances Haugen and others have demonstrated with clear evidence that they were fully informed and aware at every step—that they knew everything they denied knowing. More evidence exposing what they knew seems to come out regularly.
- **They racist lie.** In 2017, Mark Zuckerberg and his team hired a PR firm called Definers, one of many in the ecosystem of Re-

publican and MAGA media shops, to attack their critics. Definers targeted Color Of Change, circulating false claims about our funding as an organization that played on deeply troubling historical tropes. They promoted the idea that we were merely Black puppets whose strings were being pulled by a Jewish donor in service of his interests and not our own. They aimed to bury Facebook's impact on Black communities by making it seem like our claims should be treated with suspicion. It was quite clear that their goal was undermining our credibility as a Black organization, as well as our credibility in Congress and in government, which also made us a target for the racist right wing.

- **They buy people off.** Mark Zuckerberg has used his charitable foundation, the Chan Zuckerberg Initiative (CZI), to pressure critics into silence. CZI had always declined to fund Color Of Change, saying we were too radical. But as soon as our work challenging Facebook started gaining momentum, CZI suddenly offered us $1.5 million, with my takeaway being that we would need to shut up if we wanted the money. (We didn't take it. Others did.) Facebook also buys off potential future critics, not just active critics. In a host of different ways, it buys votes in Congress and buys relationships with government officials, as well as gullible journalists and media personalities, in the way that most corporations do.
- **They discriminate.** Mark Zuckerberg and his team routinely shut down people who dared to speak up about adverse racial impact, driving out people like the manager Mark Luckie, who in a 2018 memo to all Facebook employees bluntly stated, "Facebook has a black people problem."[16] At a Black History month event Facebook organized, I saw a few Black Facebook employees enter the room and take their seats. Earlier, I had asked them if there would be other Black people at the company coming to the event. They looked at me and said that what I saw in front of me was basically all of them. A Black Facebook employee once told me that there were more Black Lives

Matter signs on the Facebook campus than actual Black people.

- **They play games.** It may be hard to believe, but I was told by someone internally that Facebook executives and managers take management classes in which they explicitly learn how to run out the clock in meetings to prevent the airing of information and the discussion of topics they want to avoid or suppress. Up close, I saw how well they do this, trained or not.
- **They flood the zone.** Unsurprisingly, Meta can use its vast wealth to flood the media environment with everything from paid advertisements and marketing (e.g., $6.1 billion in the first half of 2021) to stories they plant through favorable journalists. In 2021, for example, it initiated a program called Project Amplify, which forced users to see positive news about the corporation in their personal feeds, clearly intending to drown out anything to the contrary.
- **They keep going.** Seemingly feeling invincible and unaccountable to any restraining forces at all, Mark Zuckerberg has the money to research and develop new platforms, products, and services that create injustice for profit, intentionally or not. He does this having never addressed the effects that his first-generation platforms have had on our elections, our mental health, our ability to call out and fight racism, our privacy, and our ability to access reliable information.

Meta can largely use these tactics however and whenever it wants, as individual challenges and threats to its control arise. That is the direct result of the threefold source of their power: a customer base wedded to its platforms, lack of any meaningful government regulation, and the complete decision-making control held by Zuckerberg. All three factors, taken together, make systemic corporate accountability very, very difficult to win. Yet we can take steps in moving toward the goal of curbing Meta's power. The first such step is to make an honest assessment of where we stand and where we need to go.

Airbnb: A Case of Negotiation

We might not think of the short-term rental company Airbnb as being part of the tech sector, but in functioning as an online marketplace, that's exactly what it is. It was considered an anchor of the so-called "sharing economy," a distinctly tech-rooted set of corporations that emerged in the 2000s. In at least one respect, Airbnb serves as an important example of how taking on profiteers can work. When Color Of Change confronted Airbnb in the mid-2010s about the rampant racial discrimination taking place on its platform—directly enabled and encouraged by the way Airbnb had chosen to run its business—we were eventually able to establish a negotiation.

Our own co-founder, James Rucker, had faced direct discrimination by Airbnb hosts. In trying to book a stay, he experienced one cancellation after the other, while then discovering that the hosts that canceled his booking would immediately re-list their places as being available for others. He then noticed that the platform had no protections against racial discrimination based on his profile picture—at least no policies that actually worked—and offered no recourse for those who experienced it. This was a very real thing for many Black people who far too often found that Airbnb hosts refused to rent to them. As Airbnb was promoting the benefits of its services to Black homeowners, it was ignoring the widespread discrimination its users committed against both Black renters and owners.

The corporation's grand promise of bringing us into the future was covering up the reality of how far it was actually dragging us into the past. That was typical of so many Silicon Valley corporations—and still is. Airbnb executives might want us to believe that the "old guard" hotel industry is weighed down by pesky unions and is generally in desperate need of the magic of "disruption" that only a Silicon Valley firm can bring. But that's their own mythology and we cannot buy into it.

The hotel industry does not presently discriminate against formerly incarcerated people—many of whom have felony conviction records due to being targeted unfairly by police, prosecutors, and judges—by preventing them from booking rooms. James Rucker, a Black man simply looking to book a room for a trip, is not denied rooms in a hotel because he's Black. And if he is, there are rules in place to make sure he has recourse—rules that enforce the idea that the hotels were wrong to do what they were doing. It is Airbnb that is stuck in the past, refusing any disruption.

It took time for Color Of Change to get the attention of Airbnb, especially the attention of CEO Brian Chesky. It took more time, working with allies on the inside while creating pressure on the outside, to get Airbnb to move beyond the typical corporate responses to activism, which often follows this sequence:

- **Hope that the problem goes away.** The first response of most large corporations is to ignore the people talking about the problem and hope they lose momentum, stamina, and support—or can be paid off.
- **Deny the problem causes harm.** The second response is defensive, sometimes with reasoning as antiquated and logic-defying as arguing that "separate but equal" segregation in the 1950s was perfectly fine for everybody.
- **Sell people on the upside.** The third response is to argue that things like the "sharing economy," "market disruption," and "consumer empowerment" all ultimately work in the favor of everyone, even if it's not always obvious.

Chesky probably did not like the idea of Airbnb enabling so much anti-Black racial discrimination in the hospitality and rental market, such that the escalating conversation growing around the hashtag #AirbnbWhileBlack would permanently stick to its public profile. (We at Color Of Change didn't start that great hashtag, but we certainly amplified it to gain more leverage during our fight.) He probably did not want to fight with racial justice advocates in public, and lose.

As someone with a low public profile, despite being one of the wealthiest people in the world (reaching a net worth of $9.2 billion in 2025), Chesky may also have wanted to avoid becoming popularized as a villain at a time when hostility toward unaccountable, unresponsive, and unscrupulous billionaires was growing. There was always the prospect of an upside, too: Airbnb was profiting from racial injustice, but it might profit even more if it eliminated some degree of racial discrimination.

Because Chesky saw benefits to steering through the controversy in a meaningful way, and felt constrained by some of the disincentives for ignoring the problem or merely throwing false solutions at it, we had some leverage. It was not instant, but we created that leverage over time. As we made clear that it might be in his interest to engage us with some degree of good faith, we were able to establish a negotiation.

The executives and staff we negotiated with inside Airbnb came to see racial justice advocates as partners in working toward somewhat shared goals—and eventually it seemed like Chesky did, too. Like many across the tech sector, Chesky was fully in charge of the organization: His decisions alone determined what happened at Airbnb. But he responded to people on the inside who both understood the business and understood not only how change could happen but also why it should. A willing CEO is often a necessary condition of corporate change, and an important accelerator for it. But it took a long time to get him there.

Airbnb agreed to support a racial justice audit of its business, a thorough assessment led by an outside expert. Laura Murphy, who later conducted the Facebook audit, was the one to do it. The audit, we argued, would help everyone see the problem more clearly and objectively, if the company chose to engage with it in good faith. And to some extent, it did.

We negotiated further, getting Airbnb to launch a set of initiatives that changed some of the deeper rules governing how it operated as a business, reducing racial discrimination, and making Airbnb more equitable. The corporation continued to invest in that initiative, called Project Lighthouse, and continued to take its commitment to reducing harm seriously. While we did not get everything we wanted, we won changes at Airbnb that ran deep.

Chesky was a willing partner—up to a point. He refused to address the way Airbnb profited from effectively reducing the housing stock in certain neighborhoods, especially Black neighborhoods, thereby driving up rents and displacing residents who had lived there all their lives.[17] Only the force of government regulation could change the calculus for Chesky in that regard, and force his hand. So our strategy would need to move toward targeting city councils and other regulators who could pass laws that would constrain the predatory nature of the Airbnb business model. That's what happened, thanks to the leadership and efforts of the larger movement, and Airbnb now faces regulation in certain cities that it cannot ignore.

Chesky would also not concede on the issue of prohibiting people with felony convictions from booking rooms through Airbnb. That will also likely require negotiations with government leaders, which might lead somewhere good, rather than continued dialogue between Airbnb and advocates, which might not. Though Chesky did not seem to get on board with Donald Trump and Elon Musk as his co-founder, Joe Gebbia, did, it was still clear how tenuous progress can be when it's tethered to the personal whims of an all-controlling CEO.

Real Solutions Versus Fake Solutions

Recall that earlier in this chapter I listed two questions to keep in mind when directly engaging with profiteers. The first, addressed in the preceding sections, is about knowing whether you're in a dialogue or negotiation. The second has to do with evaluating what decision-makers offer you when the concessions start coming in: Is the solution real or fake?

Corporations that oversee themselves choose what to look at and what to ignore. When we give them that power, they rarely make the right decisions to look out for the rest of us. Standard-setting, regulation, oversight, and enforcement are ideas that mean nothing if they are not rooted in independence. Only independent experts and outside authorities, accountable to real people impacted by their decisions, can truly say which changes address real needs and which avoid them.

Yet corporations want us to believe that those who abuse people—intentionally or unintentionally—should be in charge of defining what is and isn't abuse, and what will or won't stop it. That the people who cause problems are somehow best suited to solve them, and should be put in charge of doing so. They want us to believe that the foxes should guard the henhouse: that the fossil fuel industry should set environmental standards, the food industry should run health inspections, the pharmaceutical industry should determine what drugs are safe, and the banks should define what constitutes a predatory loan.

They want us to believe that the biggest threat to accountability . . . is accountability. Why is that particular lie—that problem-causers are the best problem-solvers—so profitable for them? Because that lie allows them to tell a whole lot more lies. If they are the problem-solvers, then they get to define what qualifies as a problem and what qualifies as a solution. And that lets them evade ending the real injustices they cause.

Their ultimate goal is to get us to accept fake solutions to real problems. When the social media platforms try to convince the public that "online literacy" (which places the burden of safety on the user) is the solution to online abuses, we know we're in the middle of a fake solution. They want us to believe that instead of it being Meta and Google/YouTube's responsibility to stop programming their content algorithms to aggressively bait boys into consuming (and even getting addicted to) violent and extremist content, for example, parents should somehow train their kids to defend themselves against it. What makes that a fake solution is that the social media algorithms are purposely designed to break through most people's defenses. Kids can't be expected to resist on their own. Nor should anyone. (For more on real versus fake solutions in the tech sector and beyond, see the online Appendix at rashadrobinson.com/book.)

Imagine a drug dealer who tells someone that the fatal drug they're offering won't hurt anyone who just eats well and does yoga. So many industries get away with shifting the responsibility of safety to the consumer at the same time they undermine the ability of people to protect themselves: polluters, online gambling platforms, predatory loan services, food manufacturers, the tobacco industry. Meta, Google, and others are designing tech products and platforms that have been proven to hurt people—and then telling people it's their fault if they get hurt. They want to tell us that the solution is consumers making better choices, instead of corporations eliminating the products that lure us into harmful choices and then making it nearly impossible for people to avoid them. In this way, Big Tech corporations have become experts at regulation evasion.

Our most important challenge is being able to hold the line between real solutions that reduce the ability of corporations to profit from injustice and fake solutions that mostly cover up the status quo and do not meaningfully change anything at all. If we accept their fake solutions as real, and call that a win, we play right into their hands and delay the prospects of any change that actually matters. We lose the negotiation.

To maintain their near-total control over online commerce, online content, and online social connection, Big Tech corporations lie about the contents and effects of their products. Just like Big Tobacco lied about the death and disease its products caused, and about the marketing that multiplied the harm. And just like Big Tobacco, Big Tech lies to the public, to the media, to regulators, to shareholders, and to Congress.

The challenge is to ensure that people who are affected by Big Tech's conscious choices, and people who are not dependent on its profits, get to judge what the real problem is and make sure the government and other influential institutions do something about it. We just need to skip the part where we wait forty years to do it, as we did with Big Tobacco. It's going to be hard, and with Doanld Trump in office at the federal level, it's going to be harder than usual. But it's possible.

The Challenge of Turning Big Tech Around

Winning environmental regulations for cars in California, like high-bar vehicle emissions standards, has historically resulted in benefits to residents of other states. California is such a big, important market that the auto manufacturers have had to work from the highest common denominator rather than the lowest. It's more cost-effective to manufacture only the better version of their cars—required for California's roughly 39.5 million residents, with an estimated 1.7 million new car buyers in 2025—rather than creating two different versions.

Winning regulation in California, rather than trying to win regulation in Congress, is a classic example of mapping the system to find the intervention point at which winning a victory can have a cascading effect far beyond that win—as well as knowing the arena in which the power of environmentalists was greatest and the allies for their cause were strongest. It's about *not* trying to change the direction of the entire ship with one big push, which would never work, but rather looking for the rudder. That's where the least effort is required but the maximum impact is gained.

Of course, the opposition can play the same game. For years, the corporate right wing tried to find the intervention point by which they could unravel California's standard-setting control over the car manufacturing industry. They couldn't figure it out during the first Trump administration. But they spent four years studying how they could do it if they ever came into power again, and they made quick work of it as soon as Trump took over the White House in 2025. (An article in *Politico* spells out exactly how they finally did it.)[18] A very smart strategy that worked well for environmentalists for a long time, with impressive results, was neutralized in a matter of months.

Trying to apply the same strategy to the tech sector is playing out in a similar way. In 2016, the European Union (EU) adopted a law called the General Data Protection Regulation (GDPR), which, starting in 2018, required Big Tech corporations to take specific measures to protect the privacy and personal data of individuals in Europe. In 2022, the EU enacted the Digital Services Act as a complement, to take on the problem of illegal content and ensure greater consumer protection. The hope was that if Big Tech corporations were forced to comply with stricter standards in one market, they would do so in every market—protections would expand from Europe to everywhere else.

Though many tech corporations have been forced to invest significant resources to get in compliance with the EU laws, most people in the United States have not experienced meaningful improvements. That is because it is not too costly for tech corporations that want to continue profiteering in the United States to segment their markets—establishing different rules for different users in different countries. We have not made the cost of the status quo high enough to force them to change: Injustice is still profitable for them in the United States. Moreover, the international race for dominance in emerging technologies like AI has led to the GDPR being effectively scaled back in Europe itself—if not by the written rules of policy, by the unwritten rules of enforcement.[19] Tech corporations were trying to undermine it all along the way, and they have largely overpowered the forces trying to defend it and make it as impactful as intended.

The global regulatory landscape for Big Tech is analogous (in reverse) to what happened with Big Tobacco. After decades of work, using the legal system to drive a wedge between tobacco executives and the politicians they had pocketed, American-based movements finally won meaningful regulation—in America, alone. But the new laws didn't cascade around the world. In fact, something of a deal was struck: In exchange for having higher standards in the United States (except in Black and Brown communities, where predatory marketing still continues), Big Tobacco has been allowed to sink to the lowest standards in other countries—and the U.S. government does not use any of its international influence to stop it.

When it comes to Big Tech, we in the United States will need to do this work ourselves. The Europeans have built greater power over Meta and its allies, but they haven't done our work for us. As I've learned firsthand, it will not be easy to break through. It will require a redoubling of our efforts, led by people with the most to gain by transforming Big Tech's role in our lives and marked by the ability to create incentives for politicians, investors, and others that force them to change course in favor of justice.

Big Tech: Innovation in Reverse

After his initial takeover of Twitter, I and others talked with Elon Musk. I had no illusions about his agenda or politics. But it seemed for a moment that we might be able to prevent him from rolling back all of the progress that people at Twitter had made leading up to the 2022 elections. Maybe we could preserve that. (We were worried about rampant misinformation in the election, and we did, in the end, preserve some protections, though they were later eliminated by Musk.)

But Musk kept harping on the value of a digital public square in which anyone could say anything. Without irony. Without understanding that the public squares were where Black people were bought, sold, violated, and torn from their families. He has surely delivered on his vision of a public square in which small, violent mobs freely wreak havoc on everyone else in the community. He turned Twitter, which he renamed X, into a troll-ridden cesspool of toxicity, harassment, and disinformation that riles people up to attack or discriminate against people who are not like themselves. The upgrade Elon Musk contributed: profiting financially and personally (in terms of his own "renegade" brand) from letting those trolls run the show, and from seeming to deliver more supporters and more channels of propaganda for Donald Trump.

Musk's self-styled public square is not owned, managed, or guided by the public at all—only by him, a single man. And it's hardly public in the sense of who has access to it: It seems clear that Musk routinely manipulates X to turn up the volume on his own content, as well as the perspectives he supports, and to nearly mute everyone else.[20] The platform is an authoritarian dictatorship, not a public square or democracy of any kind.

Tech platforms have become some of the most powerful forms of media we experience in our lives. They are part of the infrastructure of our lives, too: opening up pathways for interacting with people and also opening up pathways for corporations and governments to track and manipulate those interactions. They shape what we believe, how we behave, and how we think about ourselves and others.

And as with all forms of media that came before them and stand beside them, one corporate executive after the other—and one policy decision after the other—has turned these technologies into major accelerators of racial injustice and other injustices. In their quest for monopolistic dominance and limitless profit, Big Tech executives have not raised but rather lowered the standards for what's acceptable in terms of the harmful role of media in our lives.

It's innovation—for injustice.

As they drag us back into a robber-baron past in which big business dominated everything, under the guise of taking us into the future, the effects don't pay out evenly. The past is exactly where anyone who was once on the short end of equality—due to gender, geography, race, class, or anything else—cannot afford to go.

As you read this, though, you might wonder, *Why is he harping on race when he's talking about Big Tech? I don't see the problem?* Well, that's the first problem: that some of what Big Tech does is still not popularly understood as a problem at all. Remember from chapter 4 that the foundation of winning any real solution is controlling the perception of the problem. That is why it is essential to create the infrastructure needed to tell a different story that motivates both everyday people and decision-makers to challenge the people who create big problems.

Before I go on to discuss how Big Tech hurts Black people, let me say that the effects of injustice are equally devastating for girls and women, LGBT people, anyone vocal about opposing Trump, anyone with a small business that competes with Big Tech, immigrants without legal status, and employees of the vast network of businesses controlled or influenced by tech corporations who are facing unfair practices targeting them. (For a brief description of each group listed here, see the online Appendix at rashadrobinson.com/book.)

The following are a few ways that Big Tech accelerates racial injustice:

- Big Tech suppresses Black activism and legitimate, truthful political speech on the one hand, while amplifying or encouraging anti-Black violence on the other.[21]
- Big Tech makes old racism new again, providing new and often hidden tools for exacerbating voter suppression, as well as job, housing, healthcare, and other forms of discrimination that are outlawed in the offline world but are made possible online.
- Big Tech monopolies undermine and shut out minority-owned businesses, and in general suppress competition that would offer better alternative technologies.
- Big Tech's internal policies exploit and discriminate against Black workers, from tech workers in an office (e.g., Meta) to warehouse workers in the field (e.g., Amazon).[22]
- Big Tech platforms' racially biased algorithms have taken over the norms that shape our everyday lives, from algorithms in software now used across the justice system that unfairly deny bail to Black people who should get it, to unfairly devaluing Black assets and Black job-seekers, to ruining the self-image and development of Black girls. (See the work of Safiya Noble for a deep dive on these issues.) [23]

It would be easy to say that these outcomes—resulting from the decisions executives make about their social media platforms—are simply a matter of bias, and that the technical fix of auditing and correcting for that bias is the best, most effective solution. And a bias audit would, in fact, be helpful, if executives take its results seriously. But looking for mere bias does not force us to look deeper at what the problem really is.

I will not say this is a conspiracy; it's simply a matter of incentives. For example, Musk is incentivized to allow or accelerate the suppression of people he sees as his opponents, while letting his fan base run wild. The problem is not even Musk. It is the lack of any regulatory framework that would set out the most basic rules for how executives run these corporations, which would change their incentives and thereby change how they make decisions.

When we focus on Musk and his personality, instead of the incentives he operates within, we lose sight of the path to real solutions. It's easy to get distracted: Musk as a villain is more appealing and enticing than promoting "incentives" as the villain. (And I know firsthand from meeting with him: He never turns off, so it's hard to turn away.) But if we are not using the former to make progress on the latter, we will not get very far.

Those on the right wing see independent and reasonable standards as major threats, of course. The idea of standards enrages them, as much as the reality of injustice enrages us. They believe that standards aiming to eliminate unfair and harmful bias would silence their voices on social media, when such standards would simply curtail lies and incitements to violence—the same kind of standards that we have for speech in the offline world (though those standards are also under attack). People on the right wing profit so much from lying—in terms of the money that comes with having a large number of followers, and in terms of political status and power—that they see standards of truth as an existential threat.

Right-wing activist leaders don't want the rules for Big Tech to change because their unfair advantages in content promotion, their recruitment strategies, and their disinformation campaigns would fall apart. And of course, many of the right-wing billionaires who finance right-wing movements, from Peter Thiel to David Sacks, made their money from Big Tech and certainly don't want the rules that enable profiteering to change in ways that would change their net worth.[24] Both right-wing activists and their financiers are aligned with the Big Tech business model. Even as they falsely cry "unfair," they know the system is set up to benefit them. They try to convince us that standards are suppression, whereas we know what suppression really looks like: It looks like them.

Of course, the real problem underneath all of this corporate behavior is that racism, like other injustices, remains profitable. And there is nothing new or innovative about that fact. Racism has never been corrected, at any point in U.S. history, through self-regulation—that is, without strong intervention from the federal government, or state governments, to create new incentives for businesses and new standards and procedures for everyone.

Current incentives enable top executives to exploit racial profiteering as much as they can, while trying to distract us with talk of much lesser, more technical problems that they will dutifully solve—on their own timeline and by their own standards, of course. Those same incentives permeate the corporate hierarchy as well. Countless lower-level executives, managers, vendors, and others make choices every day that play by the rules set by those incentives.

Where We Go From Here

Tech corporations keep the past alive with the same business model we have seen for generations, rather than truly forging something new and worthy of the word *innovation*. But in order to stop them, we must first be clear about what the real problem is, and make sure we are demanding solutions that lead to real results, instead of getting distracted by fake solutions that lead to very little change—or none at all.

That requires regrouping. That is why I'm sharing what I have learned about challenging their power: what has worked and what hasn't.

Refusing to play along is a start—from not signing an NDA, to not being bought off by donations, to not repeating the talking points of the industry. Bringing together people passionate about changing the industry—because they're being hurt by it, because they work in it and can't stand what they see, because they see how it corrupts our political system and cannot be silent—is the next step. **It's about building a constituency in the real world, not just a constituency of policy ex-**

perts and advocates—a community of people that will reward or punish elected officials for how they engage on these issues. And doing that is a springboard to gaining the kind of leverage that can eventually lead to building enough allies in Congress and among other decision-makers so that regulation becomes possible.

All of this requires as much innovation as Big Tech itself develops to defend the status quo, and it requires the infrastructure that will give us new chances and new ways to fight.

We have just begun to open up new fronts in the fight. For instance, challenging Big Tech corporations as illegal monopolies is a different approach to government intervention than some of the regulations we tried to advance earlier. It is also a different path to accountability that finds appeal across a much wider range of the political spectrum, and may therefore have a better chance of gaining momentum. Such a legal approach may seem overwhelming. But that doesn't mean it's not winnable.

Many people thought that taking up the fight against mass incarceration and police abuse and corruption was overwhelming—a steep hill to climb, with the most powerful people in both government and the corporate sector rolling boulders down at us to make it nearly impossible to climb. But we were able to see the terrain as a winnable field, build the infrastructure required to make the impossible possible, and discover accelerators that made change happen faster than it seemed like it could. We didn't end mass incarceration or dismantle the militarization of the police—not by a long shot. But we did achieve important successes to help reduce harm in both of those areas and make more progress than many people thought we could. Those instructive lessons are what the next chapter is about.

14

Taking On Government: The Role of Prosecutors

CHALLENGE: Years of incremental progress often signal the need for a major strategic shift. You do not necessarily need to abandon what you're doing, but you need to add in something new. Despite an increased awareness about the mass injustice of mass incarceration, we weren't winning meaningful systemic change. Finding a role change that could lead to bigger rule changes was going to take us further, but it took a lot of work to get it done.

OPPORTUNITY: During the same time that Donald Trump was redefining many roles across government at the federal level, the criminal justice reform movement saw an opportunity to change the role of the local prosecutor. We could turn many prosecutor races into a referendum on the old way of doing things versus a new way of doing things, and use that momentum to free a lot of people unjustly exploited and trapped in the justice system. And there were open ears for hearing the case we made to build the infrastructure to do it.

REMINDER: A *role change* is a change in the public "job description" for a position of authority in government, business, or another system. A *role* is our shared story about what people in those positions are expected to do in their jobs and what happens if they don't. A role can change only if the people capable of enforcing those expectations believe in the new story and are motivated to hold leaders accountable. The three Rs of social change are roles, rules, and results.

Seeing the Path to Prosecutors

By the early 2010s, the fight for criminal justice reform had been stalled for a long while. It felt obvious that we were not going to break through very soon, even though clearly racist police violence (and the protests that followed) captured national attention every few years and kept the issue present in the news, in political debates, and in passionate conversations across our communities.

The legal scholar Michelle Alexander's 2010 book, *The New Jim Crow: Mass Incarceration in the Age of Colorblindness,* became an important narrative tool for expanding the number of people who clearly understood that something was deeply wrong about the system and that it was getting worse, not better. It helped people understand our system of policing and imprisoning people as a structural injustice with specific features (and results) that were being replicated over and over since slavery, even if it looked a bit different in each era. I read it during the time between leaving GLAAD and going to Color Of Change, and I remember being in physical pain as I saw an argument I thought I already knew laid out in such a clear, well-researched, insightful, and convincing way.

Even with the wind at our back—the political infrastructure of Barack Obama being in office and having the tools for changing the rules at his disposal, and the movement infrastructure of many talented, focused advocates and activists rallying people and leading important fights for change—there was little momentum building toward the point where we could change the U.S. system of policing and incarceration in any meaningful way.

Was there a strategy we could believe in? The status quo of the criminal justice system was very well fortified against us; it had withstood almost all of our efforts to change how it worked. Corporate profiteering off mass incarceration—from forced prison labor, to contracts for new construction, to surveillance technology and equipment—was rampant. Those who benefited resolved to prevent anyone from interfering. And no one in power was nervous about disappointing the people harmed by the injustices those profiteers made possible or the affected communities that desperately wanted change.

I remember talking with a few key, trusted allies at the time: grassroots leaders working in communities across the country, people working in philanthropy, academics, media personalities. What could we do that would be different? Was there some kind of lever of change that we were missing? Had we overlooked a way in, one that might spark a cascade of high-impact changes? Were we spending our time on the right fights?

Many great minds were working on these questions at the time. Following the killing of Trayvon Martin in 2012, a recharged movement for criminal justice reform quickly accelerated the development of new leaders everywhere and reenergized organizations that had been working on reform for a long time. People who felt motivated to do something started running for local office, launching their own protests, providing aid and support to victims of police violence and harassment, or just educating themselves. New and old, we all believed we were in a moment that could lead to major change, with millions more people not only believing in change but also ready and willing to work for it.

When we stepped back to think about it, we found an obvious though daunting answer to our questions: local prosecutors. Within a given jurisdiction, they decide almost everything. Often known as district attorneys, local prosecutor offices:

- Decide which violations of the law to prioritize for attention, resources, and prosecution.
- Determine if someone should be charged with a crime and what the exact charges will be.
- Decide whether or not they should get bail and how much it will be.
- Run the grand jury to secure an indictment.
- Set the terms of a plea bargain.
- Decide whether or not to believe accounts of events from police officers, forensics experts, and eyewitnesses.
- Decide whom to trust and use as witnesses and experts in making the case against the defendant.
- Recommend the sentence length to the judge, if someone is convicted.
- Recommend whether the judge should consider any other factors in sentencing.

That's just some of it. Prosecutors have enormous discretion, and that can be dangerous. They can, for example, pursue cases with no merit other than driving up their conviction rate—a perverse incentive rarely correlating with justice. The role they were playing in mass incarceration became clearer every day.

In fact, many of us had taken a renewed interest in prosecutors as the case of George Zimmerman, Trayvon's killer, played out in court. The Florida state's attorney Angela Corey had been appointed by Governor Rick Scott to be the special prosecutor for the case, and it seemed like she made many missteps, intentional or not, that led to Zimmerman's acquittal. It was clear the case should have been handled differently. There was some outrage directed at her, but I remember thinking that we didn't have the power to change how that office did their work. The continuing misdeeds of prosecutor offices in cases like the death of Sandra Bland in 2015 added more weight to the idea that prosecutor accountability was a necessary lever of change.

There were few effective ways to counteract or challenge the bias of prosecutors and their offices, and abundant evidence that many practiced blatant racial discrimination. They were getting away with it. The written rules did not guarantee effective oversight, and almost all the unwritten rules gave them permission to run the criminal justice system on their own terms, without opposition, often in service of the most regressive ideas and outcomes.

That was the real rule: Prosecutors run the show. Those who were elected rarely faced any challenge—even if someone ran against them, they weren't running against the abuse visited upon people, which just got passed on from one prosecutor to the next.

It was political but not partisan: We found few distinctions between how Democrats and Republicans viewed the role of the local prosecutor. Democrats often implemented as many ineffective and racist "tough on crime" policies as Republicans. The politics of a prosecutor's office were the politics of careerism. That is, local prosecutors built their careers on gaining the endorsement of police departments by giving them every pass and, at the same time, making a show of locking up people (especially Black people) to gain the approval of their mostly white supporters.

By the middle of the 2010s, it was clear to many of us that we could not end or at least reduce mass incarceration without challenging prosecutors. They were right in the middle of every moment of the legal process in which racism and injustice are manufactured. More than any other single actor in the system, they were responsible for making the decisions that led to unfair and unjust treatment, driving up mass incarceration.

Yet we had been letting them run that show with no accountability, certainly not in the form of a concerted, coordinated effort across the country to transform them from barriers to vehicles of reform. It was time. Maybe it was one key to unlocking new possibilities.

It could also prove a perfect example of racial justice as a strategy—using the fight against racism to win an even broader set of changes. A new kind of prosecutor might also focus on investigating high-impact crimes affecting hundreds or thousands of constituents that those who came before them ignored: corporate polluters, employers exploiting their workers, and other lawbreakers across the private sector.

Most criminal justice policies that lead to mass incarceration, police violence, and other injustices are the result of decisions made at the state and local levels. The federal government can pass criminal laws only when the Constitution gives them the power to do so; the rest is left to the states. While the federal government currently incarcerates about 203,000 people, states and local municipalities incarcerate close to 1.7 million people.[1] About 66,000 federal criminal cases were filed in 2024, and yet more than 16 million state and local criminal cases were filed that same year.[2] The difference is undeniable.

There are currently about 2,400 prosecutor offices across the country handling the majority of those 16 million cases. The federal government can investigate local officials and police departments. It can distribute—or withhold—hundreds of millions of dollars of funding for states and counties, as leverage to incentivize change. But the system is largely driven by state and local officials, some of whom are elected—like most local prosecutors.

We knew that certain communities had successfully challenged the practices of prosecutors before. But how could we do more than play whack-a-mole with individual prosecutors and individual cases? How could we instead redefine the role of prosecutors nationally—changing their behavior and therefore the rules that governed the system?

I did not think about it this way back then, but I was in the middle of a strategic insight that I now know so well: *Every major rule change requires a major role change.* To get different results, we needed different rules. And to get different rules, we needed to redefine roles.

There was clearly one achievable role change that would have the biggest impact on reducing mass incarceration and other injustices across the system. We discovered through research that this might not be an impossible uphill climb. Many races were wide open for competition, and taking place in jurisdictions where many people supported racial justice. This wasn't like conservatives spending forty years taking over the Supreme Court. We could change the role of prosecutors fairly quickly if we focused on it, so we did.

When we were doing this work back in 2016, more than 70 percent of elected prosecutors ran unopposed. Their election was mostly a formality. It was merely a way for people who thought the same, looked the same, and acted the same to pass power to one another, like handing down a family jewel.

Elections could serve as a mechanism for accountability, but we had never tried to use them in a coordinated way. Prosecutors were operating without any supervision from their boss, and their boss was us—voters. Moreover, 95 percent of them were white, with 79 percent being white men. A mere 1 percent were women of color. That made no sense to us. And we knew it would certainly not make sense to the voters in our communities, if we could highlight what was going on, give them a reason to believe change was possible, and give them a way to join together and do something about it. (As I often emphasize race and gender do not always correlate with perspective and approach. Diversifying the role would not automatically change it. But the stark, systemic lack of diversity was one clear sign that change was needed.)

The opportunity to build a movement that could forge a new kind of prosecutor focused on true justice started as a question: *What is the most effective intervention we can make?* And it soon became the undeniable answer. We knew we could build a culture of belief to bring people together in action, build the infrastructure for making ourselves powerful, engage large numbers of people with a set of stories that motivated them and kept us all focused on a goal, and then ultimately change the definition of the role of local prosecutor—so we could change the rules of the justice system.

Hope in Chicago: Electing Kim Foxx

In Chicago in early 2016, Anita Alvarez was running for reelection. She was the state's attorney for Cook County, which was populated half by Chicago and half by some of its suburbs, totaling 5.2 million people—making it the second largest local prosecutor jurisdiction in the country. A lot of people already believed that Alvarez should find a new job, but she initially had enough political power to withstand the outcry.

I knew how entrenched she was because four years earlier, in 2012, Color Of Change staff and I had tried to deliver a petition to her: sixty thousand signatures demanding that she vacate the convictions of ten men who had been exonerated by DNA evidence. She ignored us, sending out a staff person to politely send us away. Alvarez wasn't afraid of disappointing us. We had no leverage, she recognized, and we did not represent an issue or community she felt accountable to. With no consequence, she also ignored a large parallel group of protesters who'd showed up that same day.

Grassroots neighborhood groups, such as Southsiders Organized for Unity and Liberation, had been mobilizing against Anita Alvarez starting in 2013 in response to her abusive, unwarranted prosecutions of young Black and Brown men for low-level crimes. Along with the Center on Wrongful Convictions of Youth and the Innocence Project, Color Of Change had taken part in successful campaigns in Chicago to free the Dixmoor Five (five Black men falsely convicted as teens for murder and rape) and the Englewood Five (five Black men falsely accused, with four wrongfully convicted, based on coerced confessions).

Eventually, Alvarez's office petitioned the court to vacate a number of those convictions—but only because we pivoted from petitions to radio ads that exposed her much more publicly and may have even created enough heat to stall her ascent to a federal judgeship, a big aspiration for her. But it shouldn't have been that hard to overturn those bogus convictions, let alone prevent them from happening in the first place. The effort it took to win only underscored that we were losing in a much bigger way that we needed to address. Despite her subsequent claims to have tried to hold police officers accountable during her time as a prosecutor, Alvarez did not charge officers involved in at least sixty-eight killings by police during the seven years she was in office. And there was not enough pressure to force her to explain why. That was our problem—all across the country.

Then, on the evening of October 20, 2014, seventeen-year-old Laquan McDonald, the oldest child in a family in Chicago's Black community, was walking away from an encounter with the Chicago police when Officer Jason Van Dyke shot him sixteen times, killing him. As was (and still is) typical in these cases, the police lied about what happened. As was also typical, the local prosecutor accepted their claim that nothing wrong had happened, no matter how ridiculous that claim was. That prosecutor was Anita Alvarez.

Weeks later, a local law professor received a confidential tip from someone inside Chicago law enforcement that the incident had been captured on video by the police dash cam, which made the shooting look like an execution, in no way justifiable. Thirteen months later, in 2015, a court ordered the police department to release the dash cam footage, a video that Chicago's Democratic mayor, Rahm Emanuel, and others had tried to keep hidden through various procedural maneuvers and lies. (As I mentioned earlier, policing was not a partisan issue: There were differences, but far too often Democrats, just like Republicans, sided with powerful police unions at the expense of their own residents.) It seemed like Anita Alvarez had done everything to play along with the mayor, too. The limited infrastructure of local activists couldn't force the city government to release the footage, despite what the written rules mandated.

One part of the community's legal infrastructure, however, was capable of forcing a different branch of government to act: the courts. After an independent journalist filed a lawsuit against the city, the courts finally ordered the video released. The video allowed for an alternative story about what had happened to Laquan to gain momentum: The truthful story people saw with their own eyes could now compete against the story that police and politicians had established as fact (but wasn't). With little surprise but absolute horror, Chicago families and community members learned the reality of what had happened that night: It was not self-defense, not a justifiable killing—Jason Van Dyke had murdered Laquan.

Anita Alvarez then had little choice but to charge Van Dyke with murder. Even the self-serving definition of her role at the time, and the limited rules that regulated her actions, required that. In 2018, Van Dyke was tried and convicted of multiple charges.

Although Alvarez switched her position by charging Van Dyke, it was too little too late. Her political standing took a hit. It made her vulnerable as the 2016 Democratic primary election approached.

Police abuse was going to be a major campaign issue for her, despite her best efforts to distract people from it. Even so, voters in Chicago—egged on by news media and the inaccurate but ever-present narratives about crime—had always expected a tough "law and order" stance from prosecutors, which often excused wrongful police behavior. Alvarez's defeat was by no means a sure thing. Long before she took office, prosecutors had built successful careers on defending violence against Black people, and doing everything to protect racist, corrupt police. The fact of her complicity in denying Laquan McDonald justice did not necessarily destroy her image as an effective prosecutor, or break any of the expectations that defined the role of prosecutor at that time.

The strategy could not only be about Anita Alvarez the person. It had to be about voting out the type of prosecutor that had reigned for so long in that office. We had to show that Alvarez represented the worst of what a prosecutor could be. Our strategy was not only to play on who she was as an individual but also to redefine the role of the prosecutor itself. If we could achieve that, then voters could see that Alvarez was very obviously disqualified: She wouldn't meet the new definition. It could allow us to open up that seat for someone else, and to make sure that position was always filled by a new kind of prosecutor. On the other hand, it would not be a meaningful win in our fight to change the rules if we merely replaced her—different person, same role.

The candidate we backed would have to be someone who represented a new role for prosecutors overall, someone ready to redefine it, someone who would work every day to fulfill that new definition, which included:

- Recognizing and creating mechanisms of accountability, and changing incentives, to thwart the threat police posed to people going about their lives.

- Recognizing where racism was the only explanation for the way some people were treated in the system, and eliminating decisions based on that bias.
- Changing the metrics of success from maximum convictions at any cost to fairness, justice, and safety for everyone.
- Exposing and rectifying—rather than burying and denying—past cases of wrongful conviction, including opening up the records to see where the state's attorney office itself had committed wrongful acts that punished innocent people in the past.
- Charging people in ways that did not coerce them into taking unfair plea bargains, admitting to crimes they did not commit, and accepting excessive charges.
- Ending bail where it was unnecessary and kept people in jail for no good reason, just because they could not afford to get out like wealthier people did.

These and many more practices would define a generation of progressive prosecutors. And in Chicago in 2016, there was one person who fit that definition: Kim Foxx. An experienced prosecutor who had been working on criminal justice reform policy for the county board president, Foxx had grown up in Chicago and knew its rules. She also knew how the system needed to change.

The election would not be an easy one, even with Alvarez destabilized by the scandals and all her past unjust acts. But Chicago communities were ready to take action. People had had enough of battling each injustice after the fact. They wanted to get ahead of injustice, shifting from accountability to prevention. Perhaps a prosecutor set on establishing new rules for how the system worked would create disincentives for bad police behavior: raising the floor for what was acceptable and creating consequences for those whose behavior was below it.

Voter engagement related to elections was not entirely new territory for Color Of Change, but being directly involved in electoral campaigns through Color Of Change's newly minted Voting While Black political action committee was. We focused on events and engagement with Black people who did not regularly vote, testing our hypothesis that a local election rooted in local issues that felt tangible, such as police violence and mass incarceration, would bring them in. If it worked—and it was not the only such experiment we ran in 2016—then it could represent an entirely new front in the fight for major criminal justice reform.

It did work. Through this race and others, the progressive prosecutor movement crawled out of infancy and grew into a force to be reckoned with. Those who ignored the people and values our movement represented would be ignored by voters and tossed out of office. That was a new form of power. We would redefine the role of prosecutors as the main strategy for gaining the power required to change the rules.

Reaching a New Milestone

No primary race for the office of prosecutor in Cook County had probably ever elicited so much energy and had so many people involved in it. The #ByeAnita campaign was infectious. It created a platform for all sorts of community groups and networks to participate in the excitement. The turnout for the 2016 primary election shattered previous records: a 51 percent turnout rate between the primaries for both parties, higher than any primary since 1992. Over 1.1 million voters cast their ballot in the Democratic primary for state's attorney. In the end, the Cook County election results were definitive: Kim Foxx won 58 percent of the vote, exactly double Anita Alvarez's take of 29 percent.

People wanted a role change, and our movement had shifted from presence to power. What rule changes would follow the major role change we had won? How could we transition from winning political power to winning policy power?

Plenty of rules remained stacked against us. For instance, Jason Van Dyke, who murdered Laquan McDonald, was given a light sentence by the presiding judge, Vincent Gaughan, which resulted in Van

Dyke's early release from prison in 2022. That decision was even questioned by other judges. Gaughan was playing by the unwritten rules that treated crimes committed by police differently than crimes committed by others—even in the case of murder. And the written rules granting him that clearly biased sentencing discretion allowed him to make his personal opinion known—to rebel against the new rules of accountability for police. (We've since seen many Trump judges rebel against the law, from within the law, in even greater ways.)

Despite Foxx's win in the 2016 general election, it would not be an easy road to real change. Members of the local Fraternal Order of Police, the union for Chicago police officers, had been openly hostile to Foxx during the campaign and did not hide their racism and misogyny, foreshadowing a harassment campaign targeting Foxx for years to come. Judges who did not believe change was needed would use their power to stop it. The state's attorney office that Kim Foxx inherited was packed with Alvarez loyalists and adherents to the ways of the old definition of prosecutor. As longtime staff members, they were often able to use the rules of the office to obstruct reform, before Foxx could change them.

Yet Foxx did not go into hiding or fall in line, reverting to playing the role of prosecutor that the anti-reformers wanted her to play. She led amazing work—in many cases, real systems-change work. I do not have space here to chronicle her entire time as state's attorney—all the attempts to undermine her, all the successes and frustrations the community experienced, all the ups and downs. Suffice it to say that the resistance to change was no joke. The backlash to the changes she made was at times terrifying.

But at the end of the day, the results from Foxx's time in office are undeniable. She reduced Cook County's incarceration rate by nearly 20 percent and sent thousands of accused individuals to rehabilitation programs instead of throwing them behind bars. She helped clear many people who had been wrongfully convicted. By pushing to vacate over one hundred wrongfully prosecuted cases, she led the nation in exonerations. She recommended pretrial release (rather than out-of-reach bail) for people accused of low-level, nonviolent offenses, in an effort to eliminate the system's bias against people without money while still ensuring public safety. Working with community groups, she made strides to end the school-to-prison pipeline by providing services for students at risk of incarceration. The results of that election led to results that truly mattered for people's lives.

Other races the progressive prosecutor movement won that year and in the several years that followed brought about dramatic prosecutor role changes all over the country: Larry Krasner in Philadelphia, Aramis Ayala in Orlando, Diana Becton in Contra Costa, Stephanie Morales in Portsmouth, Alvin Bragg in Manhattan, Kim Gardner in St. Louis, Rachael Rollins in Boston, and many others across Florida, Texas, Virginia, Vermont, and California. Major representatives of the movement who now have many years of accomplishments behind them, such as Kim Foxx and Larry Krasner, have become public figures and public voices who can carry a larger message about reform, as well as lessons from tangling with the opposition. And they (along with progressive state attorneys general) stood in a uniquely capable and motivated position to find ways to oppose illegal federal actions directed by Trump.

In the past, many young lawyers who cared about justice would never have wanted to step into a prosecutor's office (unless they were there to negotiate on behalf of the defense). They could not have seen the role they wanted to play in the world within the definition of the role of a prosecutor. But progressive prosecutors have changed that.

They have inspired young lawyers to see the prosecutor role as one that can be dedicated to fighting for true justice—a driver rather than a blocker of reform. They have broken ground on building a new set of policies that can transform the criminal justice system and help end the plague of police abuse, among other injustices. They have also helped to expose all those standing in the way of reform—people aiming to quietly profit from keeping mass incarceration and other injustices alive and well—which has been part of weakening their grip over both the written and unwritten rules of the system.

Progressive prosecutors have also inspired the movement to keep going: not only to believe we can win but also to believe in the importance of the role of everyday people in making change. It shows the value of a coordinated inside/outside strategy. Kim Foxx would often tell me that the reform movement created the space for her to do her job, making her work possible. We were part of her infrastructure, and she was part of ours.

In that way, the role of prosecutor wasn't the only role we changed. We also changed the role of community member. People discovered who they could be:

- An agent of change fighting a system that it seemed might never change.
- Someone with the ability to unite with others to change how elections worked.
- Someone with the ability to bring others into the fight.
- An essential player in the game that followed, defending those hard-earned wins.

A community member could be a movement member—not watching society happen around them but actively taking part in changing how it works. Some people are born believing that about themselves (or grow up always being told that's who they can be). Others discover that about themselves in moments like this. Either way, the definition of someone who cared about criminal justice was starting to include someone who wins more fights than they lose.

In a relatively short amount of years, the trend of mass incarceration in the United States turned around. From 2015 to 2024, prosecutors sent 17 percent fewer people to prison (275,000), sent 13 percent fewer people to jail (84,000), and placed 25 percent fewer people on probation and parole (1.2 million). The number of incarcerated children dropped by 60 percent. And since 2000, Black imprisonment rates have dropped by nearly half.[3] Lots of factors led to those results; the movement to elect and support progressive prosecutors in making serious rule changes in major cities was one of them.

In the end, we needed to solve two big challenges to make this role change:

- Advancing media and messaging work in ways that weren't typical for a prosecutor race, so that the public would see the role of prosecutor differently and also see the promise of making major change through this race.
- Organizing people in new ways that demonstrated to prosecutors that they would need to view the role differently themselves, creating a system of rewards and consequences (electoral, reputational, professional) that shifted whom prosecutors were accountable to and what they would be held accountable for achieving.

The media work involved not only typical political ads but also documentaries, storytelling through news media, and representations on TV shows that made people feel the tide was turning (and needed to turn) on prosecutors.

The work of changing incentives for politicians included the typical ways of showing that a constituency of people was ready to vote with intention, but also getting President Obama to put his weight on the scale by talking about prosecutors publicly, showing the force of this movement by being active in between elections and not just during them, and showing prosecutors that they would no longer enjoy uncontested races—the privilege of staying in office would need to be earned.

What Came Next

Both national and local groups in the criminal justice reform movement worked together to popularize the understanding of who prosecutors were, what they did, what role they had been playing, what new role they should play instead, and, most important, how to hold them accountable, even when they are our friends. Kim Foxx and Larry Krasner were both stars in the movement for reform. That didn't mean that we didn't have to push them, or occasionally fight with them, once they were in office. But there was a set of shared values and shared goals that had never been there before.

That constant pushing from communities also helped create the space we needed to open up new possibilities. That space doesn't open up on its own. We have to push it open, to set standards ahead of where even good prosecutors may be today, so that they know they need to do even better tomorrow and can play their role of pushing the system forward, as we push them forward. Changing expectations for roles we rely on for justice is a constant process.

We've had many disappointments. We supported some people who symbolized the role change we wanted but then weren't quite up to fulfilling that role. Some prosecutors were not savvy enough to run their offices well or to successfully navigate the political environment. Some were run into the ground by attacks, including threats to their life. Some lost their way under pressure, and in many ways reverted to playing the old role. For example, Kim Ogg, who would not have won her race to become district attorney for Harris County, Texas, in 2016 without the support of our movement, largely turned her back on the commitments she had made to our communities and our cause over the course of her time in office.

Yet for every setback, we were taking more steps forward.

One story that says a lot about Kim Foxx and her dedication to real change occurred as soon as she took office. I was told that her predecessor, Anita Alvarez, had maintained a not-so-secret list of advocates whom she banned from her office. It was clear to these community members that she did not want to hear from them. In essence, she cut off their mic in terms of being able to have a voice in any negotiation about reform. Naturally, Kim Foxx did not see representatives of the communities she served as a threat, in the way Anita Alvarez had, even if there was disagreement. She believed they belonged at the table. They should be consulted. Their presence represented possibility. They certainly should have as much of a chance to share their information and share their ideas as police and politicians. These were new rules Foxx put in place.

Yet, even a simple rule change such as that was a disruption, and perceived as an existential threat by everyone who had some kind of profit to lose in the process of much-needed change. The backlash overall has been fierce, as I detailed in a piece in *The New York Times* in 2020 that does not even cover half the story.[4] The people fighting reform are well-resourced, and their power to obstruct reform, or even take us backward, is the result of formidable, well-funded infrastructure set in place over many years.

Many of the progressive prosecutors breaking new ground for criminal justice reform, and for transforming the strategic approach of these offices, were highly motivated, highly informed Black women. And so the threats, racial slurs, attacks on credibility, and aggressive disrespect coming from police unions—and even coming from other prosecutors—was intense and unceasing. One of the staff members working in Foxx's office was so harassed by police officers and their allies, including daily phone calls from people spouting the worst racist and misogynist slurs, that she was driven to take leave.

In fact, the behavior of police unions, police officers, and other unhinged people who could not handle change showed us exactly who they are. They showed exactly how much racism still pervades police departments, almost obsessively. They showed exactly what illegal, abusive, awful acts police were willing to commit when they thought no one was watching and they couldn't get caught. They showed us exactly how much they lied whenever they could gain something from it. In some ways, they made the best case for the urgency of reform. And they showed how we needed even more accountability, certainly not less.

The backlash, however, was not just a matter of individual police officers or police union officials trying to undermine accountability and ensure that police could continue profiting from the status quo in terms of financial gain and political protection. Beyond those individuals, many more people had been profiting from unchecked racism in the system: corporations losing money; politicians losing their favorite fear-mongering, fact-free policies; judges having their decisions reviewed in the most embarrassing way; assistant prosecutors losing their friendly relationships with police and their old ways of doing business; prosecutors in other jurisdictions who lost the ability to lead their offices with no questions asked, no scrutiny of their practices, and the ability to use high conviction rate numbers to advance their careers; and statewide and national politicians like Trump losing control of the narratives about crime that served their own fearmongering. Any part of the infrastructure of the system that produced injustice involved people with something to lose. A parallel set of incentives that included making villains out of liberals was increasingly profitable for anyone in the business of right-wing infotainment.

Right-wing governors and legislators have suspended or removed progressive prosecutors from office, tried to reduce the scope and budget for their work, taken cases away from them, and tried every other way they can to make progress impossible—actions that are all sponsored by endless media campaigns promoting absolute lies about who they are, what they've done, and what it led to.

When Larry Krasner took over the prosecutor's office in Philadelphia, he developed a list of police officers who would no longer be invited to testify in court due to their long histories of lying on the stand. He rejected the punitive priorities of Pennsylvania's association of district attorneys—and was shunned by them. The Pennsylvania legislature wasted more than $3 million trying to impeach and remove him, through bogus procedures and proceedings that were called out as such by a judge, before being taken up by the Pennsylvania Supreme Court.

As I discussed in chapter 9, the most effective tactics preyed on people's deeper feelings and insecurities, stories that triggered people to question whether what they were perceived to be losing from reform was worth what they were gaining (which was always underplayed or denied). Stories supporting reform are based not only on deep ideas about justice but also on a lot of new information that asks people to rethink their assumptions about our approaches to crime and punishment. Stories attacking reform are steeped in false but persuasive and intuitive narratives about race, human behavior, and other ideas that run very deep. It was easy for the old narratives to be effective and often a struggle for the new narratives to gain ground.

Yet most progressive prosecutors have won reelection despite these attacks, or perhaps because of how transparently corrupt these attacks have been. Every reelection makes our movement stronger. Holding on to power makes it possible for more and more people to feel invested in enforcing and reinforcing new sets of rules.

In some cases we weren't prepared for the backlash, but in other cases we were. We kept investing in winning people's commitment at the level required to win political power and drive change forward. We put an infrastructure in place to fight against the backlash. Even if we have not defended every issue very well in all cases, such as bail reform, we have defended the role change represented by progressive prosecutors. That is a legacy, though we must remain vigilant, active, and committed to expanding our reach and our wins every single year if we want that legacy to continue.

Part of how we know we are winning is that the opposition to progressive prosecutors is using the language of reform, rather than the language of reversion to a previous time. In Arlington, Virginia, for instance, the 2023 challenger to progressive prosecutor Parisa Dehghani-Tafti ran on a platform of "real reform" in an effort to co-opt our successful narratives and confuse voters. He lost. Voters didn't fall for it. They knew who the real reformer was. But the fact that our opposition felt the need to attach himself to a narrative of reform was a huge win. It used to be that progressives would feel the need to attach themselves to a "tough on crime" narrative in order to win. Now the reverse was true. A major turnaround. A new rule in itself.

We measure success best, however, in people's lives. What has changed for the better, and is it merely incremental and case by case, or is it systemic and transformative? The results I mentioned above are the real signs of success. And yet there is a long way to go.

The larger movement organizing to end mass incarceration and police violence provided the base of people, energy, infrastructure, and intelligence needed to launch the progressive prosecutor movement. In turn, the progressive prosecutor movement has emboldened, expanded, and empowered the larger movement for criminal justice reform. In New York City in 2024, as just one example, advocates won the elimination of solitary confinement, a proven practice of torture that has passed as reasonable for far too long, supported by propaganda everywhere that hides its reality.[5] The city council passed the law, and a subsequent mayoral veto by Eric Adams was overturned by the highest court in New York State. Ending solitary confinement has been a movement goal for decades, and now it is a reality in the country's largest city. The work on prosecutors did not play a direct role in that incredible win, but it has helped energize people, rallying people around the belief that we are not condemned to live in a world in which everyone in power is stacked against everyone who wants and needs reform. Communities can actually put reformers in office who know how pervasive and destructive the injustices are, and make government officials actually do their job to represent us and deliver the change we need.

The case of building the progressive prosecutor movement is one example of what it takes to become unignorable and make injustice unprofitable, holding decision-makers accountable whenever they enable profiteering. It focused on being able to bring about a profound *role* change capable of leading to profound *rule* changes, and thereby long-deserved changes in people's lives. It has brought some relief from the daily injustices that destroyed communities, families, and people for more than a century. It has not been perfect. We have not defended everything we won, and we have not yet won nearly enough. But we had been hitting the wall of the status quo for a long time, and this strategy certainly helped us break through it, even if we have not yet torn the entire wall down.

The Infrastructure of Winning

In taking on the role of prosecutors, infrastructure was critical. Color Of Change helped organize what became the first of a series of annual national gatherings focused on prosecutors, involving local groups and leaders across the country and also national leaders from Black

Lives Matter, labor unions, legal advocacy groups, the legacy criminal justice reform groups, and more. Those leaders included people who had already been working on prosecutor races, like Whitney Tymas, who identified key races and cultivated support for strong candidates. Other groups, like the Women Donors Network, had already been researching the incredible lack of diversity and participation in elections for different local officials, which helped us all see this opportunity.

Journalists who wrote about prosecutors included Josie Duffy Rice, and funders determined to support leaders in bringing this new strategy to life included the Open Society Foundations (created by George Soros) and Chloe Cockburn, who then worked at Open Philanthropy. Donor circles included the Solidaire Network and the California Donor Table, and political groups included the Working Families Party. Legal advocacy groups included the ACLU. All these contributions were necessary. Eventually, prosecutors themselves would join us, both seeking and offering support.

In the story about progressive prosecutors, can you see where our success was only as good as our infrastructure? Can you see where we had to build a new level of infrastructure in order to break through to a new level of results?

Infrastructure for big elections was everywhere: data systems, organizing tools, leadership development, money for media. But there had never been infrastructure built in this way that would allow true outsiders to step into such a powerful role in politics, including by challenging other Democratic officeholders. There had also never been infrastructure that enabled communities to win local elections—over and over, in a coordinated way across the country—based solely on the issue of criminal justice reform. In fact, there had never been infrastructure built to enable people who cared about reform to be consistently competitive in prosecutor elections at all.

We also needed new types of organizations in the criminal justice reform ecosystem that could accept political donations, which tax-exempt nonprofits are not allowed to accept. We needed data infrastructure to help us understand which races to get involved in and how best to do so. (Of course, plenty of data and research methods related to elections already existed but they had never been applied to prosecutor races.) We needed to build new ways for community members to rally together and reach one another, which had never been done before at this scale for these races. We also needed a new way to demonstrate the stakes of these races: People had to feel that the movement went beyond just a single race. Seeing the bigger picture was highly motivating and bolstered belief.

At the simplest level, our movement needed to build and provide the infrastructure that could achieve three goals, from which so much more would follow:

- **The infrastructure of coordination.** We needed to connect everyone working on these races across the country, bring us all together regularly so that we could share learnings and strategies, and bring us together with the prosecutors themselves.
- **The infrastructure of recruitment.** We needed to identify and support candidates capable of competing against the old-guard prosecutors, which included defending them against relentless attacks by right-wing media and others.
- **The infrastructure of follow-through.** We needed to support reform-minded prosecutors once they took office with public backing, technical assistance from experts, recruitment, communications, and other capacities that helped them move from vision to execution.

We needed to build much of the infrastructure from scratch, or adopt and adapt it from other realms of political and community engagement. Of course, many cities already had a strong network of grassroots community organizations that had been fighting against police abuse and fighting for criminal justice reform for decades. Strong leadership was everywhere.

Those groups needed shared infrastructure in the form of common resources, which they could use to unite around prosecutor races and become more than the sum of their parts: common resources for engaging the news media, for educating members and communities, and for networking with others across the country. Ultimately, all of this taken together—along with several other key elements, such as a network of committed funders—constituted the infrastructure of a new kind of political power, especially Black political power.

I can say proudly that one of our unique inventions was what the staff at Color Of Change named the text-a-thon. It was like a phone-banking event for a new era: gathering people together to send texts to voters, telling them what was going on, seeing if they had any questions, and encouraging them to register, vote, and join the movement.

These events utilized innovative telecom technology, but even more important was the cultural technology. Staff leaders at Color Of Change invented and organized text-a-thons around a big, motivating theme, one that turned out to be both attractive and effective: Black Joy. The text-a-thons were parties that allowed Black people to participate in politics in a Black environment, on their own terms, in a way that felt comfortable, authentic, and exciting for them. That was unusual for politics, which, outside of Black churches, most often required Black people to join spaces that were created by and for white liberals. During our parties, people would share space together while they worked through lists of friends and neighbors, texting them about a prosecutor election and what we could win together if we turned out to vote.

Most people at the time had never received this kind of text before. Now, ten years later, we usually dread those texts. We get too many of them from bots programmed to sound personal or authentic while actually making us feel harassed. But back when the texts came from a real person, they were a fresh idea and a good way to make people feel connected.

Our text-a-thons showed people that they counted, and they could get very specific benefits from participating in a local election—and winning. Building the infrastructure to pull off these parties helped build community and a culture of belief, creating personal and social rewards for people who were stepping into uncertain territory by being involved in an election in this way. It felt personally powerful and communally powerful at the same time.

We started in a place that was not that different from where we were in New Orleans during Hurricane Katrina: No prosecutors were nervous about disappointing Black people, and very, very few in the local, state, or federal political establishment were nervous about disappointing Black people when it came to addressing or ignoring the ongoing travesty of the criminal justice system. Prosecutors barely ever received any public criticism or attention for their role in creating so much injustice for so many people. They were so used to Black people being forced to accept injustices—such as being surveilled, persecuted, prosecuted, and convicted of crimes that white people do not even get arrested for, and being sentenced to much longer and harder sentences for the same crimes others get much lighter sentences for committing. These are life-and-death issues. But they received a big shoulder shrug from people in politics who saw both our issues and us as "lesser than."

How could Black communities, whose lack of power was exactly what the status quo thrived on, create enough political power to change the rules of that same system? How could we get to a point where local communities—voters of every race and background—were able to draw a red line for how profitable racism could be? How could multiple communities across a city or county band together and develop the power required to create a litmus test for prosecutor races—the power to define who is and isn't a legitimate candidate?

Infrastructure made power possible. Not inevitable, but possible. Role changes made rule changes possible. We are not there yet, but we are a lot closer. We cannot stop now, even if so much that's happening at the federal level is working against us.

15

Taking On Hollywood Profiteering

CHALLENGE: Cycles of outrage can lead to one-off changes, while deeper fights can lead to lasting changes in the rules. It is often necessary to respond to specific instances of injustice in order to build a base of people ready and willing to fight for the larger cause, but the challenge is knowing when to move beyond small concessions and carry people into fights meant to bring about systemic change.

OPPORTUNITY: Corporations may seem all-powerful, but many are deeply dependent on consumers whose attitudes and choices keep them in business. It is possible to force corporations to listen to people, especially when we want them to alter but not entirely rework their business model. But making corporations listen requires constantly growing our collective level of demand for change.

Changing Reality on TV

My niece Camden came into the world early in 2010. During one memorable visit to my brother and sister-in-law's home, I offered up Uncle Rashad's temporary babysitting services. This is a role I relished. And it was one of my least stressful roles in life at the time. (Or so I thought.) Back then, Camden was only a few months old and didn't do much beyond sleeping. While she dozed peacefully, I could keep up with work emails, which never felt so soothing to deal with as when Camden was softly breathing beside me. Maybe, if I wasn't too loud about it, I could even check out some daytime TV. That was something of a vacation-style pleasure that I was rarely ever able to indulge in.

Flipping through channels, though, my stress ratcheted up. My work brain turned back on. I saw talk shows with Black folks at each other's throats, literally. The crowds were delighted. In the back of my mind, I also knew that people in the industry were smiling all the way to the bank.

The Jerry Springer Show wasn't the only one. In some form, it was everywhere. Producers presented the Black characters in news shows, talk shows, reality shows, and even game shows as cartoonish and extreme, undeserving of empathy. I saw damning news reports about the Black community, full of blame, with none of the proper context or perspective that was needed, which other people in other stories were getting. I saw the complete mix-up between causes and effects. I was watching twenty-first-century minstrelsy.

Very few products on the market in 1830s and '40s—when popular minstrel shows (featuring white actors in blackface makeup) spread racist stereotypes across the United States—were still widely sold in 2010. Even fewer were popular with consumers or important profit drivers for the corporations that manufactured them. But racism was one of those products. Black stereotypes remained highly profitable.

I was far from naïve about how poisonous television could be, or who profited from selling that poison. I led the programs and advocacy work at GLAAD, charged with helping to change the rules that permitted homophobia to run wild on television and in other media. But in that moment, looking back and forth between the TV screen in front of me and my sleeping niece beside me (and all the struggles of the past behind us), I was provoked in a different way.

I went back and forth in my mind, too, between imagining how this kind of media would shape her sense of the world and imagining how this kind of media would shape the world's sense of her. Very little of what I was seeing on TV made me feel hopeful about either. On the latter point, a study from a few years later revealed how relevant my concerns were back in 2010. It showed that, on average, the people in white Americans' personal social circles were 91 percent white. Perhaps even more important, it noted that "75% of white Americans report that the network of people with whom they discuss important matters is entirely white."[1]

Where were white people learning about Black people, if most of them never talked deeply with Black people? Media. All forms of it: entertainment, news, music, memes. And, it's fair to assume, they were probably not learning anything good or real, given how much the most popular forms of media promoted stereotypes and distortions about our lives.

GLAAD's work to change media in ways that changed society, in concert with many others, had been very effective in both big and small ways. I had been at GLAAD for only a few months in 2005 when Joan Garry, then the executive director, gave me a white paper about changing media representations that had been written a decade earlier. My biggest takeaway was understanding that there were rules for changing the rules. It outlined the methods for what it referred to as cultural advocacy, separate from legal and political advocacy. That paper informed not only my sense of how to do this work but also the work we actually needed to do. (For a quick overview of the paper, see the online Appendix at rashadrobinson.com/book.)

By the early 2010s, GLAAD had created a ratings system that proved to be a powerful leverage point for forcing news and entertainment media corporations to continue improving the rules governing how they represented LGBT people onscreen—with a lot more work to be done about representing trans people. Over time, most media corporations determined they did not want to be on the wrong side of the litmus test we had established for determining whether they were doing right or doing wrong by LGBT people. That was the stick: negative incentives to stop doing bad things. And as the years went on, we raised the standards so that they had to keep improving to keep their same rating.

But there was also the carrot: the GLAAD Media Awards. That was a positive incentive to encourage doing good things, rewarding networks, studios, and individual creators and performers with public acclaim for work they did to model more accurate and authentic representations of our identities, our lives, and our experiences in society. Increasingly, more people inside these media corporations wanted their companies to be on the right side of history. As their personnel diversified, there were more people employed at these corporations who had a personal stake in the impact of the work they did every day. They saw how LGBT representations—accurate and inaccurate—affected their own lives.

We were steadily making it unprofitable for those working across the media landscape to demean us as people, blame us for the world's problems, and stoke hostility against us through their programming—all for profit. By changing the rules for media representations, we had helped accelerate protections in schools and at workplaces across the country. Other signs pointed to increasing acceptance across society, as well. We had helped make same-sex marriage much more acceptable and celebrated among millions of people whose support was needed to make it legal and protected in the real world.

Treating LGBT people fairly in news and entertainment media became more profitable for most Hollywood corporations to do, across most of their content, than treating us poorly. But it was a long, hard fight. And it is not over. Thanks to Silicon Valley profiteers, of course, more media platforms than ever are incentivizing people to create and share the most unfair and hostile content about us.

We had successes and failures and, as we see today, surges of backlash. One of the most popular reality TV shows on air today features a legendary drag queen showing up-and-comers how to be drag queens. But many forget that *RuPaul's Drag Race* started in 2009 on Logo, a niche network for queer audiences, before moving to VH1, MTV, and, through spin-offs, Paramount+ and mainstream networks in at least sixteen countries. Not only did that show build an audience of passive viewers and admirers, but it helped build a constituency of defenders who have rallied to fight back against right-wing attempts to eliminate drag queens from public view. Media power (alongside activism, organizing and political advocacy) has been critically important in the fight over political power.

But the changes we won—and the changes we failed to win—did not affect all people evenly. Take away the hostility directed at a middle- or upper-class white man because he is gay, and you then have a middle- or upper-class white man who is pretty good to go. Take away the hostility directed at a Black man because he is gay, and you still have a Black man dealing with all the other hostilities directed at him. Moreover, it may generally be harder to take away the anti-gay hostility directed at that Black man, compared to the acceptance and fairness a gay white man might receive. Take away the hostility directed at a lesbian, and you do not necessarily take away any hostility directed at a trans or nonbinary person. In an unequal society, even progress is not equal.

Many authentic representations of lesbian, gay, and bisexual people in entertainment media today are a mark of how far we've come: They show us what many LGB lives are like today, reflecting the reality of many of our experiences. The many fewer authentic representations of trans people in entertainment media, however, are generally a mark of how far we have to go: They show us what trans lives should be like, even when society is still preventing trans people from living those lives—it's aspirational.

Even changes in representations that white gay and lesbian people won did not chart a linear path of progress. The character of Will on *Will & Grace* was a milestone for representation. But Will, an attractive gay lawyer living in New York City, somehow didn't have a serious partner, let alone one featured on the show, until season six. We never even saw him have a romantic kiss until season seven. (NBC would applaud themselves for having a gay character, but it was still a fight with them to make that character a real gay man.) The coming-out episode of Ellen's eponymous sitcom on ABC was a milestone (and a ratings hit), but the show was canceled a year later.

The combination of indulging in daytime TV and babysitting my niece brought all of these thoughts to the fore of my mind that day. It was a turning point, helping me see how I should write the next chapter of my work: bringing my skills and experience from GLAAD to Color Of Change. We needed a force that could change the rules of media so that racism was no longer profitable for corporate media—ultimately, so that the influence and impact of corporate media would not be as harmful for us. We needed both carrot and stick.

The Challenge of Making Wins Real

For the first several years after I launched Color Of Change's engagement with Hollywood, we faced a constant conflict. What is a temporary or mild concession that is granted to put out a reputational fire, and what is a real, systemic change that will reduce injustice in the world? When have we made racism unprofitable for a moment, and when have we made it unprofitable permanently? When have we changed the rules they play by, and when are we just being played?

This conflict wasn't unique to taking on profiteering in Hollywood. Corporations that had announced they would no longer support ALEC, after all our work to show them the harm ALEC did in the world, joined back up again later on. Similarly, many corporations announced they would no longer donate to politicians who supported the violent attacks on Congress on January 6, 2021, or denied the results of the 2020 election. They stopped, until they started again—in many cases, just several months after they made their announcements. It's not easy to change the behavior of profiteers and establish permanent new rules.

That's because incentives are not static. One of the biggest traps

of magical thinking is assuming that the incentives we can change are the only incentives defining the environment that a corporation, politician, or other target of influence is operating in. We create financial losses for a corporation for certain behavior, and it stops that behavior. But then our opposition threatens greater losses—or creates even greater gains for resuming that behavior. Consumers who care about justice stop shopping at a chain store that's doing bad things, but then even more consumers who believe in white power or some other right-wing idea stop shopping at a chain that's doing good things.

In 2025, the retail giant Target was hit by a boycott coming from the left, led by Black communities, for caving to Trump and rolling back their racial justice and DEI policies. But a few years before, Target was hit financially and reputationally by a backlash from people on the right, led by media personalities, for displaying gay pride merchandise. Both forces wanted to influence the rules for how Target does business.

The political winds shift. The consumer winds shift. And yet corporations almost always find a way to take advantage. It is magical thinking to believe that the rules we set are the *only* rules in the game corporations are playing. Our rules can easily get overrun by rules with more force behind them, especially when we pretend the rules are static and no one else is working just as hard as we are to change them. And the opposite is also true: We can overturn our opposition's rules if we are focused and savvy about taking them on.

In addition to incentives changing around corporations, corporations can also take control of changing those incentives themselves. They can try to buy people off—for example, donating to charities in the hopes that money will get activists to shut up and go away, or providing financial perks to social change leaders by hiring them into fancy jobs. Color Of Change never took corporate donations, so we were mostly immune from the crass transactional tactics corporations might want to use against us. Mostly.

No one is fully immune. And that is what makes Hollywood particularly difficult to challenge: Entertainment corporations have a lot of very enticing incentives to offer. Granting access to the glamour and celebrity of stardom—a ticket to the Grammys or Academy Awards, an invite to a private party, the chance to be on a movie set or talk with celebrities—is hard for a lot of people to resist.

I face these choices all the time. It's been easy for me to reject corporate money and other buy-offs. But it hasn't always been easy to know whether showing up or refusing to show up at an event is the most strategic thing to do, and the allure of stardom certainly makes that harder.

Being close to power, in this case the power of stardom, is extremely seductive for most people. It might make an activist working to change how Hollywood works be a little nicer to a target than they otherwise would, or frame a change as a recommendation more than a demand, or not go too hard on an executive in other ways. I saw this play out at GLAAD. There was integrity there. But it wasn't always easy to go after certain networks that had done a lot to be so friendly and seductive, opening the door to the glamour of Hollywood, perhaps even feeding us a few minor wins along the way but always holding out on the big wins.

It is critical to be clear-minded and honest about which wins require constant work to prevent backsliding, and also which wins drive real impact. It's the distinction between real and fake solutions, and nothing can cloud our vision more than hanging around celebrities for too long.

An Opportunity at *Saturday Night Live*

In one case at Color Of Change, we jumped on an opportunity when, in 2013, the longtime *Saturday Night Live* (*SNL*) actor Kenan Thompson said he was no longer going to dress up to play Black women characters; if they wanted Black women characters on the show, then they would have to hire Black women performers. We took the baton from there, immediately launching a campaign to pressure *SNL*, owned by NBCUniversal, to end its long-running policy of largely excluding Black people from its ranks, especially Black women.

One white consultant who was working with us said it wasn't a real opportunity because those unwritten rules had been around for so long under the creator and executive producer of the show, Lorne Michaels, that they could never be changed—we should accept that it was a white show, even if it launched Eddie Murphy and Chris Rock to become huge stars. But we knew better. With the producers and network caught off guard, this was one of those moments of disarray when we might be able to change incentives we otherwise couldn't. There was a line across which even *SNL* was accountable to Black people—or at least needed to appear to be so.

Our campaign succeeded, forcing the show's producers to take the unusual step of calling for a round of midseason hiring, which led to writers and actors like Leslie Jones and Sasheer Zamata coming onto the show in January 2014. It seemed to genuinely set the show on a new path. Not necessarily a transformative one, but one in which the show slid forward more than backward when it came to Black talent—and just as important, Black perspectives.

After the change, I saw a sketch making fun of the racist double standards of Hollywood awards shows. I thought it would not have been something the writers would have addressed before the new addition of personnel and perspective. Immediately after the 2016 election, that week's host, Dave Chappelle, along with Chris Rock (making a surprise cameo), headlined a different skit that staged an election-night scene in which white people were losing their mind watching Trump beat Hillary while the two Black characters were shaking their heads with the biggest "I told you so" look imaginable.

That perspective—that America electing an out-and-proud racist to office was no surprise to Black people, and that we saw it coming even though white liberals wouldn't listen to us—was an important idea for the audiences that watch *SNL* to hear, and for everyone who was trying to get people to understand that perspective to be able to share. Another shift in perspective it offered: Black people are actually experts on American politics, given how much of politics in America swirls around race.

Both sketches were as funny as any others—or funnier. But the focus was different. It was all part of a larger shift in the rules for television comedy that so many people worked and made sacrifices to achieve, across so many intervention points in the industry, both in public and behind the scenes. If we could make those changes last, we might be able to establish a new rule: Getting laughs about racism is not about using comedy as a cover to get away with saying racist things; instead, it's about using the persuasive power of comedy to expose racism and how it works (and who benefits from it) in ways that help people see how bad it is for most of us—and ridicule it. *SNL* hasn't quite made that shift permanent, but there's far more balance now than there used to be. That can seriously influence how the show's audiences think about race, in positive ways.

That said, having the infrastructure to continue to enforce the rules and prevent backsliding requires a lot: A change is never permanent, and sometimes the patterns of behavior we see are only as good as the people in positions of authority at any given time— whether they accept those rules as the parameters for their work or break them, and whether there are any consequences for breaking them.

It is not possible for activists to keep open an entire shop dedicated to holding one show accountable for what it does, and TV producers and executives know that. As soon as we let up on our pressure or focus, they can revert to their old behaviors. All rules require enforcement—and reinforcement—in the form of enduring incentives that keep people in check. If the incentives change back, the system will change back. In fact, the 2025–2026 season of *SNL* launched without any Black women performers at all.

More Opportunities, More Challenges

In a contrasting case in 2013, we were able to force the Oxygen cable network, also owned by NBCUniversal, to abandon its plans for airing a reality show about a Black Atlanta rapper with a bunch of kids by different mothers. It would have taken the exploitation and reinforcement of Black stereotypes to new heights. (Such a show would have been a serious stray from mission for Oxygen, which was launched in

2000 by a Nickelodeon founder who wanted to offer women-focused content that provided an alternative to the largely terrible portrayals of women everywhere else.) Blocking that show was an important win. It would have done a great deal of damage, and there should have been another way to elevate local rappers without exploiting their stereotype potential. It also helped our members see their own power, and believe in this work, while putting people in the industry on notice about our strength.

But getting that show canceled did not change the course of Oxygen, let alone the course of the reality TV industry. The industry did not say, *Let's abandon distorted and harmful content.* What it said was, *Let's not get in this specific fight with Color Of Change if they have a lot of momentum and we can't win.* Making that show unprofitable was different from making the network's overall strategy unprofitable.

In fact, Oxygen turned into a police-centered programming destination for "true crime." That shift may, in fact, have had an even worse effect on Black communities than we could have imagined when we ran our campaign against that one show. It's hard to invest so much emotional and professional time working on something, only to find yourself in a "one step forward, five steps back" situation. Campaigning is hard. It's bad enough to lose. But to lose while winning—because the win wasn't what you hoped it would be and you didn't have the power to make it be something else—is somehow more difficult.

Another campaign in our earlier years of this work involved a very substantive negotiation and positive results with A+E Networks, co-owned by Disney and Hearst Communications. A+E had already begun airing another regressive show related to the criminal justice system, *Akil the Fugitive Hunter.* It was a reality series about a real-life bounty hunter, Akil Muhammad, glorifying his work. The fact that Akil was Black, from South Central L.A., made it more complicated for us. It might be harder for us to rally people against him because he had already had some positive press in Black media as someone who had worked his way out of a difficult life situation to find success. Having a Black person as the lead subject provided cover for the show. Some people found it hard to believe that such a show could still have a racist impact, and so Akil gave the network more immunity to criticism than it might otherwise have had.

We were always trying to address issues from multiple angles, based on the fact that people live in an integrated world (as discussed in chapter 12). At the time, Color Of Change was right in the middle of working to change the rules related to the profiteering and abuse enacted by bail-bond companies in the real world, including so-called bounty hunters. Those profiteering businesses, often seen as mom-and-pop shops but usually supported by global insurance corporations, coerced money from families already living on the edge financially and committed grave violations of people's privacy, safety, and legal rights.

Akil the Fugitive Hunter, we reasoned, could create a media phenomenon promoting lies about the bail-bond industry that would get a lot more attention than the truths we were promoting, and would thereby set us back. For example, it could make popular personalities or even heroes out of people at the bail shops who actually played a prime role in injustice. It could glorify violence, and violations of people's rights in the system, with the show's storylines modernizing "slave catcher" narratives that had a highly regressive impact on people's views about what was acceptable treatment of Black people in service of the rhetoric of public safety (on top of using the word *hunting* to refer to human beings).

We were able to make our case to executives at A+E, which profited from cheaply made reality shows but could sometimes show concern for their content. It was negotiation: one of those rare cases in which a conversation with reasonable decision-makers who were open to being persuaded by arguments about right and wrong, rather than promises of punishment or reward, might lead to a rule change. They heard us. They wanted to do the right thing. They moved the show online and then phased it out. Of course, it wasn't all goodwill: We made them aware of the kind of campaign we could run against them if they didn't want to negotiate. In the end, it was always a question of power—the power to shape the incentives governing decisions.

Several years into my tenure at Color Of Change, I had helped orchestrate wins going up against Disney, Viacom, Fox, NBCUniversal, and many others. In quick time we had built the expertise and infrastructure we needed to rise to a level of influence over certain kinds of decision-making that would have been the envy of other advocacy groups. But was it enough to fulfill our purpose as change-makers, sworn to deliver real results for Black people and all the people who benefit when Black people win real rule changes?

Our wins were all meaningful, aimed at raising the floor of what was acceptable. But they were also limited: They did not lead to a greater cascade of change across the reality TV industry, or win a major policy change in terms of standards and practices in one corporation that we could use as leverage with other networks to pressure them to get on board with raising standards for their programming.

We won some fights, but certainly lost others. Even A+E still did everything it could to make big hits out of *Dog the Bounty Hunter* and *Duck Dynasty,* profiting off the process of feeding audiences everything they needed to move farther to the right (and become more hostile to nonwhite people). The producers of those shows were like Jerry Springer, who used the excuse of bringing on "real people" to justify the stereotypes his show exploited, as if he were a neutral party. Big Tech plays the same game: *We're just here to let people say what they have to say, and this is what people have to say.* But behind the scenes, of course, they are picking and choosing what gets buried and what gets the spotlight. Reality TV does the exact same thing, excusing shows as being "documentaries" to justify "truth-telling" programming that is actually highly selective on their part and has a terrible impact on how audiences think about nonwhite people—even impacting how nonwhite people think about themselves.

I never saw any shows mainstreaming the views of Black radicals, or allowing Black people to broadcast anything near the kind of hateful attitudes that white people got to spend all day expressing on reality TV.

Our goal was implementing fairness, accuracy, balance, and authenticity as guidelines for developing media content that influenced millions of people. But the opposite of all of those practices was still highly profitable in ways we could not yet change. It wasn't magical thinking that got us there. We were simply up against more powerful forces. We needed an even more systemic approach to make systemic change, more than merely incremental improvements here and there. And we needed more power.

From Canceling Culture to Reshaping It

It is not easy to look back on work I had deemed successful and assess it in much more limited terms only several years later. Should I be proud? Should I be pained? It was work that required much effort and involved many smart people on our team. We pushed ourselves further than anyone thought we could go. Such work requires honesty. It requires a lot of humility. And it requires hope and commitment. I was constantly asking myself, *If that didn't work, what will? What's next?*

As with Big Tech, it can feel like Hollywood is so overwhelmingly powerful that it can be hard to change how it works (even if it's possible to hit individual shows and movies on their casting decisions or other issues). We can also get caught up in the magical thinking of assuming popular culture is always marching forward, on the side of progress—which of course is not the case. However, neither the role media channels play in justifying the status quo nor the role they play in making progress against the status quo is inevitable. Media corporations operate within incentive structures, and there is always a way to gain the power it takes to change those incentives, and therefore how they do business. Figuring out the right strategies will only become more important as decision-making in Hollywood gets concentrated among fewer and fewer people, thanks to the big mergers we have not been able to stop.

We at Color Of Change had worked successfully for several years to eliminate truly harmful, misinformation-spreading content, to raise the floor for what was acceptable and set new rules against profiteering from the worst of racist and other problematic content. We had also successfully collaborated on changing the content of shows that could model what more responsible but equally entertaining TV could look like, to raise the ceiling of possibility.

One such show was the 2018 miniseries *Seven Seconds* on Netflix, created by Veena Sud and starring Clare-Hope Ashitey and Regina King, who won an Emmy for her role in it. The show's drama focused on a cover-up within a New Jersey police department that put both racial conflict in that community and the structural racism in the justice system on full display. We wanted to help Hollywood decision-makers see that they could profit without profiteering. It was not clear, even with Regina King's Emmy, that anyone looked any differently at alternative approaches to telling stories about crime and race in a more realistic way as a result. Tapping into the feeling of realism was always in fashion. But committing to the content of realism wasn't.

I knew we were not going to win real change by working through Hollywood one show at a time. For one thing, we could not create enough momentum that way. It would be like trying to steer a cruise ship with a single wooden oar. For another thing, I knew that corporations would eventually adapt effectively to cancel culture. We could lose our power to make a difference if we kept hitting the same cancel button over and over. (That instinct about the patterns of the industry turned out to be very accurate, especially after 2020.)

I have often said that racism is highly adaptable. Racial profiteering is highly adaptable, too. Getting shows canceled was becoming a cost of doing business. The business model of Hollywood was adapting to it. Media corporations fortified their defense of the long-running, cash-cow shows that really mattered to them, including some highly problematic reality shows and scripted crime shows like *Law & Order*, and they cut others loose, as sacrifices, if they became a problem. Their stated DEI initiatives and their few "good shows" created a positive enough aura around them to protect their most prized media properties, no matter how problematic they were. They were learning the game.

The crime shows that really did so much to warp public

perception—fearmongering about people of color, cities, and police reform and beefing up support for the worst of racist policing—had exploded in number. More and more went into production every year. While many people had been calling out those shows for how problematic they were, they remained popular and profitable. Much like Big Tech, entertainment networks understood how to manipulate people's appetite for sensational content and feed it to them in ways that made them rely on it, almost as its own lifestyle. TV also had a tried-and-true formula for hooking people. And in many cases, diversifying the casting only served to excuse the content.

When it came to TV programming related to the criminal justice system, we realized we needed to set our own standards, which we could use to create a broader consensus about what was harmful and therefore what was unacceptable. That goal sat at the intersection of changes that needed to happen in entertainment media and changes that needed to happen in the justice system.

We knew that the perception of violent crime going up was the opposite of the reality, which was that crime was going down. But in the fictional world of TV, the crime rate was skyrocketing. Viewers were inundated with more and more scripted crime drama shows (and even some comedies) that were scaring the hell out of them, making it feel like violent crime was worse than ever. And they wanted to consume it.

Racist policing in the real world could not exist without the propaganda that crime dramas provided, making racism invisible. As much as these shows prided themselves on projecting the feeling of realism, their writers and producers did everything they could to erase the reality of what policing in America was really like. In fact, police in the real world were often incentivized by these shows to be more violent and abusive: They wanted to be the heroes kicking down doors, yelling "Freeze, NYPD!" and dispensing the justice they believed the scumbags dirtying our streets deserved. These shows made it seem cool to define the unwritten rules of being a "tough guy" cop as violating the written rules of the actual law—especially people's rights.

That is when we had the idea for creating the most comprehensive research study on scripted crime-related shows ever conducted, which might give us real leverage in being able to call out entire networks and media corporations in a way that would bring them to the negotiating table. We were under no illusion that data and facts would persuade people on their own. But lining up data and facts to put bad actors in the spotlight for their role in the system (and not just for one-off bad choices), and doing so in ways that made them uncomfortable and created a cost to the status quo, was an important new strategy for this area of content. We needed to show the connection between the misinformation about race, crime, and the justice system promoted on these shows and people's misperceptions and inaccurate beliefs about the real world. It wasn't just harmless entertainment: That was the lie we had to neutralize.

Although many people tried to put us in the box of "diversity," our study was not only about diversity. We certainly made the connection between a lack of diversity among decision-makers and the content on crime shows. But our real focus was demonstrating how these shows were serving as a propaganda arm for the many bad things police, judges, prosecutors, prison wardens, and others did, while many of the viewers that entertainment corporations relied on for revenue were turning against those practices. We weren't trying to increase our *presence* on these shows; instead, we were trying to increase our *power* for shaping them. As in our prosecutor work—where we were not necessarily trying to elect Black prosecutors but rather prosecutors who would do right by Black people—we weren't merely demanding to see more Black characters on these shows; we were demanding better stories and more responsible practices about issues that impacted Black people.

I had talked about taking on the deeply regressive impact of crime-related TV shows when I first interviewed to lead Color Of Change. But it took time to build up the credibility and infrastructure to move from analysis to action and from action to impact. We needed to be taken seriously as an organization in order to be unignorable on this issue, for which there were many forces working against us to make us ignorable.

In 2017, we had produced a report about the injustices women and nonwhite writers faced in Hollywood, *Race in the Writers' Room: How Hollywood Whitewashes the Stories that Shape America.*[2] That report had created a stir and had revealed that crime procedural shows were the least diverse in terms of the writers and producers who determined the stories they told and the images they showed. That wasn't the main point of the report, but it would become an effective entry point.

A Turning Point

Our comprehensive study of popular crime shows on television culminated in a report titled *Normalizing Injustice: The Dangerous Misrepresentations That Define Television's Scripted Crime Genre,* which we released in January 2020.[3] The reception was very positive, but it did not immediately lead to action. However, over the next several months, outside Hollywood, a series of brutal killings of Black people by police and vigilantes changed the context. After George Floyd was murdered in May, sparking the greatest level of energy we had seen in a generation for taking racism seriously and doing something to end it, the report played a different role. We stepped into that moment.

People wanted Hollywood—and every other industry—to take accountability for the ways it contributed to anti-Black hatred and discrimination. Many, many good people across Hollywood itself wanted to take a hard look at what they were doing and understand how they could do better, making the connection we had always wanted them to make between what we see on TV and what happens in the real world.

The report was damning and specific about how these shows worked to promote racist and regressive ideas that served as a kind of misinformation about the criminal justice system and its effects on people. We introduced new ways of looking at these shows, through metrics we developed, that got people thinking differently about them. Many of those metrics demonstrated how crime shows normalize injustice: either pretending police officers never do harmful things or pretending that the harmful things they do are justified (unfortunate but not unjust)—and may not even be that bad. Ever notice that when police characters on these shows beat people up, those people never really get hurt? When you systematically study hundreds of hours of this stuff, those patterns emerge very clearly.

For instance, we pointed out a pattern in these shows that made wrongful actions committed by white police characters look right by having Black police characters endorse those actions, and by having beloved "good guy" characters endorse those actions or even perpetrate them, too. That leaves a lasting impression with viewers: If the "hero" characters that viewers know and love are doing it, there must be a good reason, right? If Black characters are going along with it, how could it be racist? The report identified specific storytelling practices that, taken together, warp people's attitudes and understandings like the best propaganda.

In the dreadfully iconic opening of every *Law & Order* episode, the god-like narrator says, "In the criminal justice system, the people are represented by two separate yet equally important groups: the police who investigate crime and the district attorneys who prosecute the offenders." What it doesn't explain is that the people are also exploited for profit at every turn by those same two groups, in addition to several others who hide their profiteering practices by making sure they never show up on any TV shows: bail-bond corporations, telecom corporations, private prison corporations, private contractors that serve prisons and jails (e.g., food, clothing, construction), weapons manufacturers, surveillance contractors, mayors and police who explicitly target nonwhite and/or poor people for excessive ticketing, police union officials who try to cover up the wrongdoings of their worst members, and so on.

The report hit these issues deeply. And soon we saw that it gave people both inside and outside the industry new language not only to talk about these things but also to do something about them. We were invited into dozens of TV show writers' rooms, sometimes so that the producers could say they talked to us and check that box for appearances only, but often because executives, producers, writers, and actors genuinely wanted to do better.

(In 2025, we released a follow-up, *Normalizing Injustice 2,* featuring a "Copaganda Index" and the results of confidential interviews with people working across the genre.)[4]

Hollywood had spent decades collaborating (often secretly) on hundreds of movies and TV shows with police departments, the Department of Defense, the conservative Parents Television and Media Council, and even the Chinese government. In 2020, however, there was wider recognition than ever that they should get additional perspectives—and that since the work they put onscreen mattered, affecting people's lives, the shows should be more responsible about their influence. But taking advantage of a new level of goodwill was a long way from changing the incentive structures that had made Hollywood a PR machine for the police for decades.

When LGBT people were in the policy wilderness in the 1990s and early 2000s, seemingly far away from winning the changes we needed to fully take part in society and guarantee our safety, this kind of work to change the narrative environment seemed more essential, not less. Specifically when we were out of power, it became a way to take control of our presence in ways that could lead to power.

In the case of criminal justice reform, momentum had been building in the 2010s, but we needed this kind of narrative reinforcement. We knew that so much of the reforms we won could be overturned with the change of an election, despite the claims by people on the inside that everything was safe, and so it became only more important to engage Hollywood in order to invest in longer-term narrative reinforcement. But racism remained profitable—these crime-and-punishment shows were the engine of revenue for TV networks. They were a much deeper part of the business model.

Changing those incentives requires more than a report. It requires major infrastructure capable of engaging in ways that continue to adapt and never let up until we win. But the first step was trying to take a far more systematic approach—to make an attempt to change the rules for the entire industry, rather than change one show at a time. The report, especially the way that it demonstrated the extent of the problem and created a new audience for more systemic solutions, was a starting point on the path.

How to Get Away with Racism

Hollywood is more than just a little footprint within Los Angeles County, California. When I say "Hollywood" I am talking about the entertainment industry, particularly the part of the entertainment industry that produces movies, television, video games, certain kinds of marketing, and all their related extensions. Hundreds of thousands of people are involved in making Hollywood what it is and enabling Hollywood to do what it does. In addition to directors, writers, and actors, those involved include all the staff at TV networks and streaming platforms, producers, casting directors, designers, production crews and managers, lawyers, bankrollers, critics, marketers, international deal-makers, and more. The industry is deeply rooted in Los Angeles and New York, and it also has other power centers, from Silicon Valley to Atlanta. The world built around all of these people and organizations constitutes the infrastructure that makes Hollywood such a powerful force in our lives.

Yet just a few corporations and their many subsidiaries own and produce nearly all of Hollywood's output: Disney, Sony, NBCUniversal (Comcast), Paramount Skydance Corporation, Warner Bros. Discovery, Amazon, and Netflix. (And depending on when you are reading this book, there may have since been even further consolidation.) The media landscape includes many other players as well, from major corporations that are a growing force within entertainment (like Apple, and YouTube/Google), to major players in certain areas of the industry (such as Microsoft in the video game sector), to independent networks (like Starz and AMC), and many independent studios (such as Tyler Perry Studios, the largest singular film production studio in the United States).

But the great majority of television shows, movies, and video games that get produced are owned by a very few corporations. That greatly limits the possibilities for what we see in terms of formal entertainment (and TV news) content, while also making the rules that those few corporations set the de facto rules for the entire entertainment industry. **While the options for consuming entertainment media seem to have only gotten wider and wider, the owners and controllers of that media have remained very narrow.**

Hollywood and corporate profiteering have a long, entangled history, especially when it comes to racial profiteering. The most influential show in establishing the police procedural as a staple of television programming was *Dragnet,* which made the move from radio to television when it premiered on NBC in 1951, right when owning and watching a television every night was starting to become a mass phenomenon. The show followed two detectives in L.A. as they supposedly gave viewers a window into the gritty reality of investigating crimes. The fictional *Dragnet* was produced in direct collaboration with the very real Los Angeles Police Department. Police associations would soon celebrate the show and give it awards for changing public attitudes about police for the better. They were doing the work of cultural advocacy even long before GLAAD. The police themselves understood the power of representation very well.

Dragnet trained American viewers to see the world through the eyes of police—that is, to see what police departments and politicians wanted people to think the police acted like in the real world. In fact, that show and the dozens that followed its format for decades after made it much more difficult for people to see the truth of how police operated. Trying to change the criminal justice system means going up against decades of propaganda telling millions of us every night that reform is not necessary.

When viewers are "educated" extensively by fictional television, whether they notice that propaganda or not, it becomes difficult for them to accept any stories to the contrary—anything that would create a conflict between the fictional view of the world they know and love and the reality of the world that is painful to accept. Hollywood is everyone's professor of crime, but it no more deserves that authority than a professor at Hogwarts lecturing us about physics. It's all make-believe. But it's hard not to believe that what our favorite lovable characters are telling us is true. And they are still promoting stereotypes and misinformation about race, racism, poverty, and Black communities.

Many people feel, whether they recognize it or not, that the truth about policing that Black communities are telling them must be a distorted fiction, while the distorted fiction these shows are telling them must be the truth. That dynamic—that twisted logic and the legacy of police propaganda in Hollywood from *Dragnet* to *Hill Street Blues* and *NYPD Blue* to *Law & Order, Blue Bloods,* and *Chicago P.D.*—is still a major influence in preventing police reform and police accountability today. It warps perception and thereby warps people's sense of what's merely unfortunate and what's actually unjust. And it makes Hollywood, rather than everyday people, the "expert" on the lived reality of policing.

That is power. It is also in the profiteering sweet spot—the intersection of political profiteering, government profiteering, and corporate profiteering. Everyone profits from these shows: politicians get more support for their agenda, police departments get more authority and resources, and media corporations get more revenue from advertisers and streaming subscriptions. It all hinges on storytelling that either erases certain people to make us irrelevant or demeans and dehumanizes us to make us into villains and ultimately make it seem reasonable and acceptable to treat us unjustly—to normalize injustice. That is the engine of exploitation.

With Hollywood narratives at their back, politicians win elections and power over policy, governments evade accountability and increase their budgets and authority, and corporations rake in millions on building up the ever-expanding machinery of the criminal justice system. And though Black and Brown people are the impetus and excuse for running the system the way it's run, everyone suffers from the abuses that people in power trade in for profit.

Presence and Profiteering

I would never say that we have not made real progress over the last hundred years with respect to media representations of Black people. Of course we have. Black people own certain media channels and content. Black people are leading characters in certain media. Stories we have wanted told are being told in high-quality, mass-appeal, big-reach news and entertainment media outlets more than ever before—some of them even by us.

Not all of those changes in presence, however, have led to changes in power. Some of them even work against us. Everyone who's part of a group that is outside power can relate to the troubling dynamics of what happens when some of us get inside power. Black politicians, Black corporate executives, and other "Black faces in high places" do not always serve the interests of Black people overall. Sometimes, they serve as role changers who make a lot of sacrifices in order to push forward rule changes. Other times, they put a new face on the old rules in ways that benefit the status quo, for which service they are often handsomely rewarded by the people with real power whose interests they serve. And a lot of times, it's hard to tell what's going on: Someone who wants to drive change might get lost within the system, sometimes being helpful and sometimes being quite unhelpful.

It's not always clear what is helping or hurting the cause of justice when it comes to media representations. But one thing is clear: It would be hard for us to gain power in America if we were represented more often than not in toxic ways. And so changing the volume and substance of our presence was a critical step toward changing perception and changing the rules. That media infrastructure is a critical step on the path to power.

While some anti-Black stereotypes and other forms of grave misrepresentation are still accepted, many are not—at least in most media. That's good. Yet the question of strategy is not how far we have come but how far we have to go. The rules are still not what they need to be. And too many efforts focus on gaining more presence rather than gaining the power to change the rules that matter most in terms of impact.

Fox News hosts cannot explicitly rant and rave for hours on end about Asian people or Jewish people, making completely ridiculous claims about their inherent inferiority. They might tap into hateful antisemitic or anti-Asian racism when they are trying to attack someone specific, like George Soros. But they know there is an unwritten rule they can't break, which is not to go after Jewish people or Asian people as an entire group—as a people. Even if many Fox viewers are clearly anti-Jewish and anti-Asian, and would eat it up, Fox News would face consequences it does not want to face for breaking those rules. It would not be profitable overall for them. That same unwritten rule does not exist for Black people and people from Central and South America.

That reality is an example of progress being distributed unevenly: having rules that curtail media figures from breeding hate and hostility, but only selectively. Much like rules that let certain people get away with drug use while other people have their lives ruined for it, it has been difficult to change the rules for influential organizations like Fox News. Yet those rules have real consequences, and not only for Black people. The right-wing blame machine reaches a lot of people. It's tapping into those deep narratives people already carry with them, and exploiting them to turn people against criminal justice reform, workers' rights, and other forms of progress that benefit everybody, not just Black people. It's part of what keeps profiteers going: As I outlined in chapter 6, blame is a powerful weapon of distraction. It is not that hard to recognize corporate profiteering. Even when it is not obvious who is getting hurt and by how much, it is usually obvious who is benefiting. In the case of Fox News, in addition to the owners, the Murdoch family, it's right-wing politicians and everyone who benefits from right-wing policies.

In the case of those daytime television shows I was watching while babysitting my niece, like *The Jerry Springer Show,* decades of research show us how much the displays of violence and sensational stereotypes affect people's attitudes and behaviors toward Black people, and how profound those effects are. Even so, it's not always easy to see the connection, particularly in a country where this type of content is normalized and justified as "just showing the reality" of how things are.

But it is completely obvious who profits. Before his death in 2023, Jerry Springer was worth $60 million. The main producers did pretty well for themselves, too. NBCUniversal, which distributed the show (as well as *Law & Order* and *The Apprentice*), made incredible profits. And, once the old minstrel practices of exploiting sensationalized images of Black people took the new form Springer popularized, so did every other copycat show that came after it. All those hosts, producers, and media corporations made millions. That's not even counting the police departments and others in the world who profit from the idea that Black people are inherently a mess and a menace, and therefore need to be controlled.

As I said before, racism is big business. That business has a deep interest in controlling the rules. Racism is also highly adaptable, with profiteers finding ways to circumvent any new rules that might try to hold them back from exploiting racism.

The Limits of Diversity: Casting Versus Content

Two major types of decisions determine how Hollywood influences people: casting and content. By *casting,* I don't mean just actors. Rules about casting apply to every role related to producing a movie or show, from the actors to the executives, directors, writers, producers, and crew members.

Rules about *content* have to do with the creative process. The following are questions related to content:

- Are there written or unwritten rules that govern who the hero can be? If you show a nonwhite hero, do you need to offset that by showing a nonwhite villain?
- Are there rules about showing "bad" police only as individuals and never questioning the system of policing itself?

- Are there rules that say it is okay to make fun of rich people for *being* rich, but not for what they do to *get* rich, such as being part of corporations that harm millions of people?

Executives are hardly drivers of progress, but in my experience, when forced to make changes, they almost always default to changes in casting rather than content. In fact, they do whatever they can to prevent changes in content, because that's where they really make their fortunes. **In the context of profiteering, it's much easier to change the cast and maintain the content, in order to keep raking in profits from exploiting harmful representations.**

Here's a simple way to think about it: Suppose you're an advertiser. It's easier for you to change who is in your ads than it is to change the product you are selling. If you're selling cigarettes, the primary harm doesn't come from who you cast in your ads to sell them; it comes from selling them at all. If a cigarette corporation wanted to celebrate hiring their first Black spokesperson, would we take the bait and celebrate with them? Or would we only celebrate if we were able to stop them from targeting Black communities with their killer products? Casting is not progress in itself. Diversity matters most when it comes with soul, not just skin.

Similarly, Hollywood tries to convince us that if they add a few Black cops to the cast, then a cop show will no longer have a terrible effect on society. But it does. So the challenge of eliminating profiteering when it comes to entertainment is not just to change the rules of casting, but to aim for the bigger, harder goal of changing the rules of content.

Another challenge: Not only are casting changes easier for Hollywood to make, but they are easier for consumers to demand. Most audiences focus on characters (and actors) more than on the structure or substance of a story. Characters are much more visible in pass/fail litmus tests when it comes to people demanding to see something they can identify with (or demanding changes in offensive misrepresentation).

But we can't be sucked into the cancel culture strategy as our main strategy for changing culture, exactly because it focuses so much on casting and not nearly enough on content. One dangerous big lie they tell in Hollywood is that a few authentic and truthful representations somehow counteract all the other harmful content that entertainment corporations manufacture and distribute. **That is why changing the rules is so important: It's about raising the standards for all content, not just adding a few sweet candies to a bag of poisoned pills.**

When I was leading work at GLAAD, it was very clear to us what the strategy needed to be. The networks would point to one or two shows, or maybe only one or two characters, as good examples of progress on LGBT representation. We would then point them to the dozens of other homophobic characters, storylines, and dialogue running wild on their networks everywhere else. We demanded real standards, raising the floor for all content, not just here and there. That did not mean every show or movie would raise the ceiling and break new ground. It was never our goal to make every show a platform for promoting social justice. Despite the right-wing lies to the contrary, we knew that was not authentic and not what the entertainment industry was about. But it was our position that there needed to be a baseline for doing less harm, a line they could not cross, and it needed to be higher than it was.

Our goal was impact, and so we could not be satisfied if the networks planted one or two authentic queer characters on a show and let them wash their hands of the rest. The goal was to remove homophobic characters and content from *all* of their shows, everywhere—even the shows where anti-LGBT stereotypes and attitudes may have driven the content and driven the profit. And if those shows could not exist without their homophobic jokes and characters and stories, then they should not exist at all. If they could not profit without homophobia, they should not be in business at all. (The same should be true for demeaning portrayals of women or anyone else: If the show can't live without it, we shouldn't have to live with that show.)

It was not about simply making the right moral argument or phrasing our demand the right way. We needed to be able to back that up. We needed to make that profit unprofitable, in concrete terms, by making it too costly for them to continue with it. That is the goal of anti-profiteering work: to make what's currently profitable something that actually has too high a cost, even for those profiteers who never want to give it up.

Hollywood specializes in creating alternative universes. *In those universes, harms are fictional,* some people might say, *so how bad can they be?* They can be very bad. They train us to not think about consequences. They train us to focus on the moment, and then move on. They ask us to look at racism, for instance, as something that happens in a moment, not over a lifetime.

My goal in this work, whether at GLAAD or Color Of Change, was to force corporations to reckon with these harms and, whether they were willing to change or resisted change, force them to end their profiteering. How could we make that profiteering unprofitable? What power would we need to do so?

Raising the Ceiling, Raising the Floor

Entertainment content can help society move forward or it can prevent us from moving forward—or even take us backward. The same single show or movie can do both at the very same time; that is, it can challenge one stereotype while reinforcing others. Imagine, for example, seeing a movie featuring one smart Black scientist that also tells us about how that scientist was abandoned by his Black father, teased by his Black schoolmates for being smart, and then taken in by a white family who had the "good values" he needed to be taught in order to make something of himself. That movie would not provide a net benefit in reducing racial stereotypes.

That's not the kind of presence we need. Yet the rules are set up to produce one horrifying cliché after another, each amplifying cultural myths. The unwritten rules that tell writers they need to structure their characters and stories in this way are enforced quite seriously. Scripts that don't play by the rules get passed over, and careers of people who don't play by the rules get stalled. There is plenty of punishment to keep people in line.

Remember the story about Black elves I told in chapter 5? When we break both the written and unwritten rules of moviemaking to include Black elves rather than exclude them, we are raising the ceiling. When we get Hollywood to tell stories about the true Old West, which actually had Black people in it (including a significant number of Black cowboys), rather than about the fake Old West, which didn't, we are raising the ceiling. When we raise the ceiling for what is possible in Hollywood, we can open up the following:

- New jobs for otherwise excluded people as actors and writers.
- Opportunities for telling new stories.
- Opportunities for modeling new behaviors.
- Opportunities for schoolteachers to see and teach more truthful stories, and for people to rally around their true history and legacy.
- Opportunities for people all over the country to learn to be skeptical of any stories about the United States that are asking them to pretend certain people did not exist in it, did not make a contribution to it, or do not deserve to receive the benefits of those contributions today.

It's about possibility. But we cannot forget to raise the floor of what is acceptable at the very same time. We need to make space for new stories. But that has a widespread positive effect on society only if we also force certain old, untrue stories into retirement. **Telling one truth does not have the same impact if there are ten lies that come along with it. And we cannot reward media corporations that give us one truth for every ten lies.**

I have worked to challenge the rules of storytelling, especially for crime-related shows, for many years. One thing I come up against all the time: Hollywood creatives and executives always point me to what's different and special about their show or movie. But their biggest impact comes from what they all do together that is exactly the same. They want us all to celebrate the one moment in one single episode when they raised a progressive social issue in a compelling way that is different from any other show, and ignore the highly regressive rhetoric, the misinformation about the justice system, the stereotypes and glorification of police violence that we see in scene after scene, episode after episode, season after season, on every show—including theirs.

There are many examples outside of policing. For example, the Supreme Court could not have publicly assassinated affirmative action—which it did in 2023 in the broad light of day, at least in the realm of higher education—if Hollywood had not been chipping away for decades at the perceived value and credibility of providing equal opportunity to minority groups. TV shows and movies popularized labels, like calling someone an "affirmative action case," that promoted people's worst fears about the policy—namely, that unqualified people were replacing more deserving people in education, business, and government. Hollywood refused to tell the truth: Affirmative action wasn't covering over Black inferiority; it was making up for generations of white privilege.

Hollywood refused to tell the truth of affirmative action's role in gender equality as well: The single biggest beneficiaries of affirmative action were white women, not people of color. But on TV that was almost never the case. Demeaning white women as undeserving of the positions they ascended to has been a much lower-volume story. The reason? It is not as profitable of a lie. It's still profitable, for certain, but less so than it used to be. Large numbers of white women media consumers do not want to hear it and will make their opinions known. Those opinions will be heard and heeded. That is not to say white women have anywhere close to the same degree of power in Hollywood as white men, or don't face regressive representations of women at every turn. But when it comes to disrupting the lies and aspersions cast against affirmative action, they certainly had more power than Black people and could eventually take themselves out of the crosshairs of that attack.

Hollywood profits from lies about affirmative action in two ways.

As with all racist, demeaning jokes and misinformation, there is an audience just waiting to eat it up and buy into any story that tells them affirmative action is either pointless or unfair, or both. That's a moneymaker. But there is something specific to affirmative action: People in power in Hollywood greatly profit from undermining it because it's one way of protecting their own jobs. White men are overwhelmingly in charge in Hollywood, and many feel they would have a lot to lose in terms of money, reputation, access, and authority if they had to compete in a fair system in which simply being a white man no longer gave them an unfair advantage. They would love to take affirmative action down. So they are naturally attracted to creating media that helps them do that and give it the thumbs-up.

When we look at the unwritten rules—that is, how they actually function in the day-to-day—it is very hard to say that Hollywood is a liberal industry. Many people who are present as the face of Hollywood may be liberal, but many of the people who have power in the industry are not. Its profits from racism, sexism, demeaning poor people, and other injustices are vast, and its willingness to end them is extremely limited. That is just as much the case for all the other injustices in the world that Hollywood helps keep alive instead of disrupting.

The Biggest Hollywood Fiction

Hollywood is a factory for stories, and some of its biggest stories are about itself. Those stories are seductive and convincing, however inaccurate and hollow they may be.

Hollywood executives love to talk about how much of a difference they make in the world when they proudly point to something positive they did, usually an exceptional case in their portfolio. But they will deny that they have any real impact on society when someone else points to something negative they did, usually the norm of the way they do business every single day. They tell us that they have power to make an impact when they want us to pay attention, but they pretend to have no power at all when they want us to look away. In that way, they are not that different from other profiteers, such as a corporation that promotes its one semi-helpful environmental impact decision while burying the thousands of decisions it made that wreck the environment and our health.

Yet perhaps the biggest story people in Hollywood tell is the one about how we can and can't get the industry to change: *No, no, that won't work, that's not the way to change Hollywood.* That is always true of people within the systems we are trying to change. Long ago, I realized that people within a given industry are certain that only *they* know how to get that industry to change. They ask us to believe that if we just put a little less pressure on them, be a little less aggressive, be a little less demanding, it'll all work out much better. But it never works out. **Whether you're trying to change a major corporation, a local school board, or a county government, the people on the inside will always tell you a story about how to do it that makes life easier for them and makes change less successful for you. Their proximity doesn't make them right.**

The first step of winning change is to be grounded in a strong, credible, verifiable theory of change: knowing how a system does and doesn't change. That means, first and foremost, being an expert on how power works. People on the inside can sometimes offer a lot of insight and support. But the reality may be the exact opposite of how people in that system tell you (and themselves) it will or won't change. Sometimes even people who have been working on the outside to change a system will tell you the opposite of what's true.

In chapter 14, I discussed the process that we at Color Of Change went through in realizing that prosecutors were likely to be the most effective lever for reducing mass incarceration and police violence. Of course, few people in the system were telling us that, in part because they were experts in the status quo and not actually experts in making change, and in part because their own assumptions and mythology about how the justice system worked served their own interests (even unconsciously) and not ours. Some people who had been working on criminal justice reform for a very long time, perhaps decades, also could not see or believe in the prosecutor strategy. For instance, there were those who believed we could just sue our way to justice through the courts, even though that strategy had been slow and limited.

The same process plays out when thinking through strategy for changing Hollywood. Imagination is critical. Not accepting other people's assumptions at face value is also critical, even if those people have a lot of valuable insight in other areas of the industry. We must believe that a faster pace and a more effective method of change exists, in the face of approaches that are not meeting the moment of urgency and delivering change fast or comprehensively enough.

Unwinding Our Own Attachments

The first step in building the infrastructure needed to tackle corporate media is a bit different from that needed in other areas of infrastructure. It starts with belief—but not the belief that the strategy requires serious infrastructure and it is possible to build it, or the belief in the upside of the impact that infrastructure could help achieve. Rather, it starts with the belief in the goal of the change itself, the belief that you can be part of achieving that goal, and the belief that there are going to be some things you need to let go in order to get there.

Hollywood shows and movies are popular—with everyone. And that means that even people in our movement can feel very attached to a set of characters and stories that have played the role of their companion for their entire lives. It's hard to let go. It's hard to hear that a show you love may be standing in the way of racial justice, that it may be racial profiteering incarnate. It's actually very revealing. Criticizing a TV show that people know and love can understandably make them defensive. They feel judged, like they're participating in the racism themselves, or even in the racial profiteering, just by watching or being a fan.

But responses to criticism reveal how deep people's commitments go. Some people who love a certain TV show can easily give it up if they become aware of its negative effects. Or they may refuse to give it up because, in some way, it's part of them—or because, in some other way, they profit from it.

Many years back I was at a retreat in the mountains, a chance for people working across the fields of politics, art, and media to come together informally and build relationships, while also learning about one another's work. I had given a short talk about changing police and crime narratives in Hollywood, offering up some of my ideas as the relatively new head of Color Of Change. Most people in the audience loved it—though not everyone.

Later that afternoon, as several of us were packed on a raft floating down the river (for what they called recreation), one of the conference participants, someone who had worked in Hollywood for a while, challenged my views on crime shows. She explained to me how terrible it would be if I talked about these uninformed ideas in public because I'd be showing how uneducated I was about how good crime shows actually were in terms of social impact. It was like something out of the movie *Dear White People*. There we were, trapped on a raft with the bright sun beating down and making the orange of our life preservers glow an alien color, as a white woman berated a Black man for being uneducated—about racism. The fact that I had worked so long at GLAAD, one of the most successful drivers of cultural strategies, didn't seem to matter, either.

I made the mistake of getting defensive and arguing with her. Everyone else on the raft was visibly uncomfortable. In fact, the only person who seemed completely at ease with the situation was her. But her disagreement with me wasn't simply a difference of opinion over whether crime shows were good or bad in terms of social impact. Since transitioning out of Hollywood marketing, she had become a credentialed progressive, staunchly fighting for good causes, and eventually taking part in the resistance to the right wing and Trump. She even started promoting the idea that the forces of culture, like TV shows, were an important lever for influencing outcomes in politics—good or bad.

Yet, for whatever reason, she was so personally attached to the crime genre that she could not apply that same thinking to some of the most influential shows on air. It was such a clear example of the many ways in which we can be attached to defending what we hold dear, rejecting any rational conversation about it, while also missing the central role that race plays in the relationship between American culture and American politics. Those attachments can get in the way of understanding all the drivers of injustice we need to take on, seeing opportunities to do so, and picking the most effective targets to create the impact we need.

After a while, everyone got really quiet while we continued floating along the river—and floating along the tensions that can make that first step of building belief so hard: agreeing on the problem and what will solve it. Not long after, many activist groups wouldn't give me the time of day as I tried to explain how dangerous Donald Trump was becoming and how important it was to do everything we could to cut down the platform on which he was rising—that is, *The Apprentice.* (I tell that story in chapter 16.) As I faced a combination of indifference and resistance, I remembered that conversation from the raft—it felt like I was still on it.

Some people loved using Trump as a punching bag. And yet many people simply couldn't see or believe how racism and racists on television could pose such a great threat to our real-world lives, or what an integral role entertainment television played in creating the platform for him to establish legitimacy and attract so much support—specifically because he was engaging people through popular culture and not just politics. For whatever reason, they didn't want to believe it.

Today, people who once denied its influence are happy to talk about the problems of crime shows on TV. But here we are, another decade into the dominance and entrenchment of those shows as a profit driver for Hollywood, and they are harder to uproot now than they would have been if people had come around to these beliefs when the time was best to strike.

16

Failing to Take On Racial Profiteering and Cultural Power

CHALLENGE: It is not always easy to see a threat in the moment when it is most possible to do something about it—before it gets out of control. Missing those moments is not usually about having access to the right information but about breaking out of the patterns of magical thinking that prevent us from seeing what is right in front of us.

OPPORTUNITY: Racial justice is always a helpful wayfinder. Whenever racial profiteering is gaining ground, it is a sign that greater injustices will soon follow—affecting everyone. It's a helpful way of seeing how and when to invest energy and resources in fights that are both winnable and highly valuable—for everyone.

Trump's Pop Culture Revolution

The intersection between culture and politics is strongest when it opens up a new path for gaining power that wouldn't be there without it. As I mentioned in the chapter about magical thinking, to understand the Donald Trump era, both how we got here and how we get out of it, we need to look beyond politics.

When I took the helm at Color Of Change in 2011, I saw how antidemocratic ideas were rising across several powerful and popular channels that reached millions of people. At the time, we weren't yet facing today's full-blown ecosystem of media channels and technology platforms aligned with the sole purpose of recruiting and converting people into right-wing ideology. But it was well into development, and it was clear where it was going. The effort would move from the confines of purely political spaces like Fox News into the everyday lifestyle and infotainment media that a wide array of people consume every day. And "star" personalities outside of politics would be critical to its growth.

All of the ideas I saw gaining steam were rooted in race in some way—from questioning who gets federal funding, to redefining who counts in the census and who votes in elections, and even to questioning who is loyal to the country and who is a traitor. Having seen the backlash against LGBT rights, and having grown up learning about the backlash to the civil rights and women's liberation movements, I knew these forces were powerful enough to turn a defensive backlash against President Obama into a highly offensive assault on progress, democracy, and freedom overall—one that could drag us down for a long time. The Tea Party always felt like it was a cultural phenomenon, uniting people from different walks of life around a certain set of values, rather than a typical political fad. And it was evolving to become even more powerful.

Many of the grievances that would unite this emerging movement were rooted in conspiracy theories. Name a political issue, and there was a conspiracy theory that would encourage outrage for it. Birtherism, for example, gave members of this right-wing world a way to bond over their hatred of Barack Obama. It was the idea that Obama was not a legitimate president because instead of being born in Honolulu, Hawaii, he was born in a country in Africa that most of these people couldn't even point to on a map. The standards of truth were inverted in this world: Instead of increasingly outlandish ideas creating skepticism and dismissiveness, they created loyalty and passion.

Birtherism had many voices: right-wing talk radio, Fox News, Tea Party activists, and white nationalists. But they all had a limited popular profile. They were not household names in most households. It was difficult for all the believers to see themselves as being part of a national movement when their ideas were being recognized only in very niche media. But their cause gained new life—and new momentum for trying to undermine Obama heading into the 2012 election cycle—when a household name became their biggest spokesperson, someone whose media profile was experiencing a national revival: Donald Trump.

Trump's entire life was built on his willingness to stir up a blatantly racist frenzy for personal gain and political profile-building, whether in his business dealings or in the tabloid media. Many of us remember Trump's very public call to "bring back the death penalty" in New York after the arrest of the Central Park Five: five Black teenagers falsely accused of heinous crimes against a white woman in New York City, all of whom were later exonerated. (Trump, in his first term, ended the moratorium on federal capital punishment and went on to kill more Black men than any other president in the modern era through federal executions. He's triggered by Black people.)

His racist attacks on President Obama were no different. It wasn't subtle. Trump mainstreamed birtherism, hounding Obama until the racist question of his "true" origins and disqualifying "otherness" became a regular topic of conversation among much wider groups of people. Demands to see Obama's birth certificate—as if a document would ever satisfy a conspiracy mob—gained serious momentum. It was no less imaginary than saying lizard people secretly control the world, but more and more people with influence gave it acceptance every day. People in politics were already starting to follow Trump's lead. But it all could have been prevented.

Trump might have been dismissed as a washed-up and irrelevant tabloid character, with a string of failed businesses and false promises trailing him, had he not gained a platform late in life that would restore and expand his national profile.

Years before, as president of NBCUniversal, Jeff Zucker decided that NBC could cash in on the faded Trump brand by building an entire TV series around him. *The Apprentice* launched in 2004, and its first-season finale drew twenty-eight million viewers, among the best viewership numbers of any entertainment show that year. *The Celebrity Apprentice* launched a few years later, getting celebrities involved and leading to iconic clips circulating widely, as online video traffic grew rapidly during those years. The show's ratings declined greatly in the 2010s, but it remained a popular and highly recognizable brand.

It's amazing, however, that the show even made it out of the gate. *The Apprentice* was a somewhat real, somewhat fake, and thoroughly ridiculous reality show that featured Trump sitting in judgment as different teams of people competed in various business-related challenges, with the hope of winning a yearlong contract working for one of his businesses. Each week, as losers would be dismissed, Trump would entertain viewers with what became a pop culture catchphrase: "You're fired."

No matter what Trump did or said, or how he used his profile to give legitimacy to birtherism in 2011, in the run-up to Obama's second election in 2012, Jeff Zucker's successor, Steve Burke, kept him going. Every week, NBC enjoyed its profits while *The Apprentice* positioned Donald Trump as a serious, competent, and judicious businessman—someone to trust and take seriously. In reality, he was a failure at business and on the decline, but the show promoted the exact opposite image as a fiction that people loved, which Trump then used to actually become rich again.[1]

Taking On Pop Culture While There's Still Time

Brand power can create a cover for doing things that would otherwise be punished. Being a hero in a larger pop culture context allows someone to get away with acting like a villain in a much smaller context. It drowns out the noise of criticism, confers forgiveness for sin, and casts doubt on the legitimacy of the rules that designate that sin to be a sin in the first place. However it works in a given situation, brand power at that level can trump the rules of politics and, by doing so, redefine them.

Trump's political screen test worked: It demonstrated that the TV networks had no rules or limits when it came to giving credence to racism. The executives allowed their networks to be used as vehicles for race-based attacks on Obama, despite all the progress on racial equity they claimed to have made. It also tested well in the electoral context, re-popularizing racism as a powerful organizing platform for driving dangerous changes in political power in local and state races during the 2012 and 2014 elections.

Just as I was arriving in 2011, Color Of Change launched a campaign to pressure NBC to stop putting Trump on the air, aiming to end the legitimacy it was giving to both birtherism and Trump himself. Yet it was extremely difficult to get other progressive organizations to engage in our campaign. They could not see outside the world of pure politics and take on *The Apprentice* as a dangerous political vehicle in the making.

You can't see the impact of pop culture on politics if you look only at the impact of politics on politics. Liberals in general were comfortable with Fox News being the enemy, but not NBC. One was politics, the other was pop culture. They didn't get the connection. Liberal political consultants would spend months and months, and millions upon millions of dollars, focused on the thirty-second political ads that would air during a prime-time TV show's commercial break, convinced they could make or break a campaign. But few outside the LGBT, feminist, and climate movements seemed to care at all about the political impact of what was happening during the forty-two minutes of programming that captivated viewers for the overwhelming majority of that same hour—the part viewers actually watched.

Many progressive groups, especially white-led groups, simply did not understand the power of pop culture to shape politics—especially when playing on issues of race. They also did not see the threat that Trump posed back then. But it was not a fight we could win alone, especially at that time, and so we were not successful holding NBC accountable for what it was doing. That meant we could not interrupt the political rise of Donald Trump or disrupt the dangerous pattern of racist political rhetoric he was popularizing as an insurgent, entertaining, and seemingly legitimate form of "truth telling" that could not only help win elections but drive major public policy, too.

Obama won the 2012 election in part due to a very different political force crossing over into the popular consciousness late in 2011. The Occupy Wall Street protests, along with their "We are the 99%" refrain, helped put economic inequality on the table as one of the framing issues of the election. Mitt Romney, the Republican challenger, was deeply experienced in politics but also hailed from the world of private investment. He was not going to win an election that required a pledge to address inequality.

But while Occupy put inequality into people's minds far more than even Trump could put birtherism into people's minds, Trump was figuring out how to one day be on everyone's mind: be extreme, break every rule, say what no one else will (or should), find the base of diehard fans just waiting for someone like him to come along, build a popular force focused entirely on lifting him up, and take over the Republican primaries. To some degree, Obama had crossed over from pure politics to become a pop culture phenomenon. It was clear that Trump could be next, raising the game to the next level.

By 2015, and certainly by 2016, years after Color Of Change was forced to end its campaign against NBC and *The Celebrity Apprentice* in 2011, it was not hard to get leaders of progressive organizations to invest time thinking about how to defeat him. But by that time, it had become a much harder question to answer. **It may seem obvious now, but the time to stop Trump was before he became unstoppable.**

A clear line separates the people who saw what was happening in the years leading up to 2016 and the people who didn't, in terms of both political donors and advocacy leaders on the left. For many people with influence in politics, and within the nonprofit advocacy sector, pop culture didn't factor into how they thought about politics. And to be clear, the politics of racism didn't matter to many of them, either. Their interpretation of Obama's success was to think that the country was past the point of explicit racists being able to gain ground in major elections. We were in the "post-racial era," they believed, with all its new rules. They thought all those crass appeals to anti-Black racism or any form of racism by politicians were behind us, not in front of us. Those politicians would fail. This describes a lot of white people with influence in liberal politics and commentary at the time, but by no means only white people.

Black leaders generally knew different. We were painfully aware of how race, politics, and democracy have always been intertwined. We were blamed for every crime, for every failing school, for every downturn in the economy, and for every possible downturn in anything that might come along. We also knew that every rule that was supposed to create a fairer and less hostile world for us was capable of being broken by profiteers, opportunists, and anyone else who saw a way around needing to be nervous about disappointing us. But having that analysis—that racial attacks had a more serious political impact than many people wanted to believe—didn't necessarily mean having the answer for what to do about it. Some people may have understood that culture had an impact, but they did not understand how to impact culture themselves—at least not in the case of Trump.

Many thought racist attacks on political leaders and on whole communities would dissolve into irrelevance. Others believed racism was a threat but didn't know what to do about it. One rule the former group believed in: We couldn't go backward, only forward. In this variety of magical thinking, the floor could not sink back down to where it had been before. Progress was inevitable. Whether or not they should have known better, they didn't. These folks in decision-making roles across the realms of philanthropy, advocacy, media, and politics didn't see that Trump was a rule-changer, and that the role he would redefine in politics would allow him to invent and play by a whole new set of rules. They would draw us into playing a new game in which we were massively unprepared to compete.

Many of those same leaders often speak—today—about the importance of "culture change." But not then, when we really needed them to understand it. I can honestly say that many simply would not listen to anything having to do with high-level political strategy, let alone deep trends in American culture, coming from a Black leader like me (or anyone else)—even though I had come from leading culture-change work in the LGBT realm, representing some of the biggest wins against difficult odds that liberals had achieved in decades.

In July 2015, during a roundtable on ABC's *This Week,* the host George Stephanopoulos chuckled, and *New York Times* journalist Maggie Haberman laughed out loud, at the suggestion made by then U.S. House Representative Keith Ellison that Trump could win the Republican primary.[2] The following year, of course, Trump became president. Ellison, a Black man who was also the first Muslim ever elected to Congress and to a statewide office in Minnesota, later said, referring to that moment:

> Yes, I thought Trump could win. I also thought that Democrats weren't taking him seriously enough. . . . The [Jesse] Ventura win [in the 1998 Minnesota governor's race] taught me not to dismiss the long shot. There is an appeal to someone who is portrayed as an "outsider" who will speak for working families. Donald Trump is no working-class hero, but he played one pretty well on TV. He is a billionaire who is just filling his cabinet with other billionaires and lobbyists. The idea that he is going to help working Americans is founded on TV hype and PR.[3]

Ellison understood not only the persistent connection between race and politics but also the connection between celebrity and politics.

When voters in Minnesota made Jesse Ventura governor, they put the first WWE star into a governor's mansion for a long-term stay. In truth, we had all lived through Ronald Reagan making the move from Hollywood to politics and, a generation later, Arnold Schwarzenegger doing the same. It shouldn't have been a surprise.

But even so, in 2011, people who dismissed our efforts to launch a serious campaign aimed at neutralizing Trump would all say the same thing: *Donald Trump? You take all that pop culture stuff way too seriously. He's just a joke on TV. This is not worth our time. What damage could he possibly do?*

It's just TV. It's just pop culture.

Every once in a while, I think about what would have happened if Color Of Change's 2011 campaign to kick Trump off NBC had gained momentum, if more groups had seen what was at stake: Establishing a rule that people could not keep their platform on a major media network if they were promoting outrageous racist lies—a standard Trump would not have been able to violate at that point in his power. What would have happened if the corporate brands that sponsored *The Apprentice,* the celebrity participants on the show, and its producers and network executives had decided they no longer wanted their names associated with it because they faced real consequences in their lives for allowing someone to use a show in that way? Would Trump have turned into a sideshow with a minimal following rather than a major celebrity brand able to make the transition to major political power?

Giving People Permission to Be Who They Want to Be

Ever since I was a kid and saw Jesse Jackson run for president in 1988 with the slogan "Keep hope alive," I realized that candidates had to give something to you if they wanted to get something from you. Jesse was reminding us that nothing was hopeless, that his campaign would mean something big, even if he lost big. A vote for him was like a roll call for Black people: *Yes, I am here, I am present. Count me in.*

His was the first campaign I remember my parents donating to. I remember seeing his speeches and believing something was possible up there on that screen that didn't seem possible in the rest of the world around me. The constant cheers I heard—"Run, Jesse, run!"—made me feel like I was part of a culture that wanted Black men to succeed, which was not the norm of the culture I lived in every day in Long Island. Jesse gave us a way to stay in a fight that no one wanted us to be in. And to stick together no matter how that fight turned out. If he could keep fighting, we could keep fighting. Someday, he seemed to promise us, we would all trade in that hope for something real. (Just twenty years later, that dream came true.)

It was clear to me early on that Trump offered something big, too. But it was a very strange version of aspiration: If he could be terrible, you could be terrible. If he could be racist out loud, you could finally say what you really wanted to say out loud, and worry about the consequences later. And maybe there wouldn't even be any consequences. Shoot first, ask questions later. Or maybe don't ask any questions at all. Just keep shooting. It was like Stand Your Ground for political identity.

Trump offered a new culture to step into, like an ongoing carnival with many different activities to participate in, and many prizes to win. His campaign was at the center of that culture, but the culture was much larger than the campaign.

People being immersed in the world of Trump enabled conservatives to maximize their power. This is why Republicans still won't let him go: Trump makes things possible for them that are not possible without the culture, the motivation, and the engagement he creates. There's always something to buy, someone to blame, someone to threaten into silence, some content to pass around that takes people on a journey away from reality. The difference between the Trumpian culture and other political cultures is that it all feeds into making Trump more powerful, funneling him more money, whether from everyday people or from corrupt business people and government leaders across the globe, to create even more infrastructure for engagement. He combines politics and profits expertly. If he didn't, Republicans would eventually drop him.

The way that he translated that power into billions of dollars for legalizing tax evasion and for building up an infrastructure that unleashed newly empowered right-wing agents to chase immigrants all over the country, as if setting up some national paintball course for them to play in, makes the stakes of his power all too real.

Trump gave people a moment. He showed people they did not have to back down, that it was an "American value" to stand your ground and fight—not to win the peace or better anyone's lives. He wanted to deputize millions in the war against liberals, making *himself* the ultimate cause. He gave people the tools to fight that had been safely locked away in the closet. *Enough of this Black president, or this white woman in waiting. Let's party like it's 1969.*

In trying to build momentum among people to repeal Stand Your Ground laws, many progressives tried to rename them "Shoot First" laws as a way of shifting blame to the perpetrator rather than blaming the victim. But that did not stick. For the activists who were already with us, the term *shoot first* communicated the existential danger of these laws. But in the larger public environment, it only added to the celebration of the newfound privileges of gun owners. They were happy to finally get permission to shoot first. They had been waiting their whole lives for it. It would allow them to break the rules of the larger society they lived in every day, and perhaps one day come to shape those rules around themselves. Many attempts to oppose Trump failed in this same way: Somehow, the way we challenged him only reinforced the story about him that he wanted people to believe—and only got his followers more excited to defend him.

In 2016, I knew we were headed for major disappointment when Trump fully stepped into his groove as the Republican nominee and showed what he would bring to the table in his race against Hillary Clinton for the presidency.

In his convention acceptance speech he said, "Her campaign slogan is *I'm with her.* You know what my response to that is? *I'm with you.*" That was not a lucky shot. It was a slam dunk. It was exactly what his supporters needed to hear to feel liberated to be themselves and finally say what they thought (loudly). And to feel seen. It was exactly what people in the middle needed to hear in order to feel that it was worth gambling on a wildcard. He didn't just have people's votes, he had their behaviors.

A Culture That Compels People

It is critical to understand that tying activist behaviors into the very fabric of someone's identity is the hardest work to do but that it yields the biggest payoff. That is what's gained the most from operating at the cultural level in politics: embedding with people more deeply and enduringly.

You don't have to convince people to vote in every single election if voting is a behavior that their identity already compels them to perform. You don't have to beg for donations every time you need to fund your work if donating to activist causes is already what people do as a function of their self-identity. Being able to link participation in your campaign to culture is the most important stage of building cultural power—it fuses the personal identity that defines that culture with personal behaviors that define participation.

Some people cannot keep their cultural identity, or their self-identity, if they do not vote. They cannot walk away from that behavior without walking away from their entire sense of who they are as a person. My Grandpa Charlie was a perfect example: He was dedicated to voting as an expression of all that Black people had achieved and could achieve, and all his family had achieved, and he knew he was part of that story when he voted. As a kid, he would take me into the old manual voting booth to pull the lever on election day. He didn't miss an election. He was driven to that behavior by the story of his identity. The force of culture carried him, and carried me with him.

That is what it means to get culture on your side. Ultimately, many people felt in 2008 that in order to keep seeing themselves as a good person, or a forward-thinking person, they not only had to vote but had to vote for Barack Obama. Much was made of the idea that, initially, people thought Obama couldn't win because even though *they* could vote for a Black man as president, they didn't think *anyone else* on their block would do it. But one way the election was won was by inverting that belief: making people act as if they would lose part of who they were by *not* voting for Obama. They couldn't do that, even if they may have had doubts or may have had reasons not to vote for him.

In 2020, the Black Lives Matter movement similarly developed a level of cultural power that allowed people to change how they talked about race and racism. All of a sudden—and though decades of work had preceded it, it did feel like it was all of a sudden—people were not worried about what would happen to them if they said "Black lives matter." They were worried about what would happen to them if they *didn't* say it. Once that identity set in, and the incentive structures shifted, new behaviors were required.

By becoming a cultural phenomenon, the movement was able to compel a level of participation that would have taken ages to achieve, or might not have been achieved at all, if we had been relegated to fighting over laws and policies instead of forging new identities. Even if not too many big rule changes across society materialized, the new social identity compelled many new behaviors and, for a while, big and tangible new investments in time, money, and policy change related to doing something about racism.

Recall what I said in chapter 9: Narrative is about motivation. It's not about getting a story out, it's about getting a story in—inside people. Getting the story of Black Lives Matter into culture meant getting it into the deepest stories we have about ourselves—our identities—and therefore into our behaviors, not just onto our T-shirts.

Conclusion

Sometimes we are blessed with being able to choose the time, and the arena, and the manner of our revolution, but more usually we must do battle where we are standing.

—Audre Lorde, *A Burst of Light*

A couple of times each year, I'm stopped by an older Black woman—in a jazz club, at a crowded restaurant, in the busy concourse of an Amtrak station. She will compliment me on an outfit or tell me she liked what I had to say on TV. She'll smile at me and tell me I remind her of someone. It always feels past tense: a brother or uncle she lost, a cousin, a friend. There's often something unspoken in these exchanges—a warmth edged with loss. I continue on my way, wondering who she's holding in her heart in that moment, imagining my own backstory for him. Did he feel safe? Could he be who he wanted to be in his time? Was the freedom I have today possible for him back then?

As we part ways, I often get the impression that these women are trying to tell me something deeper: *Keep him in mind. Don't give up on fighting for him—for all of us. He ain't heavy.* I think about what more I can do, and what each of us can do, to win the changes that matter for the people they're thinking about. I think about the Black students just a few years ahead of me when I was growing up in Riverhead,

Long Island, who were forced into that police lineup, and the Black students just a few years behind me in Jena, Louisiana, who were nearly convicted and ruined by false charges. I think about the people still recovering from the L.A. fires of 2025 and the people forever living with the fallout of the New Orleans floods of 2005. I think about everyone under attack right now, and what it will take to make something different possible for them. I think about the challenges of our time.

During the disorienting first months of 2025, I heard the author Ta-Nehisi Coates talk about how many millions of Black people lived and died without knowing freedom, and yet they still dreamed, hoped, loved. The scholar Melissa Harris-Perry, a dear friend of mine, has underscored that same hard truth many times. Neither she nor Coates offers this perspective as permission for giving up, or for simply focusing on the small things right in front of us that can make life a little better, here and there. Rather, it's a challenge to us to stay in the bigger fight for freedom while also seeing our place in it—to remember that we can make a contribution both in our lifetime and beyond it, no matter what our starting point is. It's a reminder that while our starting point does affect our choices, any choice based on declaring a situation hopeless is a choice made in error—the very error our opponents hope we will make.

We don't choose the time we are born. But we often do choose the moment we enter history—the moment we decide to act, to risk something, to fight back, to work toward a dream of justice.

And there is a relationship between the two. People born into a time when momentum for positive change is strong, who learn about what it means to participate during that period, can have a difficult time adjusting when the tides turn and they find themselves living through a wave of backlash. For example, many people who developed their strongest political consciousness and found a role for themselves in activism during Obama's historic, hopeful run for president, and learned about the process of making change during the time of his administration, got used to a certain set of rules for making change, and a certain pace of progress.

Those who participated in activism for the first time during the Nixon and Reagan eras, when the country was dominated by a conservative, business-led, racially rooted backlash to the social and economic rules that had been established during the Progressive Era of the 1920s, the New Deal of the 1930s and '40s, and the civil rights and gender equality era of the 1960s and '70s, developed a very different sense of what it takes to win—defending the progress they inherited while trying to gain new ground for urgent issues emerging during their time.

Those who became active in the age of Obama may have trouble making the deep compromises and embracing the defensive plays required during a backlash, which can lead to losing more than they should. Those who became active in the age of Reagan may have trouble seeing the opportunities for rapid acceleration that open up during a period of momentum, getting lost in unnecessary compromises and failing to win as much as they could. One mindset is based on being propelled by winds at your back, with opportunities for progress abounding. The other is based on facing powerful headwinds, with barriers to progress along every route to change.

No matter which way the winds blow, adjustment is challenging. It's hard to let go of the past, and it can be easy to give up on the future. But we cannot let our starting point dictate our destination, or the paths we take to get there. **In particular, we cannot depend on having the wind at our back to believe that achieving power is possible.**

In reality, we mostly live in a climate of shifting winds, in terms of both speed and direction: Whichever may feel most present in the wider cultural vibe, the reality is that there are always forces pushing us back and opportunities allowing us to leap forward. In fact, as I've shown, sometimes a period of progress may mask a quieter, behind-the-scenes effort to undermine that progress, and we can often fail to perceive the backlash brewing until it's too late. That makes it harder for us to change our approach when we need to as the winds themselves change.

In 2024, when the New York Liberty won the WNBA finals, I watched the championship game at a bar not far from the arena in which it was being played. A young brother with both style and personality wandered in, looked at the score, and soon declared for everyone's benefit, "Offense sells tickets, defense wins games." Both obvious and revelatory, the comment made everyone turn around to look at him, and then at one another. They took it in with thoughtful nods.

As convincing as it sounded, however, I'm not sure it's always true. But it's clear that the right combination of offensive and defensive mindsets, strategies, infrastructure, and actions can make all the difference when it comes to the games we need to play, and the fields we need to play on, to win progress.

Being effective means playing offense and defense—constantly. It means never thinking that the momentum we have achieved cannot turn against us, but it also means never thinking the forces stacked against us make our work hopeless. We must equally push ourselves to give the burst of energy required to play today's game effectively while also sustaining ourselves for the long game. Some running the sprint. Others running the marathon. At the same time, on the same team.

If we ever doubt what we have to offer and whether or not it's worth it to fight, we can look to stories of success featuring characters just like ourselves, from any era, for inspiration and lessons. Not to replicate their strategies, but to find fuel in their spirit and vision, and sometimes to translate their best insights into terms that make sense today. That can mean looking for lessons around the corner, not across the world.

As my friend LaTosha Brown of Black Voters Matter teaches, authoritarianism isn't new to the South—it's been the operating system for centuries. Some people want to focus our attention on models of defeating authoritarianism in Europe or on other continents over the last decades, while deprioritizing (or even ignoring) the victories over authoritarianism that Black people achieved—in lockstep with many others—right here in our own country, from slavery to the civil rights era to going up against MAGA governors, local officials, and corporate leaders who aim to dominate their communities.

That's one reason I keep coming back to race throughout this book. Certainly, any oppressed group with a history of successes and failures fighting seemingly all-powerful forces has a lot to offer to our shared struggles today. But it's more than that.

Racism is so central to the operating system of America that if it's possible to reprogram it, it's possible to reprogram anything. Racial justice is a living testament to possibility. There is also no escaping the fact that MAGA's success would not have been possible without exploiting racism, and defeating MAGA is not possible without neutralizing their ability to continue that exploitation.

Either we see the power of race and win, or they do. Treat race as a side issue, and you get bad strategy (and often bench your best players). Understand what it takes to overcome racism, and the secrets of social change become clear. Wherever it is possible to change the rules to prevent racial profiteering, for example, the path to preventing profiteering overall opens up.

Racism has been a powerful organizing force since the founding of the United States. Every sector in the new nation was organized to profit from it and to consolidate power as a result of it: politics, commerce, civil society, education, religion. Today, we see a consolidation of power across media, government, and corporations that is equally dangerous, and equally rooted in a set of values that put profiteering (of all kinds) at the center of the strategy for dominance. The various forms of backlash to COVID-19 policies, the Black Lives Matter movement, gender equality, environmental sustainability, and so many other points of progress have helped advance this consolidation.

There is no sugarcoating the situation we are in today. It will take serious power to reverse its effects and turn us toward a better future. But the first and most consequential thing we can change is our mindset: from despairing to believing, from maintaining outdated assumptions about social change to honestly analyzing power, from accepting racism in our country to calling it out, and from searching for a perfect leader to investing in our own individual and collective leadership—and in our own power.

As strange as it may sound, changing our thinking—and catching ourselves in the thinking that holds us back—is the first step toward justice. Some of us have relied on freedoms we now fear losing. Some of us have never had those freedoms but refuse to live without them any longer. In both cases, seeing the world through the lens of power gives us a way to move forward. The biggest threat is feeling defeated, because that is how we fall behind.

Feeling Alone in the Wilderness Is Part of the Struggle

Many of us in the LGBT rights movement felt like the winds were turning against us in 2004, carrying us far off course—perhaps irrevocably. The previous year, the Massachusetts Supreme Judicial Court had approved marriage for same-sex couples, following Vermont's civil unions law in 2000, which created the first statewide legalization of same-sex partnerships. But the progress in those two liberal states, and a few others, helped fuel a concentrated, coordinated backlash across many states in a single year, one that threatened to leave us worse off than we started.

Leading up to the 2004 elections, Republican religious ideologues and operatives placed eleven state constitutional amendments on the ballot that would define marriage as being between one man and one woman only. They had been aiming to settle the rules of marriage for decades, and to motivate people to vote in the presidential election who might otherwise skip it if there wasn't something as contentious as same-sex marriage on the ballot. Voters in all eleven states approved the bans, and George W. Bush won the election.

The strategy was partially devised and coordinated by Ken Mehlman, a closeted gay man who served as the head of the Bush reelection campaign and, subsequently, as the White House political director for most of Bush's first term. Mehlman's strategy included targeting Black churches, aiming to turn out just enough Black voters against same-sex marriage and LGBT people more broadly to create a winning coalition rooted in large numbers of white churches and social conservatives. It was difficult to watch the cynical engagement of Black churches play out that year against the backdrop of Barack

Obama's electrifying speech on the national stage at the Democratic National Convention and the high-profile Democratic primary run of the Reverend Al Sharpton, a Black religious leader outspoken on behalf of LGBT people. But the backlash ran deep across the political spectrum: Gavin Newsom, then mayor of San Francisco, had his speaking role at the DNC taken away because he had issued marriage licenses for same-sex couples and Democrats wanted to cut that issue loose.

At the beginning of 2005, the country was sinking deeper into the immoral, fruitless, multitrillion-dollar war in Iraq, while becoming more beholden to religious conservatives, Big Oil corporations, and right-wing conservatives at every level. I joined GLAAD because I saw that those of us in the LGBT movement were not only facing our own major setbacks but also being blamed for the loss of the 2004 election and the setbacks that loss would bring for others. We were at the beginning of a long-term backlash that would be hard to neutralize and that brought with it dire consequences. Even many GLAAD supporters did not see our work as needing to be integrated into the larger civil rights ecosystem or to contribute to dethroning the reigning conservative regime.

But we had our role to play: Don't take on everything at once, fight the cultural fights around representation that we were born to win, and see how those fights change the calculus for political leaders down the line. I invested in my own ability to make our movement more powerful, deepening my practice related to conducting research, running campaigns, and engaging people across the media landscape—including corporate media. And others were hatching a comeback. Working with grassroots activists and a network of movement leaders across multiple disciplines and sectors, Evan Wolfson at Freedom to Marry and Matt Coles at the ACLU mapped a path through the backlash: scoring state-by-state wins, changing national norms, and taking it all to the courts. It wasn't as linear as it sounds. It depended on a lot of different pieces falling into place in the right way, and adapting or even starting all over again when they didn't.

But by maintaining hope and maximizing the few wins we got, we created belief, then momentum, then success. By the time I left GLAAD to lead Color Of Change in 2011, just six years later, much had shifted.

LGBT representation in both news and entertainment media had become more regular and much fairer. We could fight for representations that moved us forward on issues like same-sex marriage, rather than just fighting to eliminate terrible stereotypes and dehumanizing portrayals. By raising the floor, we gained opportunities to raise the ceiling. Corporations were marketing inclusion. Kamala Harris, as California's attorney general, was marrying gay and lesbian couples. And Ken Mehlman, the architect of the 2004 anti-gay ballot strategy to win Bush's reelection, was not only out of the closet but also in GLAAD's offices offering to help achieve the exact opposite result he had once orchestrated.

I certainly realized in that moment that building power isn't about purity. It's about creating ways for more and more people to join in as time goes on, if it moves us to our ultimate goals—even if I gave Ken a bit of side-eye at the time. It's about addition, not subtraction.

We know that backlash follows progress, almost inevitably. But the question is whether progress can follow the backlash. That is not inevitable at all. Progress requires preparation, leverage, discipline, and participation: A critical number of people must never give up. A critical number of people must contribute whatever they can and adapt to the changing winds rather than being swept away by them. They are the people who keep investing in the thinking, the practices, and the infrastructure that will enable us not only to take advantage of the next opportunity, whenever it comes, but also to force opportunities into existence. I have always been one of those people. And if you have read this far, so are you.

We Can't Go Forward and Backward at the Same Time

New strategies are a response to failed strategies. If we do not concede failure, at least internally, we will never be able to do new things.

And we cannot build strategies for the present as if we are still living in the past.

But the instinct to go backward—to return to plans developed for a different time, to rely on the thinking that's most familiar—runs deep in moments of crisis. When the ground shifts this fast, it is natural to reach for what once felt stable. But nostalgia is not a strategy. And as a Black gay man, there's no time machine I want to step into, no myth of a bygone era I want to return to (except maybe going back for some good music and fashion). The Civil Rights Movement did not fight to return us to an earlier version of the United States. Its hundreds of leaders and millions of followers fought to force the nation to become something it had never been before. That is still our task.

I think about that task when those women stop me in the Amtrak station and thank me for standing for something. I push myself to stand for the right thing, not only in terms of what we're fighting for but also in terms of how we fight, and to correct course when I get it wrong.

Some of the institutions and infrastructure we relied on to defend progress and advance justice are now gone or severely unstable. Others have been captured outright by people hostile to justice and to democracy itself. This is not a temporary disruption; it is a structural transformation, and it requires us to transform, too.

This book argues that we all have a role to play. Raising your voice at work, at your community club, at your school, in your religious organization, or even within your family can set things in motion that might not have been possible in a different time. But the flip side is being able to do that with savvy and in service of a purpose that's more than just making your opinion present. Giving $5 to a cause or candidate, when millions of people are doing the same, can be game-changing for that cause or candidate. But the flip side of that is making sure you can evaluate whether that cause or candidate really has a chance. My goal in this book has been to demystify political dynamics and make that assessment easier. Everyday people and up-and-coming leaders have more opportunities to contribute to progress than ever, and can learn how to do so effectively—whether as an individual, as part of a small group, or as part of a large organization.

At the very beginning of this book, I talked about how the right wing has shown people new ways to get involved in politics and social change. They have trained people to obsess over capturing certain levers of power, like the courts. They have motivated people to fight for radical, often absurd policy changes (like fiercely attacking healthcare, clean water, drag queens, vaccines, funding for science, and the teaching of factual history) that come to symbolize their values, building entire social identities around them. They have encouraged people to embrace the mindset of going on offense and to devote endless time and effort to getting organized—breaking and remaking whatever rules they need to along the way, making the most of every opportunity they can find to use their voice. They have given people a way to tap into their own personal power and turn their outrage into action, even when it felt new and uncomfortable. They have told people that they deserve to win—and that they can.

The strategy driving their movements was clear: Feeling that attending a protest was a meaningful and satisfying act in itself wasn't good enough. They pushed people beyond the experience of merely feeling part of history, to focus on what needed to be done to *make* history. And the billionaires funding their movements were often more radical than the people in them—not only encouraging extreme action but leading the way.

That same passion, drive, and ingenuity is also on display all the time among people who fight for justice and progress. So many everyday people have stepped up in new ways just since the beginning of 2025. But we need more people, more committed, and more focused on the right goals. And we need to eliminate the barriers that hold them back.

We're at a time of enormous disruption and possibility in terms of how power works—for example, how stories move through media, culture, and people's lives. We must invest in the power of individual media creators who can help power our movements, even if they operate in unfamiliar ways. That means amplifying them, supporting them financially, helping them stay on course when they falter, or even becoming one of them. And it certainly means helping to connect them so that they can become more than the sum of their parts, and we are not reliant only on celebrities, traditional news outlets, and traditional TV hosts to do all our engagement for us. The traditional media no longer reach into people's lives and influence them at the deepest level, the way that social media influencers, on-the-ground organizers, religious leaders, and other engaging people can.

For leaders of organizations (and the wealthy individuals and institutions that support them), that means bringing forward talented people who can invent new forms of leverage while also creating ecosystems that elevate high-impact messengers. **It means accepting that influence now travels through human beings just as much as it does through logos, and that building power in this era means investing in a chorus of individual voices.**

The new communications reality will make some people in leadership positions uncomfortable. We are used to funding institutions, not individuals. We are used to measuring reach through mailing lists, not relationships. We are used to thinking about staff capacity, not storytelling power. But we need to turn our thinking around if we want to turn this country around.

If all of this feels daunting, it should. But it should also sharpen us, not freeze us in place. We are not the first people to face a moment when democracy felt fragile and the future felt uncertain. What is different is the terrain: digital, accelerated, fragmented, flooded with lies that travel faster than truth, and full of more high-stakes fights affecting our lives than we can even track. But the underlying challenge is the same: Will we allow a very few people to continue concentrating power in their own hands, or will we get organized enough to claim that power for ourselves—and for the benefit of the many? The answer is in finding the specific ability you can add to make a movement more powerful—whether you are part of the offense or part of the defense.

James Baldwin once wrote, "Not everything that is faced can be changed, but nothing can be changed until it is faced." That is where we are. Just as we cannot romanticize the past, we cannot wish away the present; we can only decide how seriously we are willing to meet it.

The road ahead will reward those who are willing to organize differently, fund differently, lead differently, build infrastructure differently, and participate differently. It will not reward those who cling to methods that once worked but no longer do. We are not going back to what was. The question at the heart of this moment is not whether the future will be different—it already is. The question is: Who will internalize the essential lessons for becoming powerful enough to shape it?

I've argued here that presence alone will never produce power; that visibility without leverage is a trap; that storytelling without strategy is mere performance; and that real change is made not by being seen, but by being organized. I have also argued that injustice is not just ideological—it is economic. Racism is not only a cultural problem—it is a business model. Authoritarianism is not just a political threat—it is an investment strategy. If we want a different future, we must change the incentive structures that make harm profitable and humanity optional—doing whatever it takes to convert presence into power.

Many of us are here, living in this country today, despite people having tried to deny our existence or even prevent us from continuing to exist at all. In many moments of history, we were not supposed to survive. It may have seemed inevitable that we wouldn't. But we did. And we made the world better. Today's America couldn't have been made without us, even though its rules are still not made *for* us. Because we have not yet completed that work, we now stand again in the middle of another challenge of survival—knowing we must do more than merely survive while others force us to live under the constant threat of their dominance.

One belief that a history of survival can give us, if we embrace it, is that contributing to the betterment of ourselves and the world is our special purpose as a people. I see the power of that purpose whenever I look at all the ways neighbors stood up for neighbors in Minnesota and everywhere Trump's violent, illegal police force tried to break up communities—fighting not only for their neighbors to survive but also for their idea of America to survive. I see it when journalists and other storytellers leave the corporate media outlets that won't let them speak the truth and set up shop on multiple other platforms, committed to reaching and building audiences without that interference. Ministers demonstrate that purpose, and what it takes to beat the odds, when they buck the trend of their peers by promoting love over hate and showing that the way forward in faith runs through solidarity and not division, exclusion, and the convenient blotting out of all the words in scripture that have to do with justice. It's the young person launching a new effort to organize young people and change the trajectory of their generation's contributions, and the older person recommitting and reinvigorating efforts to organize their families, communities, and industries. It's the lawyers, businesspeople, healthcare professionals, and others who reject the training and incentives of their fields that tell them to fall in line, and instead find ways to expand the boundaries of the change they can advance.

Those are the efforts that help illuminate the path to the power we all need to walk to ensure our existence and our fulfillment as a people—and as a country. My hope is that this book has helped chart that path, helped you find your place on it, and helped you make sure you never walk it alone.

Acknowledgments

I first started thinking about writing this book after the 2016 election. I had just come off a series of winning issue campaigns and an election cycle where I helped develop a strategy to defeat a number of regressive prosecutors and support candidates running on progressive platforms—at the same time that Donald Trump was elected president.

I sat in rooms full of magical thinking, where leaders from the last campaign tried to place themselves at the center of the "resistance." During that time, I put forward a new framework for how to think about our work—an opposition strategy that laid out how the Trump administration differed from previous Republican administrations, and how we would have to organize our time, resources, and advocacy not just to resist but to win.

That document became the framework for a new piece of infrastructure I helped co-found: the Fight Back Table, a progressive collaboration that is still operating today.

In those rooms, I began to recognize a familiar pattern: Some people in our movement get to be the "thinkers" and the "strategists," while others are cast as the "boots on the ground." To be clear, there is nothing wrong with being boots on the ground—but the real decisions so often happen in strategist spaces, and the people in those rooms rarely have to produce receipts to get there.

I came to realize that if I didn't get my ideas onto the page, I would continue to be invited to tell stories of success while others decided how those wins would be interpreted, replicated, resourced, and led going forward. One of the goals of this book is to make an intervention in how strategy is shaped going forward.

This book is also the product of more people than I can possibly name, and a lifetime of work, collaborations, partnerships, and conversations. It reflects decades of learning, arguing, organizing, listening, staying close to brave people, and trying—again and again—to understand how power actually works in service of winning real change.

Collaborators, Readers, and My Sounding Board

Movements don't happen alone—and neither do books like this.

To my collaborators and co-conspirators across organizations, campaigns, and cycles of progress and struggle: Thank you for trusting me, building with me, and believing in this project.

First and foremost, my friend and longtime partner in strategy and idea generation, Ryan Senser. He was the first person I sat with when I began mapping the ideas for this book—and the last person I talked to before I hit send to the publisher. Ryan didn't just believe in the concept; he believed in me as a leader and thinker. He brought his own talent and experience as we wrestled with the ideas at the heart of this work.

To my creative, curious, and incredibly encouraging editor, Elizabeth Méndez Berry: You made me believe I would finish this book even when I didn't. You were patient as I pushed back on your smart recommendations, only for me to return later and realize you were right. At the very beginning, you told me you would be an advocate for the reader—and this book is better because you kept that promise. Thank you for believing in me and this project.

To my literary agent, Gail Ross, who had my back from proposal to rollout—you encouraged me when things stalled and told me the truth when they got hard. I'm grateful for both.

There are many brilliant thinkers, researchers, and strategists who gave me advice, support, and careful eyes along the way: Sophia Tu, Eleanor Morison, Josie Duffy Rice, and Theo Emery, who gave incredible assistance with research; Dorian Warren, who generously "interviewed" me for hours of recorded conversations I was able to transcribe and shape; and the fact checkers Alexa O'Brien and Howard Cohn.

There are also people I cannot imagine surviving the last several years without, a crew that celebrated my achievements, held me through challenges, and inspired me through their work and commitment: Alicia Garza, Heather McGhee, Michael Smith, Andre Banks, Anthony Romero, Michael Bell, Ai-Jen Poo, Robert Raben, Sarah Williams, Alexis McGill Johnson, Brandon Sharp, Safiya Noble, Trishala Deb, Alphonso David, Monifa Bandele, Angela Rye, Katherine Grainger, Chloe Cockburn, Ashley Allison, Jeremy Heimans, Wayne Jordan, Tricia Rose, Yolanda Caraway, Jenn Stowe, Alvin Starks, Kendrick Sampson, Keith Boykin, Jose Antonio Vargas, and dream hampton.

My thinking has also been informed by a long list of friends, collaborators, supporters, and sparring partners who have and continue to push me, provide feedback, and give me hope that we will win: Joy Reid, Melissa Harris-Perry, Janet Dewart Bell, Pamela Shifman, Vanita Gupta, Judith Browne Dianis, Darren Walker, Tanya Coke, Sherrilyn Ifill, Laura Murphy, Charles Blow, Evan Wolfson, Seema Sadanandan, Deepak Bhargava, Felicia Wong, LaTosha Brown, Erica Corbin, Bridgit Antoinette Evans, Vivian Schiller, Dr. Rev. William Barber II, Congresswomen Ayanna Pressley and Lateefah Simon, Senator Elizabeth Warren, Emil Wilbekin, Prince Harry and Meghan, the Duke and Duchess of Sussex, Lori Bezahler, Sabeel Rahman, Rupa Balasubramanian, Héctor Sánchez Barba, Tamika Mallory, Rob Richie, Ellen Dorsey, Laleh Ispahani, Patrisse Cullors, Cristina Jiménez, Michael Vachon, Rami Nashashibi, Clarence Patton, Nina Turner, April Verrett, Keesha Gaskins-Nathan, Kim Anderson, Gara LaMarche, Tarana Burke, Sarah Elizabeth Lewis, Anna Galland, Maurice Mitchell, Marisa Franco, Carmen Rojas, Michele Jawando, Linda Sarsour, Christina Greer, Warrington Hudlin, Noorain Khan, Charmaine Mercer, Fatima Goss-Graves, Margaret Huang, Damon Hewitt, Mutale Nkonde, Mara Brock Akil, Braeden Lentz, Desmond and Sheena Meade, Tom Perriello, Alexander Soros, Sanjay Pinto, Imara Jones, Roland Martin, Rev. Mark Thompson, Adrianne Shropshire, Terrance Woodbury, Gina Belafonte, Lola West, Anurima Bhargava, Steve Bumbaugh, David Coleman, Ava DuVernay, Lumumba Akinwole-Bandele, Kirsten West Savali, Emily Jenda, Marianne Manilov, Jane Fonda, Annie Leonard, Tavis Smiley, Lena Waithe, Darnell Moore, John Legend, Nadine Smith, Tiffany Cross, Don Lemon, Asha Bandele, Nii-Quartelai Quartey, Samiya Bashir, Kendra Fox-Davis, Quinn Delaney, Patty Quillin, Scott Budnick, Alison Morgan, Molly Munger, Alan Jenkins, Kirsten Levingston, Darlene Nipper, Tara McGowan, Cliff Albright, Chris Hughes, Derrick Johnson, Rev. Al Sharpton, Melanie Campbell, Nikole Hannah-Jones, Glynda Carr, Clay Cane, Veena Sud, Tracey Sturdivant, L. Joy Williams, Malkia Cyril, Jessica Brand, Jessica González, Joe Torres, Becky Pringle, Whitney Tymas, Marisa Renee Lee, Kevin Jennings, Kevin Hager, Justin Krebs, Tess Hetzel, Yasmine Yu, Shane Martin, Darlene Nipper, Marcus Littles, Sherrie Deans, Nick Turner, John Meigs, Cristóbal Alex, Maya Harris, Craig Aaron, Meredith Sumpter, Christina Hollenback, Rashida Bumbray, the team at Sunshine Sachs Morgan & Lylis (SSM&L), Leigh Chapman, Micaela Fernandez Allen, Binaifer Nowrojee, Gina Clayton-Johnson, Christal Jackson, Lorella Praeli, Colin Williams, Joan A. Davis, Patricia Jerido, Michelle Coffey, Patrick Gaspard, Laura Silber, Yasin Yaqubie, Peter Murray, Kavitha Mediratta, Roz Lee, Beverly Tillery, Baron Vaughn, Janiece Evans-Page, Mary Kay Henry, Randi Weingarten, Michael B. Jordan, René Spellman, Alicin Reidy Williamson, Michelle Ringuette, Ryan Coogler, Sarah Jones, Janos Marton, Bruce Cohen, Rinku Sen, Helena Huang, Becky Wasserman, Tiffany Warren, Edgar Villanueva, Nina Shaw, Caroline Edwards, Kate Kendell, Marc Solomon, Rodney McKenzie, Carrie Twigg, Adrienne Warren, Mara Verheyden-Hilliard, David Mitrani, Joe Sandler, Valerie Berlin, Alberto Means, Deon Jones, Trymaine Lee, David Johns, John Basnage, Brady Walkinshaw, Taryn Higashi, Adey Fisseha, Tonya Allen, and so many more.

And colleagues who helped me hone my leadership across years and institutions—at FairVote and Right to Vote Campaign, GLAAD (Joan Garry, Neil Giuliano, Glennda Testone, Sean Lund, Cindi Creager, Tom Ogletree, Diana Rodríguez, Rich Ferraro, Daryl Hannah, Aaron Walton, Cordey Lash, Yvette Burton, Shana Naomi Krochmal, Sean Piazza, and more); and Color Of Change (James Rucker, Heidi Hess, Van Jones, Gabriel Rey-Goodlatte, Valerie Brown, Arisha Hatch, Ian Fuller, Sarah Min, Rashid Shabazz, Alicia Meeks, Jennifer Edwards, Amanda Brown Lierman, Alana Mayo, Erica Williams Simon, Archana Sahgal, Paul Butler, and more).

Editorial Gratitude

In addition to Elizabeth, there was an extraordinary team at One World Penguin Random House, led by Chris Jackson—someone I admired long before we ever worked together. His leadership, insight, and editorial rigor made this book stronger, clearer, and more focused.

Oma Beharry—thank you for your grace with my bumpy landings into deadlines.

To the entire One World team: thank you. On the production and editorial team: Evan Camfield, Janet Renard, Allison Fox, Jennifer Backe, Kevin Quach, and Michael Morris. And on the publishing team: Milena Brown, Raaga Rajagopala, Katryce Campbell, and Jocelynn Pedro.

Family

Everything I know about responsibility, discipline, and possibility began at home.

To my parents, Everett and Shirley: Thank you for raising me with expectation and love—for believing in me early and loudly, and for teaching me that success isn't just about achievement, but about hard work.

To my partner, Amin Gates: I have never met anyone like you. You are fully your own man, with clarity and confidence, and you make space for me to be big without ever shrinking yourself. You have not only made my life better, but you've also been so patient through late nights and even vacations—while I sat at the computer typing—a witness to this process, a sounding board to my ideas, and a fountain of support and love when I needed it most.

To my brother, Jamar, one of the most hopeful and optimistic people I know. Most people wouldn't know what to do with half of what you've faced, yet you've built a home with your hands, a thriving business with your talent and hard work, and a beautiful family with my incredible sister-in-law Christina, raising some of the best kids I've ever known—Camden, Elon, and Cairo—it is inspiring. Thank you for making Beewell Farms in Vermont feel like another home.

To my late maternal grandparents, Charlie and Matilda; my paternal grandmother, Mary Robinson, who proudly shows visitors the photo she keeps of me with President Obama and still, at ninety-three, cuts me a slice of her famous pound cake even when I pretend I don't want dessert; and my late grandfather, Eugene, who—along with her—attended recital after recital, speech after speech as I grew up.

To my Aunt Theo and late Uncle Arnold; my Uncle Gene and late Aunt Caulie; my late Uncle Gerald, whom I never got to really know but think about often; my cousin Jason Jackson; my godsiblings Erica and Antonio Rodriguez; my godson Riaz; and the many other aunts, uncles, cousins, family friends who supported my activism from the very beginning and walked with me as I grew into myself—thank you.

I am deeply blessed to be held up by a community of love.

Friends Who Held Me Through It

Writing a book is a strange kind of vulnerability.

To the friends who checked on me, made me laugh, sent voice notes, and refused to let me disappear inside my anxiety—you were as essential as any footnote:

Jason Cooper, Malia Lazu, Danielle Moodie, Devon Johnson, Nathan Hale Williams, Aisha Mills, Cassim Shepard, Ryan Palsrok, Alphonso Morgan, Phillip Osaki, Taj Brown, Yemi Dele Akinyemi, Randy Calle—and so many more.

This list could go on for pages. You know who you are. And I hope you know how deeply I love and appreciate you.

Notes

Introduction

1. For the story of the Central Park Five, see the TV miniseries *When They See Us,* directed by Ava DuVernay (Netflix, 2019).

1. Presence Is Not Enough

1. U.S. House of Representatives, Select Bipartisan Committee to Investigate the Preparation for and Response to Hurricane Katrina, "FEMA Preparedness," in *A Failure of Initiative: Final Report of the Select Bipartisan Committee to Investigate the Preparation for and Response to Hurricane Katrina* (U.S. Government Printing Office, February 15, 2006), 151–61, nrc.gov/docs/ML1209/ML12093A081.pdf.
2. U.S. House Committee on Homeland Security Democratic Staff, report prepared for Congressman Bennie G. Thompson, *Trouble Exposed: Katrina, Rita, and the Red Cross: A Familiar History* (U.S. House of Representatives, 2006), democrats-homeland.house.gov/imo/media/doc/redcrossreport.pdf.
3. For more on State Farm and the way insurance corporations make climate disasters worse for Black and other targeted

communities, including bluelining (the practice of saying there is too much fraud in Black communities to insure people in them, when it's the insurance corporations themselves that are committing the fraud), see Lindsey Fenlock, Charles Slidders, and Nikki Reisch, "Is Bluelining the 'New' Redlining? How Insurance Discrimination Deepens Climate Disparities," Center for International Environmental Law, August 9, 2024, ciel.org/bluelining-insurance-discrimination-climate-crisis; "State Farm Subsidiary to Pay $100M for False Katrina Claims," Associated Press, August 24, 2022, apnews.com/article/lawsuits-mississippi-hurricanes-legal-proceedings-d8ca251ec9f6e6ead832c7b6577bd9a3; Emily Flitter, "Where State Farm Sees 'a Lot of Fraud,' Black Customers See Discrimination," *New York Times,* March 18, 2022, nytimes.com/2022/03/18/business/state-farm-fraud-black-customers.html; Emily Flitter, "New Suit Uses Data to Back Racial Bias Claims Against State Farm," *New York Times,* December 14, 2022, nytimes.com/2022/12/14/business/state-farm-racial-bias-lawsuit.html.

4. On racially biased and inaccurate news media coverage related to Hurricane Katrina, see Rhonda Sonnenberg, "The Picture of Prejudice: Media Portrayals of Black Survivors in Katrina's Wake," Southern Poverty Law Center, September 2, 2025, splcenter.org/resources/reports/hurricane-katrina-racial-stigma; and Samuel R. Sommers, Evan P. Apfelbaum, Kristin N. Dukes, Negin Toosi, and Elsie J. Wang, "Race and Media Coverage of Hurricane Katrina: Analysis, Implications, and Future Research Questions," *Analyses of Social Issues and Public Policy* 6, no. 1 (2006): 39–55, spssi.onlinelibrary.wiley.com/doi/epdf/10.1111/j.1530-2415.2006.00103.x.

2. Power Is Making (or Breaking) the Rules

1. Adrienne Cobb, "Project 2025 Tracker," project2025.observer/en. See also Center for Progressive Reform, "Project 2025

Executive Action Tracker," progressivereform.org/tracking-trump-2/project-2025-executive-action-tracker.

2. Edwin Meese III, Stuart M. Butler, and Kim R. Holmes, *From Tragedy to Triumph: Principled Solutions for Rebuilding Lives and Communities* (Heritage Foundation, September 15, 2005), 1, web.archive.org/web/20051115014950/https://www.heritage.org/Research/GovernmentReform/sr05.cfm.
3. See "Danziger Bridge Shootings," *Wikipedia,* en.wikipedia.org/wiki/Danziger_Bridge_shootings; and *Times-Picayune,* ProPublica, and *PBS Frontline,* "Law & Disorder: An On-Air and Online Investigation into Questionable Police Shootings by the New Orleans Police Department in the Wake of Katrina," *PBS Frontline,* August 25, 2010, pbs.org/wgbh/frontline/documentary/law-disorder. Many are familiar with the New Orleans Police Department killings and woundings of unarmed people on the Danziger Bridge and the subsequent cover-up, but police violence was revealed to be even more systemic—the *Frontline* documentary reported that "new evidence shows that an order was given authorizing officers to shoot looters."
4. John R. Wilke and Brody Mullins, "After Katrina, Republicans Back a Sea of Conservative Ideas," *The Wall Street Journal,* September 15, 2005, https://www.wsj.com/articles/SB112674719461641356.
5. Naomi Klein, "GOP Opportunity Zone," *The Nation,* October 10, 2005, thenation.com/article/archive/gop-opportunity-zone.
6. Lisa Myers and Richard Gardella, "$229,000 FEMA Trailers," NBC News, November 15, 2007, nbcnews.com/id/wbna21824609. "The agency spent more on trailers as temporary housing for hurricane victims than it would have cost to buy new houses."
7. Paul Kadetz, "New Orleans: A Lesson in Post-Disaster Resilience," *Forced Migration Review* 45, February 2014, fmreview.org/crisis/kadetz. "Disasters can effectively create a blank

slate for states and venture capitalists to take advantage of and potentially make permanent the displacement of marginalised people," Kadetz writes, citing Naomi Klein, *The Shock Doctrine: The Rise of Disaster Capitalism* (New York: Henry Holt, 2007). He then provides the destruction of the affordable housing units in post-Katrina New Orleans as an example.

8. Certain members of Congress (and voters across the country) raised many questions about the bailout at the time, objecting to its terms. See Sheryl Gay Stolberg, "Constituents Make Their Bailout Views Known," *New York Times,* September 24, 2008, nytimes.com/2008/09/25/business/25voices.html.

3. How to Make Injustice Unprofitable

1. David D. Kirkpatrick, "The Number: How Much Is Trump Pocketing off the Presidency?," *New Yorker,* August 11, 2025, newyorker.com/magazine/2025/08/18/the-number.
2. In her book *Race for Profit: How Banks and the Real Estate Industry Undermined Black Homeownership* (Chapel Hill: University of North Carolina Press, 2019), a finalist for the Pulitzer Prize in History, Keeanga-Yamahtta Taylor provides a very clear example of how governments can facilitate and accelerate racial profiteering, even under the deceptive guise of racial progress: "[In the late 1960s], new policies meant to encourage low-income homeownership created new methods to exploit Black homeowners. The federal government guaranteed urban mortgages in an attempt to overcome resistance to lending to Black buyers—as if unprofitability, rather than racism, was the cause of housing segregation. Bankers, investors, and real estate agents took advantage of the perverse incentives, targeting the Black women most likely to fail to keep up their home payments [due to the many other factors of racism they faced] and slip into foreclosure, multiplying their profits. As a result, by the end of the 1970s, the

nation's first programs to encourage Black homeownership ended with tens of thousands of foreclosures in Black communities across the country. The push to uplift Black homeownership had descended into a goldmine for realtors and mortgage lenders, and a ready-made cudgel for the champions of deregulation to wield against government intervention of any kind."

3. "Why Critics Are Alarmed About the Influence of PragerU's Educational Videos," *PBS News Hour,* September 15, 2025, pbs.org/newshour/show/why-critics-are-alarmed-about-the-influence-of-pragerus-educational-videos.

4. Perceptions Define Solutions

1. Ivan Penn, Peter Evans, and James Glanz, "How PG&E Ignored Fire Risks in Favor of Profits," *New York Times,* March 18, 2019, nytimes.com/interactive/2019/03/18/business/pge-california-wildfires.html.
2. Scott Waldman and Thomas Frank, "Trump Refused to Give California Wildfire Aid Until Told How Many People There Voted for Him, Ex-Aide Says," *Politico,* October 3, 2024, politico.com/news/2024/10/03/helene-trump-politics-natural-disaster-00182419.
3. Lauren Sommer, "Kerr County Struggled to Fund Flood Warnings. Under Trump, It's Getting Even Harder," *All Things Considered,* NPR, July 10, 2025, npr.org/2025/07/10/nx-s1-5461091/texas-flooding-warning-system-fema.
4. Kailong Ji and Tierra S. Bills, "Wildfire Recovery and Resilience Strategies for Resource-Constrained and Vulnerable Communities," University of California Los Angeles Institute of Transportation Studies, February 28, 2025, its.ucla.edu/publication/wildfire-recovery-and-resilience-strategies-for-resource-constrained-and-vulnerable-communities.
5. UCLA Latino Policy & Politics Institute, "UCLA Analysis

Finds Altadena Faces Uneven Wildfire Recovery," press release, October 17, 2025, luskin.ucla.edu/ucla-analysis-finds-altadena-faces-uneven-wildfire-recovery.

6. Liz Landers and Doug Adams, "How Trump Is Using Presidential Pardon Power in New Ways," *PBS News Hour,* PBS, December 3, 2025, transcript: pbs.org/newshour/show/how-trump-is-using-presidential-pardon-power-in-new-ways.

5. The Written and Unwritten Rules

1. For a brief history of the meaning of the colors pink and blue—and how pink was once designated for boys and blue for girls—see Susan Bell, "Pink for Boys and Blue for Girls: The Colorful History of Things Designed for Kids," University of Southern California, December 22, 2017, today.usc.edu/pink-for-boys-and-blue-for-girls-the-colorful-history-of-things-designed-for-kids; and Jeanne Maglaty and Meilan Solly, "Unraveling the Colorful History of Why Girls Wear Pink and Boys Wear Blue," *Smithsonian Magazine,* April 23, 2025 (originally published April 7, 2011), smithsonianmag.com/history/unraveling-the-colorful-history-of-why-girls-wear-pink-and-boys-wear-blue-1370097/.
2. "GOP Marks Women's History Month with Bill Restricting Women's Votes," Defend the Vote, March 6, 2025, wedefendthevote.org/gop-marks-womens-history-month-with-bill-restricting-womens-votes.

6. Outsmarting the Blame Game

1. Anahad O'Connor, "How the Sugar Industry Shifted Blame to Fat," *New York Times,* September 12, 2016, nytimes.com/2016/09/13/well/eat/how-the-sugar-industry-shifted-blame-to-fat.html.
2. Chelsea Brasted, "New Orleans Used to Have a Strong

Teachers Union. Then Katrina Happened," *Axios,* April 24, 2024, axios.com/local/new-orleans/2024/04/24/new-orleans-teachers-union-hurricane-katrina.

3. Rashad Robinson, "The People Who Undermine Progressive Prosecutors," *New York Times,* June 11, 2020, nytimes.com/2020/06/11/opinion/george-floyd-prosecutors.html.
4. Olivia Land, "Fuming Joe Scarborough Blames Racism, Misogyny from Black and Hispanic Voters for Harris' Loss," *New York Post,* November 6, 2024, nypost.com/2024/11/06/us-news/fuming-joe-scarborough-blames-racism-misogyny-among-black-and-hispanic-voters-for-harris-loss.

8. Building the Infrastructure of Power

1. I was able to keep learning about Bayard Rustin thanks in part to *Boycott,* directed by Clark Johnson (HBO, 2001), hbomax.com/movies/boycott/a2909c85-8ff3-476c-a1c0-91c284525852; *Brother Outsider: The Life of Bayard Rustin,* directed by Nancy Kates and Bennett Singer (PBS POV, 2003), pbs.org/pov/films/brotheroutsider/; John D'Emilio, *Lost Prophet: The Life and Times of Bayard Rustin* (Chicago: University of Chicago Press, 2004); and *Rustin,* directed by George C. Wolfe (Netflix, 2023). I also contributed to a book of essays about Rustin; see "The Art of the Actual," in *Bayard Rustin: A Legacy of Protest and Politics,* ed. Michael Long (New York: New York University Press, 2024), 190–92, jstor.org/stable/jj.13944164.
2. Bayard Rustin, "Memo to Dr. Martin Luther King, Jr." The Martin Luther King Jr. Research and Education Institute, Stanford University, December 23, 1956, kinginstitute.stanford.edu/king-papers/documents/bayard-rustin-0.
3. "March on Washington for Jobs and Freedom," National Park Service, last updated November 20, 2023, nps.gov/articles/march-on-washington.htm.
4. Matthew Cooper, "5 Secrets of the March on Washington,"

National Journal, August 22, 2013, yahoo.com/news/5-secrets-march-washington-061706458.html.

5. "Bayard Rustin: The Gay, Black Civil Rights Activist," Illinois Public Media, January 16, 2026, will.illinois.edu/dialogue/episode/bayard-rustin-the-gay-black-civil-rights-activist. The quote is from a 1963 speech in New York City.
6. Douglas MacMillan and Jonathan O'Connell, "ICE Documents Reveal Plan to Hold 80,000 Immigrants in Warehouses," *The Washington Post*, December 24, 2025, washingtonpost.com/business/2025/12/24/ice-immigrants-detention-warehouses-deportation-trump.
7. Tim Walker, "Educators Fight Back Against Gag Orders, Book Bans and Intimidation," National Education Association, July 28, 2022, nea.org/nea-today/all-news-articles/educators-fight-back-against-gag-orders-book-bans-and-intimidation.
8. "Project 2025 and Unions," AFL-CIO, betterinaunion.org/project-2025.

9. Building Winning Narratives

1. Rashad Robinson, "Changing Our Narrative About Narrative," Color Of Change, April 2018, rashadrobinson.com/narrativepower.
2. Dan P. McAdams, "Truth," in *The Strange Case of Donald J. Trump: A Psychological Reckoning* (New York: Oxford University Press, 2020), 96–118.
3. *Fresh Air*, "Whistleblower Explains How Cambridge Analytica Helped Fuel U.S. 'Insurgency,'" NPR, October 8, 2019, transcript: npr.org/transcripts/768216311.
4. President Donald J. Trump, "Remarks by President Trump," Vice President Pence, and Members of the Coronavirus Task Force in Press Briefing, The White House, April 23, 2020, transcript: trumpwhitehouse.archives.gov/briefings-statements/remarks-president-trump-vice-president-pence-members-coronavirus-task-force-press-briefing-31.

5. Daniel T. O'Brien, Chelsea Farrell, and Brandon C. Welsh, "Broken (Windows) Theory: A Meta-Analysis of the Evidence for the Pathways from Neighborhood Disorder to Resident Health Outcomes and Behaviors," *Social Science & Medicine* 228 (2019): 272–92, doi.org/10.1016/j.socscimed.2018.11.015.
6. Terry-Ann Craigie and Ames Grawert, "Bail Reform and Public Safety: Evidence from 33 Cities," Brennan Center for Justice at NYU Law, August 15, 2024, brennancenter.org/media/13174/download/bail-reform-public-safety-report.pdf?inline=1. This report outlines bail reforms and their effects across the country from 2015 to 2021. It concludes:

    > This report discredits theories linking bail reform to recent increases in crime. We find no evidence to support such a connection, even after testing different types of reform in jurisdictions across the country. This finding should not be surprising: Claims that bail reform increases crime incorrectly assume that it requires the release of people who may threaten the community. In fact, in most cases judges retain broad discretion to prioritize public safety—without the distorting influence of money. It follows that the best explanations for the midpandemic spike in violent crime lie beyond bail policy, as do the best solutions to reduce violent and property crime.

7. Kimberly Kindy, "Insurers Force Change on Police Departments Long Resistant to It," *Washington Post*, September 14, 2022, washingtonpost.com/investigations/interactive/2022/police-misconduct-insurance-settlements-reform.

11. Avoiding the Traps of Magical Thinking

1. Ryan J. Reilly and Julia Craven, "Federal Bureau of Prisons Fires Head of an Obama-Era Education Effort, Putting Reform Under Trump in Doubt," *Huffington Post*, May 19, 2017,

huffpost.com/entry/bureau-of-prisons-education-reform_n_591f2289e4b094cdba53c398.

2. Exec. Order No. 07790, 90 FR 18765 (2025), federalregister.gov/documents/2025/05/02/2025-07790/strengthening-and-unleashing-americas-law-enforcement-to-pursue-criminals-and-protect-innocent.
3. Sam Raim, "Trump's First 100 Days: Friend or Foe to Criminal Justice Reform?," Vera Institute of Justice, May 13, 2025, vera.org/trumps-first-100-days-friend-or-foe-to-criminal-justice-reform.
4. For further reading on Russian interference in both the 2016 and 2020 elections, including the role of Facebook in facilitating that interference, see Alliance for Securing Democracy Staff, "Fact Sheet: What We Know About Russia's Interference Operations," German Marshall Fund of the United States, undated, gmfus.org/news/fact-sheet-what-we-know-about-russias-interference-operations; Young Mie Kim, "New Evidence Shows How Russia's Election Interference Has Gotten More Brazen," Brennan Center for Justice, March 5, 2020, brennancenter.org/our-work/analysis-opinion/new-evidence-shows-how-russias-election-interference-has-gotten-more; Kaitlyn Tiffany, "Nobody Look at Mark Zuckerberg: Facebook Doesn't Want Attention Right Now," *The Atlantic,* November 4, 2024, theatlantic.com/technology/archive/2024/11/meta-election-policy-2024/680532; and Hailey Reissman, "A New Study Uncovers How Information Spread on Facebook in the Lead Up to and After the 2020 Election," Annenberg School for Communication, University of Pennsylvania, December 11, 2024, asc.upenn.edu/news-events/news/new-study-uncovers-how-information-spread-facebook-lead-and-after-2020-election.
5. Rachelle Hampton, "The Most Underplayed Story of the 2016 Election Is Voter Suppression," *New Republic,* October 19, 2017, newrepublic.com/article/145387/underplayed-story-2016-election-voter-suppression.

6. Kevin Morris, Peter Miller, and Coryn Grange, "Racial Turnout Gap Grew in Jurisdictions Previously Covered by the Voting Rights Act," Brennan Center for Justice, August 20, 2021, brennancenter.org/our-work/research-reports/racial-turnout-gap-grew-jurisdictions-previously-covered-voting-rights.
7. Colin Dwyer, "Donald Trump: 'I Could . . . Shoot Somebody, and I Wouldn't Lose Any Voters,'" NPR, January 23, 2016, npr.org/sections/thetwo-way/2016/01/23/464129029/donald-trump-i-could-shoot-somebody-and-i-wouldnt-lose-any-voters.
8. Ten front-page stories by *The New York Times,* published right before the election and amplified by the entire news ecosystem, along with irresponsibly ignorant intrusions into the election by FBI Director James Comey, made sure that enough people wanted Hillary Clinton to be canceled to sway the election. See Duncan J. Watts and David M. Rothschild, "Don't Blame the Election on Fake News. Blame It on the Media," *Columbia Journalism Review,* December 5, 2017, cjr.org/analysis/fake-news-media-election-trump.php.

12: Corporations and the Landscape of Power

1. I've heard similar comments from people in labor unions talking about how many workers across America—including their own members—see the safety rules, health coverage, overtime, sick time, and other benefits they get as coming from benevolent employers who choose to give them all the good things they deserve. The truth is that it was the labor unions that organized and dragged corporate executives, kicking and screaming, to the bargaining table—to force them to implement rules of work that worked for workers. It's a powerful story, but it's not one everyone knows.
2. Terri Gerstein, "How District Attorneys and State Attorneys General Are Fighting Workplace Abuses: An Introduction to Criminal Prosecutions of Wage Theft and Other Employer

Crimes Against Workers," Economic Policy Institute, May 17, 2021, epi.org/224957.

13. Taking On Big Tech Profiteering

1. See "A Look Behind the Screens: Examining the Data Practices of Social Media and Video Streaming Services," Federal Trade Commission, September 2024, ftc.gov/system/files/ftc_gov/pdf/Social-Media-6b-Report-9-11-2024.pdf; and Natasha Singer, "What You Don't Know About How Facebook Uses Your Data," *New York Times,* April 11, 2018, nytimes.com/2018/04/11/technology/facebook-privacy-hearings.html.
2. Donald Trump is even going after his own niece, using a claim about an NDA to do it. See Kit Yona, "Trump v. Trump Allowed to Proceed as Judge Refuses to Delay Trial," FindLaw, June 10, 2025, findlaw.com/legalblogs/courtside/trump-v-trump-allowed-to-proceed-as-judge-refuses-to-delay-trial.
3. Paulina Villegas, "NDAs Have Long Been Used to Silence the Abused, Advocates Say. A New Law May Change That," *Washington Post,* February 8, 2021, washingtonpost.com/business/2021/02/08/california-silenced-no-more-act.
4. Access Now et al., "An Open Letter to the CEOs of Facebook's Largest Institutional Shareholders," May 2, 2018, static1.squarespace.com/static/57693891579fb3ab7149f04b/t/5ae9e204aa4a99634fa0a213/1525277190443/Open+Letter+to+Facebook+Investors_FinalFormat.pdf.
5. Mike Isaac, "Facebook's Decisions Were 'Setbacks for Civil Rights,' Audit Finds," *New York Times,* July 8, 2020, nytimes.com/2020/07/08/technology/facebook-civil-rights-audit.html. For the full audit, see *Facebook's Civil Rights Audit—Final Report,* led by Laura W. Murphy and Megan Cacace (Facebook, July 8, 2020), about.fb.com/wp-content/uploads/2020/07/Civil-Rights-Audit-Final-Report.pdf.
6. Quoted in Craig Timberg, Elizabeth Dwoskin, and Reed Albergotti, "Inside Facebook, Jan. 6 Violence Fueled Anger,

Regret over Missed Warning Signs," *Washington Post*, October 22, 2021, washingtonpost.com/technology/2021/10/22/jan-6-capitol-riot-facebook.

7. Craig Silverman, Craig Timberg, Jeff Kao, and Jeremy B. Merrill, "Facebook Hosted Surge of Misinformation and Insurrection Threats in Months Leading Up to Jan. 6 Attack, Records Show," ProPublica and *Washington Post*, January 4, 2022, propublica.org/article/facebook-hosted-surge-of-misinformation-and-insurrection-threats-in-months-leading-up-to-jan-6-attack-records-show.
8. For details on Mark Zuckerberg and Facebook's role undermining democracy across the globe, see Catherine Tsalikis, "Maria Ressa: 'Facebook Broke Democracy in Many Countries Around the World, Including in Mine,'" Centre for International Governance Innovation, September 18, 2019, cigionline.org/articles/maria-ressa-facebook-broke-democracy-many-countries-around-world-including-mine.
9. "Independent Rights Expert Says Emerging Technologies Entrenching Racism, Discrimination," United Nations, July 15, 2020, news.un.org/en/story/2020/07/1068441. This article cites a report by Tendayi Achiume, a special rapporteur (i.e., independent expert) on racism: "'Corporations such as Facebook, have economic and business models that mean they actively profit from misinformation, discrimination and intolerance,' [Achiume] said, adding that many governments have adopted algorithms which discriminate against marginalised groups."
10. For further discussion of how tech corporations program their platforms and services in ways that amplify racism and its effects on people, see Safiya Umoja Noble, *Algorithms of Oppression: How Search Engines Reinforce Racism* (New York: New York University Press, 2018).
11. See *Holding Big Tech Accountable: Targeted Reforms to Tech's Legal Immunity: Testimony Before the House Energy and Commerce Subcommittee on Communications and Technol-*

ogy, 117th Cong. (2021) (statement of Rashad Robinson, President of Color Of Change), democrats-energycommerce.house.gov/sites/evo-subsites/democrats-energycommerce.house.gov/files/documents/Witness%20Testimony_Robinson_2021.12.01.pdf; and Katie Couric, Chris Krebs, and Rashad Robinson, *Commission on Information Disorder: Final Report* (Aspen Institute, November 2021), aspeninstitute.org/wp-content/uploads/2025/05/Aspen-Institute_Commission-on-Information-Disorder_Final-Report.pdf.

12. See Rachel Siegel and Elizabeth Dwoskin, "Facebook Employees Blast Zuckerberg's Hands-Off Response to Trump Posts as Protests Grip Nation," *Washington Post,* June 1, 2020, washingtonpost.com/business/2020/06/01/facebook-zuckerberg-donation-trump. According to the article, one employee wrote, "People have been murdered this weekend at the protests and we've hosted content encouraging it."
13. For more on the Facebook practice of deliberately programming feeds to amplify dangerous content, see Karen Hao, "How Facebook Got Addicted to Spreading Misinformation," *MIT Technology Review,* March 11, 2021, technologyreview.com/2021/03/11/1020600/facebook-responsible-ai-misinformation; Elizabeth Dwoskin, "Misinformation on Facebook Got Six Times More Clicks Than Factual News During the 2020 Election, Study Says," *Washington Post,* September 4, 2021, washingtonpost.com/technology/2021/09/03/facebook-misinformation-nyu-study; and Naomi Nix, "Facebook Bans Hate Speech but Still Makes Money from White Supremacists," *Washington Post,* August 10, 2022, washingtonpost.com/technology/2022/08/10/facebook-white-supremacy-ads.
14. For more on the Facebook practice of allowing bad actors to spread hate and lies, see Mike Isaac and Cecilia Kang, "Facebook Says It Won't Back Down from Allowing Lies in Political Ads," *New York Times,* January 9, 2020, nytimes.com/2020/01/09/technology/facebook-political-ads-lies.html; Brian Fung,

"Facebook Allowed Hundreds of Misleading Super PAC Ads, Activist Group Finds," CNN, September 23, 2020, edition.cnn.com/2020/09/23/tech/facebook-super-pac-ads; "Facebook Profits from White Supremacist Groups," Tech Transparency Project, August 10, 2022, techtransparencyproject.org/articles/facebook-profits-white-supremacist-groups; Sam Biddle, "Facebook Allowed Advertisers to Target Users Interested in 'White Genocide'—Even in Wake of Pittsburgh Massacre," *The Intercept,* November 2 2018, theintercept.com/2018/11/02/facebook-ads-white-supremacy-pittsburgh-shooting; and Julia Angwin, Madeleine Varner, and Ariana Tobin, "Facebook Enabled Advertisers to Reach 'Jew Haters,'" ProPublica, September 14, 2017, propublica.org/article/facebook-enabled-advertisers-to-reach-jew-haters.

15. Quoted in *The Facebook Dilemma,* part 1 (*PBS Frontline,* 2018), time stamp 4:11, pbs.org/wgbh/frontline/documentary/facebook-dilemma.
16. Mark S. Luckie, "Facebook Is Failing Its Black Employees and Its Black Users," Facebook Notes, November 27, 2018, facebook.com/notes/3121422367961706/
17. For two reports on the impact of Airbnb in New York City related to gentrification, see Murray Cox, "The Face of Airbnb, New York City—Airbnb as a Racial Gentrification Tool," *Inside Airbnb,* March 1, 2017, insideairbnb.com/research/face-of-airbnb-nyc/; and David Wachsmuth et al., *The High Cost of Short-Term Rentals in New York City* (School of Urban Planning McGill University, January 30, 2018), mcgill.ca/newsroom/files/newsroom/channels/attach/airbnb-report.pdf.
18. Alex Nieves, "How Trump Broke California's Grip on the Auto Market," *Politico* December 22, 2025, politico.com/news/2025/12/22/trump-california-electric-vehicle-mandate-00701691.
19. Johnny Ryan and Georg Riekeles, "The EU Has Let US Tech Giants Run Riot. Diluting Our Data Law Will Only

Entrench Their Power," *The Guardian,* November 12, 2025, theguardian.com/commentisfree/2025/nov/12/eu-gdpr-data-law-us-tech-giants-digital?CMP=Share_iOSApp_Other.

20. See David Ingram, "How Elon Musk Turned X into a Pro-Trump Echo Chamber," NBC News, October 31, 2024, nbcnews.com/tech/social-media/elon-musk-turned-x-trump-echo-chamber-rcna174321; Zoë Schiffer and Casey Newton, "Yes, Elon Musk Created a Special System for Showing You All His Tweets First," *The Verge,* February 14, 2023, theverge.com/2023/2/14/23600358/elon-musk-tweets-algorithm-changes-twitter; and Caitlin Dewey, "Elon Musk's X May Be Giving Right-Wing Content the Upper Hand," *Vanity Fair,* October 30, 2024, vanityfair.com/news/story/x-has-disproportionately-pushed-right-wing-content-since-elon-musk-took-over-reports.

21. See Cinoo Lee et al., "People Who Share Encounters with Racism Are Silenced Online by Humans and Machines, but a Guideline-Reframing Intervention Holds Promise," *PNAS* 121, no. 38 (2024): doi.org/10.1073/pnas.2322764121; Jessica Guynn, "Facebook Says It's Stopping Hate and Violence Against Black Americans. Its Own Research Shows Otherwise," *USA Today,* October 25, 2021, usatoday.com/story/tech/2021/10/25/facebook-papers-whistleblower-hate-speech-black-americans-trump-floyd/6156418001/?gnt-cfr=1&gca-cat=p; and Pat de Brún, "Meta's New Content Policies Risk Fueling More Mass Violence and Genocide," Amnesty International, February 17, 2025, amnesty.org/en/latest/news/2025/02/meta-new-policy-changes.

22. See U.S. Equal Employment Opportunity Commission, "EEOC Research Finds Unequal Opportunity in the High Tech Sector and Workforce," press release, September 11, 2024, eeoc.gov/newsroom/eeoc-research-finds-unequal-opportunity-high-tech-sector-and-workforce; and Lauren Rosenblatt, "Amazon's Audit Found 'Perceptions' of Racial Inequity in its

Warehouses," *Seattle Times,* September 29, 2024, seattletimes.com/business/amazon/amazons-audit-found-perceptions-of-racial-inequity-in-its-warehouses.

23. See Zachary Small, "Black Artists Say A.I. Shows Bias, with Algorithms Erasing Their History," *New York Times,* July 4, 2023, nytimes.com/2023/07/04/arts/design/black-artists-bias-ai.html; Julia Angwin, Jeff Larson, Surya Mattu, and Lauren Kirchner, "Machine Bias: There's Software Used Across the Country to Predict Future Criminals. And It's Biased Against Blacks," ProPublica, May 23, 2016, propublica.org/article/machine-bias-risk-assessments-in-criminal-sentencing; David Wheaton, "Fighting Appraisal Bias: How the Government and Housing Industry Can Better Address This Discriminatory Practice," Legal Defense Fund, May 19, 2023, naacpldf.org/appraisal-algorithmic-bias-racial-discrimination; Dawn Zapata, "New Study Finds AI-Enabled Anti-Black Bias in Recruiting," Thomson Reuters, June 18, 2021, thomsonreuters.com/en-us/posts/legal/ai-enabled-anti-black-bias; and Avi Asher-Schapiro, " 'Algorithms of Oppression': Big Tech Urged to Combat Discrimination," Reuters, November 11, 2020, reuters.com/article/world/algorithms-of-oppression-big-tech-urged-to-combat-discrimination-idUSKBN27R02J. For a deeper dive, see Safiya Umoja Noble, *Algorithms of Oppression: How Search Engines Reinforce Racism* (New York: New York University Press, 2018).
24. See Jonathan Mahler, Ryan Mac, and Theodore Schleifer, "How Tech Billionaires Became the G.O.P.'s New Donor Class," *New York Times,* October 18, 2024, nytimes.com/2024/10/18/magazine/trump-donors-silicon-valley.html.

14. Taking On Government: The Role of Prosecutors

1. Prison Policy Initiative, *Mass Incarceration: The Whole Pie 2025* (Northampton, Mass.: Prison Policy Initiative, 2025), prisonpolicy.org/reports/pie2025.html.

2. Administrative Office of the United States Courts, "Judicial Caseload Indicators," in Federal Judicial Caseload Statistics 2024, United States Courts, uscourts.gov/data-news/reports/statistical-reports/federal-judicial-caseload-statistics/judicial-caseload-indicators-federal-judicial-caseload-statistics-2024; S. Gibson, N. Waters, M. Hamilton, E. Stevens, M. Novitt, H. Caspers, and E. Taylor, eds., "Trial Court Caseload Overview—Criminal," CSP STAT, National Center for State Courts, last updated October 2024, accessed February 26, 2026, ncsctableauserver.org/t/Research/views/Trial Dashboards/Criminal.
3. See "Turning the Tide on Mass Incarceration," Fwd.us, December 2023, fwd.us/wp-content/uploads/2023/12/Turning-the-Tide-on-Mass-Incarceration.pdf; and Peter Wagner and Bernadette Rabuy, "Mass Incarceration: The Whole Pie 2015," Prison Policy Initiative, December 8, 2015, prisonpolicy.org/reports/pie2015.html. It's important to note that while certain aggregate numbers may seem stable over the years, the changes by percentage of population are significant.
4. Rashad Robinson, "The People Who Undermine Progressive Prosecutors," *New York Times,* June 11, 2020, nytimes.com/2020/06/11/opinion/george-floyd-prosecutors.html.
5. See United Nations Office of the High Commissioner, "United States: Prolonged Solitary Confinement Amounts to Psychological Torture, Says UN Expert," press release, February 28, 2020, ohchr.org/en/press-releases/2020/02/united-states-prolonged-solitary-confinement-amounts-psychological-torture; Adam Haar Horowitz, "Amicus Brief: Solitary Confinement and Brain Damage, United States Court of Appeals, First Circuit," MIT Media Lab, March 11, 2022, media.mit.edu/publications/amicus-brief-solitary-confinement-and-brain-damage; Erica Bryant, "Solitary Confinement Is Torture, Not COVID Medical Care," Vera, March 25, 2022, vera.org/news/solitary-confinement-is-torture-not-covid-medical-care; Tiana Herring, "The Research Is Clear: Soli-

tary Confinement Causes Long-Lasting Harm," Prison Policy Initiative, December 8, 2020, prisonpolicy.org/blog/2020/12/08/solitary_symposium; and Laura Dimon, "How Solitary Confinement Hurts the Teenage Brain," *The Atlantic,* June 30, 2014, theatlantic.com/health/archive/2014/06/how-solitary-confinement-hurts-the-teenage-brain/373002.

15. Taking On Hollywood Profiteering

1. Robert P. Jones, "Race, Religion, and Political Affiliation of Americans' Core Social Networks," Public Religion Research Institute, August 3, 2016, prri.org/research/poll-race-religion-politics-americans-social-networks.
2. Darnell Hunt, *Race in the Writers' Room: How Hollywood Whitewashes the Stories That Shape America* (Color Of Change Hollywood, October 2017), at rashadrobinson.com/narrativepower.
3. Color Of Change Hollywood and the USC Annenberg Norman Lear Center, *Normalizing Injustice: The Dangerous Misrepresentations That Define Television's Scripted Crime Genre,* updated complete version (Color Of Change Hollywood, January 2020), at rashadrobinson.com/narrativepower.
4. Color Of Change, *Normalizing Injustice 2: How Most Of Hollywood's Scripted Crime Shows Are Still Spreading Dangerous Misinformation About Crime, Race and the Legal System* (Color Of Change, November 2025), at rashadrobinson.com/narrativepower.

16. Failing to Take On Racial Profiteering and Cultural Power

1. See Patrick Radden Keefe, "How Mark Burnett Resurrected Donald Trump as an Icon of American Success," *New Yorker,* December 27, 2018, newyorker.com/magazine/2019/01/07/how-mark-burnett-resurrected-donald-trump-as-an-icon-of-american-success; and Tom McCarthy and Daniel Strauss,

"How Trump's Apprentice Earnings Helped Rescue His Failing Empire," *The Guardian* (U.S. edition), September 29, 2020, theguardian.com/us-news/2020/sep/29/trump-tax-returns-the-apprentice-empire.

2. "Maggie Haberman: GOP Embraced Trump in 2011" (roundtable segment featuring Maggie Haberman, Ana Navarro, Matthew Dowd, and Rep. Keith Ellison), *This Week with George Stephanopoulos,* ABC.

3. Keith Ellison, quoted in Philip Bump, "The Real Story Behind That Viral Clip of Keith Ellison Predicting a Donald Trump Victory," *Washington Post,* February 22, 2016, washingtonpost.com/news/the-fix/wp/2016/11/29/the-real-story-behind-that-viral-clip-of-keith-ellison-predicting-a-donald-trump-victory.

About the Author

FOR MORE than two decades, Rashad Robinson's strategic campaigns, narrative interventions, and movement leadership have played a critical role in winning real change for real people. Today, he advises foundations, nonprofits, and leaders across media, politics, government, and business as they work to improve their impact on the world, design effective campaigns, develop innovative media strategies, help their organizations grow and change, and unlock the power of communities to bring about progress.

Rashad's work and insights are regularly featured in broadcast, print, and social media, in outlets as varied as CNN, MSNBC, BET, NPR, NewsOne, OWN, *The New York Times, USA Today, The Washington Post, Essence, The Hollywood Reporter,* and *The Guardian.* He has also been profiled by *Fast Company, Ebony, The Root,* and the *Stanford Social Innovation Review.*

In 2020, Rashad co-led the largest advertising boycott in history: a thousand-company boycott of Facebook and Instagram. Before same-sex marriage was legal nationally, he led the successful effort to get more than one hundred local and regional newspapers to accept same-sex wedding announcements. He has worked to bring about more authentic portrayals of LGBT people and ensure more accurate representations of both Black people and the criminal justice system across news and entertainment media. He took on financial and media corporations that enabled right-wing extremists to gain political power, while helping to increase the turnout and power of Black voters in critical elections, and co-founding a coalition of progressive organizations in the aftermath of the 2016 election that proved essential for staging a comeback in the 2018 and 2020 elections. Starting in 2015, Rashad was instrumental to launching the movement to elect a new generation of local prosecutors, leading to dozens of victories across the country and subsequent reforms that measurably reduced mass incarceration and many other injustices that have been foundational to the system. He continues to build and lead projects designed to reach more people, build more power, and win more change for communities across the country.

Rashad also served as co-chair of the Aspen Institute's Commission on Information Disorder. He won a Webby Award for Best Political Podcast in 2020 and has received numerous other honors from organizations across the social change sector. He received honorary doctorates from Georgetown University and St. Mary's College of Maryland. Under his leadership, Color Of Change was featured multiple times on *Fast Company*'s list of Most Innovative Companies.

For nearly fourteen years, Rashad led Color Of Change, transforming the organization from a small start-up into a powerhouse of Black activism and a national force for social change driven by millions of members—capable of winning change in Silicon Valley, Wall Street, and Hollywood. Before COC, he led the advocacy and programmatic work at GLAAD during a period of achieving major cultural and political progress for LGBT people. In every role, his passion is helping people make sense of the moment and how to take strategic action.

For more information on Rashad's work, *From Presence to Power,* and his other writings, visit rashadrobinson.com.